# OmniGraffle 5 Diagramming Essentials

Create better diagrams with less effort
using OmniGraffle

**Ruben Olsen**

BIRMINGHAM - MUMBAI

# OmniGraffle 5 Diagramming Essentials

Copyright © 2010 Packt Publishing

All rights reserved. No part of this book may be reproduced, stored in a retrieval system, or transmitted in any form or by any means, without the prior written permission of the publisher, except in the case of brief quotations embedded in critical articles or reviews.

Every effort has been made in the preparation of this book to ensure the accuracy of the information presented. However, the information contained in this book is sold without warranty, either express or implied. Neither the author, nor Packt Publishing, and its dealers and distributors will be held liable for any damages caused or alleged to be caused directly or indirectly by this book.

Packt Publishing has endeavored to provide trademark information about all of the companies and products mentioned in this book by the appropriate use of capitals. However, Packt Publishing cannot guarantee the accuracy of this information.

First published: October 2010

Production Reference: 1191010

Published by Packt Publishing Ltd.
32 Lincoln Road
Olton
Birmingham, B27 6PA, UK.

ISBN 978-1-849690-76-8

www.packtpub.com

Cover Image by Wishkerman, Asher (a.wishkerman@mpic.de)

# Credits

**Author**
Ruben Olsen

**Reviewers**
Thomas Cherry

Kevin Jeong

Ian Piper

Timothy Reaves

Andrew Schechterman, Ph.D.

**Acquisition Editor**
David Barnes

**Development Editor**
Wilson D'souza

**Technical Editor**
Arani Roy

**Indexers**
Monica Ajmera Mehta

Rekha Nair

**Editorial Team Leader**
Aditya Belpathak

**Project Team Leader**
Lata Basantani

**Project Coordinator**
Vincila Colaco

**Proofreader**
Jacqueline McGhee

**Graphics**
Geetanjali Sawant

**Production Coordinator**
Arvindkumar Gupta

**Cover Work**
Arvindkumar Gupta

# About the Author

**Ruben Olsen** has been making "visual stuff" since he touched his first computer, a Commodore PET 20, back in the late 70s. Since then he has played, worked, loved, and cursed almost any computer system commercially available. He is no stranger to either the old IBM VM/SP or to the latest edition of the Apple Macintosh operating system.

Ruben received his M.Sc. in Information Technology from the University of Liverpool. He is currently the co-founder and CTO of Azuralis AS—a company providing advanced telecommunication solutions.

The first time he created a diagram to illustrate an important fact was when he was taking his first university courses back in the early 90s. He hand-coded a simple diagram in Adobe PostScript and fed it directly to a laser printer, whereupon the printer crashed horribly. Back then he learned the importance of having excellent diagrams to substantiate any argument.

For nearly two decades he has used diagrams and diagramming tools to illustrate important points and facts.

A few years ago he was working as a "technical hit-man" at a VoIP service provider—and this was the first time he came in contact with OmniGraffle. He fell deeply in love with the program and this is a love that never has lessened even as the years have passed by.

When not behind the computer designing and programming telecommunication solutions, he spends his time with his three cats, reading a good book, listening to some extraordinarily good music, cooking tasty food, and watching a nice movie with his lovely fiancée (by the time you are reading this – they are newly wed).

# Acknowledgement

Writing this book involved one particular cat named Magika who never left the side of my laptop, one soon-to-be-wife who exercised more patience than expected, and two cats named Amanda and Cassie begging for attention when the writing became obsessive.

Also a great thanks to the OmniGraffle SupportNinjas—especially Paul Palinkas. They answered a whole bunch of silly questions.

This book was written under the influence of Alan Parsons, Barry Adamson, Mark Knopfler, Dean Martin, Diana Krall, Erykah Badu, Faith Hill, Fenton George, Gwangwa Jonas, Johnny Cash, Georg Händel, Leonard Cohen, Lily Allen, Mary Chapin Carpenter, Myléne Farmer, Nanci Griffith, Nick Cave, Tchaikovsky, Pink Floyd, Ramstein, Richard Wagner, Simon & Garfunkel, Tanita Tikaram, Taylor Swift, Terry Garland, Tom Waits, and Kitaro.

# About the Reviewers

**Thomas Cherry** is a software developer with over 15 years of experience in writing applications for Macintosh, PC, the web, and recently, the iPhone, and iPad. As a contractor for NASA, he utilizes OmniGraffle to design and document development projects for both himself and his team. He currently resides in Baltimore, MD with his wife Melissa, son Leo, poodle Nyxi, and cat Senyeh.

**Kevin Jeong** is a user experience specialist with over 15 years of experience in the Internet field. During this time, he has excelled in various roles including creative designer, developer and user experience architect. His passion for creating engaging and effective designs has been applied to websites, mobile applications, and interactive installations. He has done work for Adobe, Frito-Lay, Hewlett-Packard, NBC Universal, Sprint, and Walmart.

**Ian Piper** is a veteran Mac user and developer, having laid hands on his first Mac in 1985 and has rarely been seen without one since.

Ian runs Tellura Information Services (`www.tellura.co.uk`), an information management technology company. He spends most of his day pulling information systems to pieces and rebuilding them to make more sense for users. His particular interest is information architecture, designing and building navigation systems, and taxonomies for large complex websites. He has been using OmniGraffle as an essential tool in the information architect's chest since its earliest versions.

Ian's earlier writing work includes books on Xcode development tools and AppleScript, and he has edited books on Ruby on Rails and Joomla.

**Timothy Reaves** is active in the Open Source Software world, as well as being interested in the sciences, math, and reading. He lives in rural Ohio on a horse farm, with his wife and son.

**Andrew Schechterman**, Ph.D., is a hybrid medical psychologist, interaction designer, design-planning strategist, and principal user experience architect, and with his colleagues has researched, designed and delivered a breadth of GUI's, desktop applications, embedded software-hardware interfaces, and web applications. Providing applied expertise in the research and design of both digital and analog products and services, his approach integrates user requirements while balancing business goals and technical feasibility. This iterative process incorporates cognitive, emotional, and behavioral variables, promoting offerings that are relevant, desirable, and successful. His methods, processes, and case studies have been presented at multidisciplinary conferences, published in international design management journals, and cited in articles written by his peers. Though much of his writing-editing has been in medicine and healthcare, he has increasingly contributed to topics relevant to human-centered experience design and architecture. Among many applications, as well as simply sketching, OmniGraffle Professional is one of the software applications he uses almost daily in his work. Dr. Schechterman holds undergraduate and graduate degrees in the Social, Behavioral and Cognitive Sciences, with post-doctoral training and application in Behavioral Medicine, Design Management, Design Planning and User Experience Design. He can be found at `www.LinkedIn.com/in/andrewschechterman` and `www.andrewschechterman.com`.

# Table of Contents

**Preface**                                                                 **1**

**Chapter 1: Getting Started with OmniGraffle**                             **5**

**What OmniGraffle is—and what it is not**                                  **6**
**What's in a name?**                                                       **7**
**Setting up OmniGraffle before you start**                                 **7**
**The OmniGraffle workspace**                                              **8**
  The canvas                                                      8
    The toolbar                                         9
    The inspector bar                                   9
    The drawing area                                    10
    The style tray                                      10
  The inspector palettes                                         11
    Selector and keyboard shortcuts                     11
  The stencils                                                    12
**Your first diagram**                                                     **13**
  Step 1: Start with a blank canvas                              15
  Step 2: Add the first task                                     16
  Step 3: Add task—writing article                               17
  Step 4: Connecting shapes                                      18
  Step 5: Adding another workflow step: Done editing             20
  Step 6: Moving a shape                                         22
  Step 7: Adding the editor check                                24
  Step 8: Workflow step—publish on the front page                32
  Step 9: Workflow step—publish on the front page                35
  Step 10: Publishing!                                           39
  Step 11: The icing on the cake—making your diagram spring into color   41
    The Canvas Style Tray                               45
**More on moving shapes around the canvas**                                **47**
**Saving diagrams**                                                        **49**

| | |
|---|---|
| **Exporting diagrams** | **51** |
| **Handy tips regarding inspectors** | **52** |
| **Tips and pitfalls—tips on how to make great visual diagrams** | **53** |
| Tip 1: Do some planning before you start | 54 |
| Tip 2: Colorize gently | 55 |
| Tip 3: Use few fonts | 55 |
| Tip 4: Consider your output media | 56 |
| Tip 5: Symmetry is better than asymmetry | 56 |
| Tip 6: Have one, and only one, focus point | 57 |
| Tip 7: Apply the Golden Ratio to stand alone diagrams | 57 |
| Tip 8: Use titles, figure captions, and legends | 57 |
| Tip 9: Be liberal with white space | 58 |
| Tip 10: Be consistent | 58 |
| **Summary** | **58** |
| **Chapter 2: Stencils** | **59** |
| **Defining a stencil** | **60** |
| **The stencil library** | **60** |
| **Overview of the Stencils palette** | **61** |
| **Built-in stencils** | **61** |
| Common stencils | 62 |
| Maps stencils | 62 |
| Organization charts stencils | 62 |
| Science stencils | 63 |
| Software stencils | 63 |
| Space planning stencils | 63 |
| **Your first stencil-based diagram** | **63** |
| A helping guide | 64 |
| The incoming cash flow | 65 |
| Adding expense buckets | 66 |
| **External stencils** | **69** |
| Omni Group downloads | 69 |
| Graffletopia | 69 |
| Commercial stencil sources | 70 |
| Importing MS Visio stencils and templates | 70 |
| **Searching and importing stencils from Graffletopia** | **70** |
| The manual method of importing any stencils | 70 |
| The automatic method of importing stencils from Graffletopia | 72 |
| **Amending your income flow diagram** | **74** |
| **The details of the Stencils palette** | **75** |
| Overview of the palette sections | 75 |

The Stencil Library Controls                                             76
   The Stencil View Mode buttons                          76
   The Stencil Action button                              77
   The Stencil Search function                            79
The Stencil Folders pane                                                80
   The Stencil Library                                    81
   The Recent Stencils section                            81
   The Favorite Stencil section                           82
**The selected shapes Style Tray**                                      **82**
**Creating your own stencil**                                           **83**
**Creating stencils with cool graphics**                               **85**
The vector side of things                                               85
The legal side of using third party graphic files                       86
Creating a stencil with fancy graphics                                   87
   Using svg Detective to convert the SVG file            93
   Using InkScape to convert the SVG file                 96
**Exporting your stencil**                                              **99**
**Importing Microsoft Visio Templates**                                 **100**
**Organizing stencils**                                                 **105**
**Summary**                                                             **106**
**Chapter 3: Shapes, Building Blocks for Diagrams**                     **109**
**Differences from other software**                                     **110**
**Compound shapes**                                                     **111**
Shape types                                                             111
Adding a text caption to a shape                                         113
Drawing a copy of an existing shape                                      113
Favorite shapes and styles                                               114
**Singular shapes – lines**                                             **115**
The Line Style inspector                                                 117
Midpoints on lines                                                       117
Line types                                                               119
Bézier lines in detail                                                   121
Line endings—tails and (arrow) heads                                     122
Reversing a line                                                         123
Line Hops                                                                123
Favorite line styles                                                     125
Line labels revisited                                                    126
**Text shapes**                                                         **128**
Favorite text styles                                                     131
**Shape style properties**                                              **132**
Shape stroke inspector and the color of a stroke                         132
Fill color and fill type                                                 137

| | |
|---|---|
| Shadow type, color, and size | 140 |
| Text type (font), color, and size | 143 |
| Placing images inside shapes | 148 |
| **Ordering shapes** | **154** |
| **Grouping shapes** | **156** |
| Creating a group of shapes | 157 |
| Ungrouping a group of shapes | 158 |
| Resizing shape groups | 159 |
| **Adjusting shapes with the Geometry property inspector** | **160** |
| Line Label controls | 164 |
| **The Rulers and Inspector Bar** | **167** |
| The Shape Inspector Bar | 167 |
| The Text Inspector Bar | 169 |
| The Canvas rulers | 170 |
| **Connecting shapes** | **171** |
| **Summary** | **177** |
| **Chapter 4: More Tools for Editing Diagrams** | **179** |
| **The Expanded Canvas Toolbar** | **180** |
| The floating Canvas Tool palette | 180 |
| Customizing the Canvas Toolbar | 181 |
| The Canvas Toolbar preferences | 181 |
| **Keyboard shortcuts for the Canvas Toolbar** | **182** |
| **Using the Pen Tool to create your own shapes** | **184** |
| **Fast diagramming using the Diagramming Tool** | **188** |
| Diagramming Tool Modifier keys | 190 |
| **Style replication using the Style Brush Tool** | **190** |
| **Replicating shapes using the Rubber Stamp Tool** | **193** |
| **Editing magnets using the Magnet Tool** | **194** |
| **Zooming the Canvas** | **197** |
| **Moving around the canvas** | **199** |
| **Using the Action Browse Tool and the Action Property Inspector** | **200** |
| The Action Property inspector | 201 |
| The Jumps Elsewhere action in detail | 203 |
| **Using Automatic layout** | **210** |
| **Mouseless Editing** | **217** |
| Keyboard shortcuts and OmniGraffle | 217 |
| Your brain may thank you for using keyboard shortcuts | 222 |
| **Using the Outline and List functions to create diagrams** | **223** |
| The Outline function | 223 |
| The List function | 231 |
| **Diagram Styles** | **232** |

| | |
|---|---|
| **Diagram Templates** | **236** |
| **Summary** | **238** |
| **Chapter 5: More on Editing Diagrams** | **239** |
| **Creating your own shapes the easy way** | **240** |
| The Subtract Shapes menu command | 240 |
| The Union Shapes menu command | 242 |
| The Intersect Shapes menu command | 242 |
| The Make Points Editable menu command | 243 |
| The Big Wedge Experiment | 244 |
| **Subgraphs** | **250** |
| **Tables** | **254** |
| **Using OmniGraffle as a presentation tool** | **259** |
| Creating a presentation | 259 |
| Starting, navigating, and stopping your presentation | 259 |
| Advanced presentation mode | 260 |
| Actions and presentation mode | 261 |
| Changing the color and behavior of the presentation highlight | 262 |
| **The ColorSync support** | **263** |
| **Summary** | **265** |
| **Chapter 6: Making your Diagram Look Good** | **267** |
| **Manually adjusting diagram elements** | **268** |
| **Resizing shapes** | **269** |
| Size to Fit Image | 270 |
| Make Natural Size | 270 |
| Making shapes the same size | 271 |
| **Gridlines** | **273** |
| Enabling gridlines | 274 |
| Adjusting gridlines | 274 |
| **Aligning shapes to the document grid** | **275** |
| **Aligning shapes to each other** | **284** |
| **Easy shape selection** | **287** |
| What OmniGraffle defines as similar shapes | 288 |
| Selecting connected shapes | 291 |
| **Easy re-styling of shapes** | **294** |
| **Color picker tricks** | **297** |
| **The color picker in detail** | **300** |
| The Color Wheel | 302 |
| The Color Sliders | 302 |
| The Color Palettes | 303 |
| The Image Palettes | 304 |

| | |
|---|---|
| The Crayons Palette | 304 |
| The Patterns Palette | 305 |
| **Summary** | **305** |
| **Chapter 7: Property Inspectors** | **307** |
| **The Grid Property inspector revisited** | **308** |
| **The Canvas Size Property inspector** | **312** |
| More on scaling your diagram | 315 |
| **The Document Property inspector** | **316** |
| More on file format options | 317 |
| **The Data Property inspector** | **319** |
| **The Note Property inspector** | **320** |
| **Summary** | **323** |
| **Chapter 8: Canvases and Canvas Layers** | **325** |
| **Canvases** | **326** |
| Naming your canvases | 328 |
| Adding, deleting, and rearranging canvases | 329 |
| **Canvas layers** | **330** |
| A visual explanation of canvas layers | 331 |
| **Working with layers** | **333** |
| Adding a new layer | 333 |
| Duplicating and copying a layer | 333 |
| Rearranging and moving a layer | 335 |
| How to merge two layers | 335 |
| Deleting a layer | 336 |
| **Layer settings** | **337** |
| Visibility | 337 |
| Printing | 337 |
| Locking a layer | 338 |
| **Working with shapes on layers** | **338** |
| **Shared layers** | **340** |
| **When to use layers** | **344** |
| **Summary** | **344** |
| **Chapter 9: OmniGraffle workspaces** | **345** |
| **Your workspace** | **345** |
| **Summary** | **349** |
| **Index** | **351** |

# Preface

This book will teach you how to make eye-popping visuals using a lot of useful, step-by-step examples. It begins with covering concepts that beef up the basics of using OmniGraffle. The earlier chapters will teach you to prepare dazzling diagrams from scratch with the many stencils, shapes, and fonts that are included in OmniGraffle. As your understanding of OmniGraffle broadens, the book will go even deeper to explain the less understood features of the software. It also covers some handy time-saving techniques such as workspaces and keyboard shortcuts.

By the time you reach the end of this book, you will have mastered OmniGraffle to turn your ideas into diagrams.

## What this book covers

*Chapter 1, Getting Started with OmniGraffle*, will teach you the very basics of using OmniGraffle. You will need to know this so that you can move on to create your very first diagram from scratch. You will also learn how to save your diagram for other OmniGraffle users to enjoy.

*Chapter 2, Stencils*, will extend your OmniGraffle proficiency by showing you that Stencils are great time savers. We'll go through a few simple, easy to remember, rules that will make your diagram stand out from the crowd. The chapter will continue with extending your knowledge into managing and creating your own Stencils.

*Chapter 3, Shapes, Building Blocks for Diagrams*, will continue to expand your knowledge about the shapes in OmniGraffle. It will teach you how to operate on shapes, such as changing their behavior and appearance, fill the shapes, add text to your diagrams, and so on.

*Chapter 4, More Tools for Editing Diagrams*, will teach you how to use time saving tools when working with your diagrams. These tools are found in the Expanded Canvas Toolbar.

*Chapter 5, More on Editing Diagrams,* will teach you about the few diagramming functions that are exclusive to OmniGraffle Professional. It will teach you how to make new shapes using binary operations on shapes, divide your diagram into subgraphs, apply ColorSync profiles to your document, and so on

*Chapter 6, Making your Diagram Look Good,* will teach you several methods and techniques of quickly styling your diagram. It will cover how to efficiently align shapes to each other, resizing shapes based on existing shapes on your canvas, various color picker tricks and so on

*Chapter 7, Property Inspectors,* will teach you about all the available properties in OmniGraffle. It will cover the Grid, Canvas Size, Document, Data, and Note property inspectors.

*Chapter 8, Canvases and Canvas Layers,* teaches you how to deal with situations when you have to work with more than one canvas for your diagram. You will learn about naming and managing your canvases, managing your canvas layers, and other topics.

*Chapter 9, OmniGraffle workspaces,* will teach you how to set up your workspace, as having different workspace configurations tailored to various diagramming tasks can be a real time saver.

# What you need for this book

You will need OmniGraffle version 5 to follow the examples in this book. Also, the Author has suggested that you put on some smooth jazz while reading this book.

# Who this book is for

This book is written for both beginners and seasoned users of OmniGraffle. If you are new to the software, then this book will teach you everything you need to know to make stunning diagrams. For seasonedOmniGraffle users, this book contains a lot of tricks and techniques that will save you work and time.

# Conventions

In this book, you will find a number of styles of text that distinguish between different kinds of information. Here are some examples of these styles, and an explanation of their meaning.

File and folder names in text are shown as follows: "please open the file named `your second diagram.png` found in the `Chapter 2` folder in the download bundle."

**New terms** and **important words** are shown in bold. Words that you see on the screen, in menus or dialog boxes for example, appear in the text like this: "clicking the **Next** button moves you to the next screen".

> Warnings or important notes appear in a box like this.

> Tips and tricks appear like this.

# Reader feedback

Feedback from our readers is always welcome. Let us know what you think about this book—what you liked or may have disliked. Reader feedback is important for us to develop titles that you really get the most out of.

To send us general feedback, simply send an e-mail to feedback@packtpub.com, and mention the book title via the subject of your message.

If there is a book that you need and would like to see us publish, please send us a note in the **SUGGEST A TITLE** form on www.packtpub.com or e-mail suggest@packtpub.com.

If there is a topic that you have expertise in and you are interested in either writing or contributing to a book on, see our author guide on www.packtpub.com/authors.

# Customer support

Now that you are the proud owner of a Packt book, we have a number of things to help you to get the most from your purchase.

> **Downloading the example diagrams for this book**
>
> You can download the example files for all Packt books you have purchased from your account at http://www.PacktPub.com. If you purchased this book elsewhere, you can visit http://www.PacktPub.com/support and register to have the files e-mailed directly to you.

# Errata

Although we have taken every care to ensure the accuracy of our content, mistakes do happen. If you find a mistake in one of our books—maybe a mistake in the text or the code—we would be grateful if you would report this to us. By doing so, you can save other readers from frustration and help us improve subsequent versions of this book. If you find any errata, please report them by visiting http://www.packtpub.com/support, selecting your book, clicking on the **let us know** link, and entering the details of your errata. Once your errata are verified, your submission will be accepted and the errata will be uploaded on our website, or added to any list of existing errata, under the Errata section of that title. Any existing errata can be viewed by selecting your title from http://www.packtpub.com/support.

# Piracy

Piracy of copyright material on the Internet is an ongoing problem across all media. At Packt, we take the protection of our copyright and licenses very seriously. If you come across any illegal copies of our works, in any form, on the Internet, please provide us with the location address or website name immediately so that we can pursue a remedy.

Please contact us at copyright@packtpub.com with a link to the suspected pirated material.

We appreciate your help in protecting our authors, and our ability to bring you valuable content.

# Questions

You can contact us at questions@packtpub.com if you are having a problem with any aspect of the book, and we will do our best to address it.

# 1
# Getting Started with OmniGraffle

In this chapter, you will learn the very basics of using OmniGraffle. You will need to know this so that you can move on to create your very first diagram from scratch. You will also learn how to save your diagram for other OmniGraffle users to enjoy. However, if your co-workers, friends, or family do not have OmniGraffle, you will learn how to export your diagram to a more common format for them to enjoy.

This chapter will cover the following topics:

- What OmniGraffle is and is not
- The naming conventions for shapes
- The OmniGraffle workspace
- A step-by-step guide to your very first diagram
- Basic operation of the software
- Tips regarding the efficient use of inspectors
- Tips regarding how to make great visual diagrams

# What OmniGraffle is—and what it is not

OmniGraffle is perhaps the easiest diagramming program available for the Macintosh. As with a lot of productivity tools, the program can be used for more than its intended purposes. You can use OmniGraffle to write a letter to your aunt, or a business report to your boss—as you could use Microsoft Word to create diagrams.

There is a good reason why you should let OmniGraffle do your diagramming (and consequently let your word processor do your reporting), and the simple reason is that OmniGraffle specializes in diagrams! OmniGraffle is exceptionally good when it comes to good-looking diagrams. Not only do the diagrams look good, they are easy to make, manipulate, and reuse.

Hopefully, you have other productivity tools on your computer such as iWorks Pages™ and Microsoft Word™ which are excellent for writing reports, books, and other texts, so you do not need to use OmniGraffle for writing your texts.

There are a few important reasons why you should try to avoid creating diagrams with Microsoft Word, or to a lesser degree, OpenOffice Writer:

- It's cumbersome to lay out shapes—there's a lot of clicking involved
- You are limited to the size of your page, and you need to carefully plan your diagram as changing it afterwards can become very work intensive
- You cannot connect shapes to each other—thus remodelling your diagram involves moving everything around by hand
- You do not have automatic layout settings—every alignment, every adjustment must be done by hand (and measurement must be done by eye)
- You have only a limited number of shapes at your disposal
- It's very cumbersome to adjust shape settings like shadow, line stroke, filling, geometry, and so on, to more than one shape at a time
- You have limited export options for your diagram

If you indeed have created diagrams with a text processor, you'll soon realize that in comparison using OmniGraffle is a walk in the park on a hot summer day with a handsome person by your side. You'll love it so much that you're going to beg anyone to let you create their diagrams for.

# What's in a name?

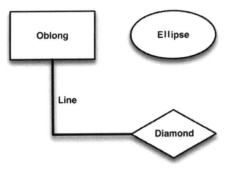

In the previous diagram we have an oblong, an ellipse, a diamond, and a line connecting the oblong to the diamond.

There are several names for the various parts of this diagram. Some people will call these diagram **objects**, others will call them diagram **elements or shapes**. In this book, we will primarily use **shapes**, but you will encounter all three words.

# Setting up OmniGraffle before you start

When you start OmniGraffle, or if you issue the **File | New** command and get prompted with the **Template Chooser** as seen next, you should select the **Blank** template and then click the **Set as Default** button.

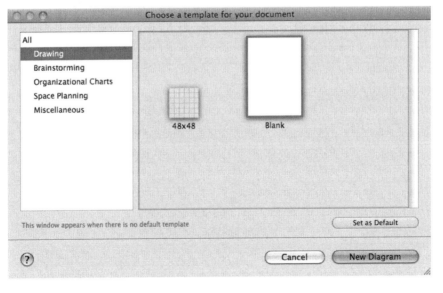

By doing this, you'll always get a new blank canvas ready for use instead of having to go through the Template Chooser.

If you feel more comfortable always being prompted by the Template Chooser, then you do not have to do anything except click on the **New Diagram** button.

You'll learn everything there is to know about the Template Chooser, including making your own templates in *Chapter 9, OmniGraffle workspaces* of this book.

# The OmniGraffle workspace

Before you continue your quest to become the best OmniGraffler around, we'll have to take a look at the OmniGraffle workspace. The reason for this, is that you need to learn a few *OmniGraffle terms* that will be used throughout the book.

When working in OmniGraffle your workspace will normally consist of three parts: The **canvas**, the **inspectors**, and the **stencils**.

# The canvas

If your **canvas** does not look exactly like the one you see next, don't panic as this is just for illustrative purposes. In *Chapter 2, Stencils* you will learn in great detail about the canvas.

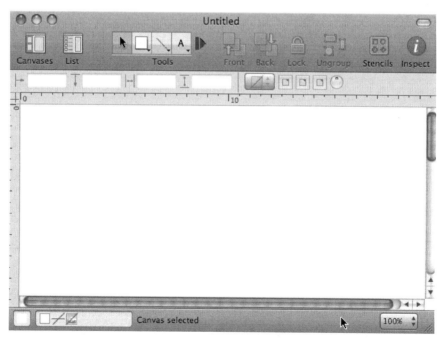

The canvas consists of four parts: The **Canvas Toolbar**, the **Inspector Bar**, the **Canvas View**, and the **Style Tray**.

 Even if the canvas consists of several parts, for simplicity's sake this area is also known as the area where you do your diagram drawings.

# The toolbar

The toolbar contains not only access to drawing tools, but also quick access to commonly used functions such as ordering drawing objects. This is how your toolbar may look—if it does not look exactly like this, do not panic—the details will be revealed in Chapter 2.

In the toolbar, you should for now, concentrate on the **tools-selector**:

From left to right we have the **Selection Tool** (arrow), the **Shape Tool** (square), the **Line Tool** (line), and the **Text Tool** (A). Depending on the current configuration of the shape, line and text tools, the symbols may differ from what you see in the picture.

# The inspector bar

We'll only show you what the **inspector bar** looks like. We mention this inspector bar here without getting into details about this tool as it is covered in great detail in *Chapter 3, Shapes, Building Blocks for Diagrams*.

# The drawing area

The drawing area is the actual canvas where you will draw your diagrams. It may be confusing to have the same name for what may seem like two parts of the program—but this is how the Omni Group, the makers of OmniGraffle, have decided to name things.

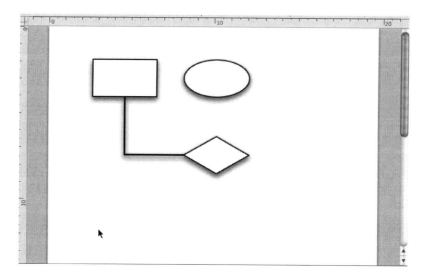

To make things less difficult for you, the book will use the term canvas for the actual drawing area. This is also consistent with what the majority of users will call the area where they are drawing stuff.

The drawing area is 100% **WYSIWYG—What You See, Is What You Get**. If you draw a circle, and print your diagram, a circle will appear on your printed paper. If you want to move your circle around the canvas, just point to the circle and drag it to its new location.

# The style tray

The style tray, found in the lower left of the OmniGraffle window, shows you the current style of a drawing shape such as a circle, square, oblong, and so on. Later in this chapter, we'll use the style tray to quickly copy the look of one shape onto another shape.

# The inspector palettes

You have four selectors available in the **Inspector Palettes**. Each selector will have several tools belonging to the selector.

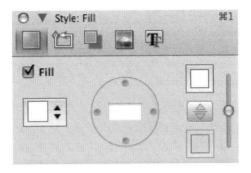

The property inspectors will aid you when you need to change the appearance and properties of your shapes. There are also inspectors for changing the properties of the canvas, and the document you are working on. Shown here is the Style inspector.

There are several ways to open up the style inspector. You can use the **Inspectors | Style** menu command, or simply issue the ⌘+1 keyboard combination.

Most of the inspectors are explained as you learn to use the various tools and techniques. In *Chapter 7, Property Inspectors* you will learn about the various property inspectors that have no corresponding tools, but still are a important factor of your diagrams.

# Selector and keyboard shortcuts

| Shortcut | Selector name | Description |
|---|---|---|
| ⌘+1 | Style | Changes the style of a shape. You can change the filling of the shape, the line style, the amount of shadow, and the text style. You can even fill a shape with a picture. |
| ⌘+2 | Properties | Amends the geometry and the connections of a shape. There are also two advanced functions (action and note) that will be covered later in this book. |
| ⌘+3 | Canvas | You can change the size of the canvas, alter the grid, change the layout and alignment of shapes, and quickly find selected shapes. |
| ⌘+4 | Document | There are only two document properties available: Document information and file format options. |

You may also use the inspector symbol (ⓘ) on the toolbar to show and hide the inspector palette. If you decide you have a favorite location in the OmniGraffle window where you like to have your palette show/hide, this acts as a quick toggle.

# The stencils

**Stencils** are collections of ready-made shapes. These shapes can be simple or they can be complex. They are great time savers when working on diagrams with more complex shapes than squares and circles.

If you cannot see the stencil palette shown on the right, you can use the ⌘+0 keyboard shortcut, or click on the stencil symbol (⊞) on the canvas toolbar. Note that this can function as a palette show/hide, similar to the inspector, previously.

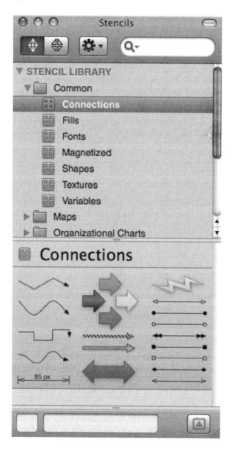

A stencil often has a name denoting its theme. OmniGraffle comes with a few of these *themes* like a stencil with ready-made furniture you can use for planning your living room—or if you need to create a really good looking organizational chart, there are stencils for this also.

When you install OmniGraffle, you will have a nice starter set of stencils available. These are very suitable for getting you going, and even the most seasoned OmniGraffle users, will often create their diagrams using only these basic stencils.

As we will see later in the book, there is a huge library of ready-made stencils that you can import directly into OmniGraffle, making your diagramming even more efficient, and specific to your personal and work needs.

In Chapter 2, you will go into great detail regarding stencils. You will even learn to create your own stencil.

Using a stencil is very easy: Just find the right stencil from the **Stencil library**, select the shape you want to use—and then drag it onto the canvas.

# Your first diagram

The saying goes: *a picture is worth a thousand words*. When dealing with diagrams, the same point is true: *a good diagram saves a thousand words*.

In this section, you will draw your first diagram. We'll build the diagram from scratch to a finished product, and along the way explain what you need to do. If you follow each step without deviation, you will get a good background on a lot of the possibilities that are present in the OmniGraffle program. It is thus better to experiment after the diagram is done, rather then when you are working your way through the various steps.

Our first diagram is going to describe the workflow for publishing information on an imaginary company's web page.

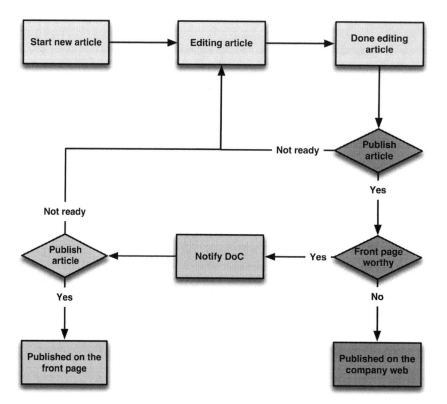

To set the stage we need to introduce some actors and publishing rules. First out is *the writer*. This person is actually writing content to be published. However, a writer is not allowed to publish information on the web without being checked by *the editor*. Unless the article being published is to be put on the front page, the editor does not need any permission to publish. If the article is to be published on the front page, then the *Director of Communication* needs to give her consent.

What we have here is a common workflow for publishing information on a company website. However, often these workflows are described in many more words and in language confusing to the reader. Using a diagram will help the reader to understand how the workflow is really going.

We are now going to make a diagram that clearly shows the workflow described in the previous section.

# Step 1: Start with a blank canvas

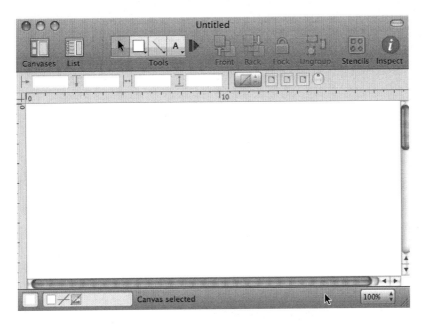

If OmniGraffle is already running, you can use the **File | New** command.

If you need to start OmniGraffle you may either have a new blank document at your disposal, or you may be presented with the **Template Chooser**.

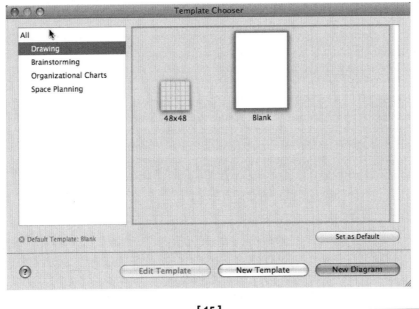

The template chooser contains a few ready-made templates for various tasks.

For this task, choose the **Blank** template and hit the **New Diagram** button.

# Step 2: Add the first task

The first task for a website author is of course to start a new article. We'll use an oblong to denote this.

In the tool-selector, you click on the **Shape Tool**. You will notice a blue circle with the number 1 inside. This indicates that this tool has been selected to perform once.

This means that after you have used the tool once, OmniGraffle will revert back to the selection tool. If you want to draw more than one particular shape, double-click on the corresponding icon, and it will not change until you select another tool to use.

Now, draw an oblong shape on the canvas. Notice that the blue circle over the shape tool is gone—and the selection tool has been automatically selected.

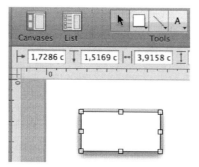

Double-click inside the oblong shape. You will now have the ability to put text inside the shape. Type in **Start new article**.

If your version of the oblong and the text does not exactly look like what you see in the book, this is not important right now. We are going to fix this later. Do not spend time trying to get your oblong looking 100% like what you see here.

When you are done press the *Esc* key (or click anywhere on the canvas, outside of the shape). You will now notice that the shape is selected since the shape has got eight "handles":

Just leave it like this.

The handles you see on the shape are what you use when you want to resize the shape using your mouse.

# Step 3: Add task—writing article

The next task is of course to write the actual article.

With the **Start new article** box selected, press the ⌘+*D* keyboard shortcut combination to duplicate the shape. You should now have one box on top of the other:

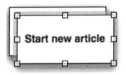

Move the selected (copied) oblong to the right of the one underneath. Try to leave a good amount of space between the boxes. You will now have two rectangles with the same content next to each other.

Double-click inside the box on the right side to edit the text, and enter **Editing article**.

# Step 4: Connecting shapes

Since you are in fact documenting a process, using an arrow from one point in the workflow to the next point makes sense. What we want is an arrow going from the **Start new article** box to the **Editing article** rectangle.

To achieve this, click on the **Line Tool** in the tool-selector on the canvas toolbar. You will notice a blue circle with the number 1 inside. This indicates that this tool has been selected to perform once.

Next, place the cursor over the **Start new article** oblong. You will notice that the shape is now glowing with a colored hue.

The glow is to indicate that you can start (or end) a line on a shape. The color of the glow depends on which version of OmniGraffle you are using. If you are reading the PDF version of this book, you will notice that the glowing color is red. Usage of the red color is also reflected elsewhere in the text.

Click once, and move the cursor over to the Editing article oblong. You will notice two things: The **Editing article** oblong is now glowing; and there is a straight line between the two shapes.

When you click on the **Editing article** oblong, the line becomes permanent. The line is also selected, which is a good thing, as you now will put on an arrow to indicate the direction of the workflow.

To add an arrow to a line, you need to use the **Lines and Shapes inspector**. If the style palette is not shown, press the ⌘+1 keyboard combination. The style palette is now visible. Click on the line style and you have access to line properties.

As you notice in this inspector, there are several properties you can use to alter the appearance of a line. In fact, you can alter certain properties on all drawn shapes (lines, circles, oblongs, and so on).

The important widget for you right now is the following part of the inspector:

The left selector controls the appearance of the start of the line.

The right selector controls the appearance of the line ending.

The middle selector is what kind of line you want to have. Between the two shapes we are now working on, you can leave this selector as it is.

Change the right selector to an arrow head:

Now you have an arrow between your shapes:

# Step 5: Adding another workflow step: Done editing

We need to add the step where the writer is done editing the article. This is done by adding a new oblong, entering the **Done editing article** text, and finally connecting the **Editing article** oblong with the **Done editing article** oblong.

Instead of repeating Step 3 and Step 4, we will duplicate the last box we created along with the arrow. Then we'll re-connect the new arrow to the **Editing article** oblong.

Hold down the *Shift* key and click on the arrow and the **Editing article** box. Both should now be selected.

Use the ⌘+D keyboard shortcut command to duplicate these shapes:

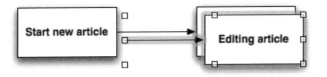

Move the selected arrow and oblong below the existing diagram. You will now for all practical purposes have two diagrams, which need to be connected to each other.

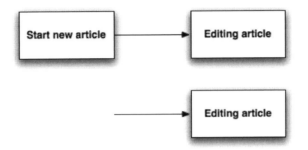

Double-click inside the newly created oblong and change the text to **Done editing article**.

To connect the "loose arrow" to the upper diagram, click on the arrow. You will notice the arrow has a small red diamond on the right side, and a small green circle on the left side (where you now have the arrow point). The red ring is an indication of the starting point of the line, and the green ring is an indication of the endpoint of the line.

Click on the red circle and drag it over the **Editing article** oblong. Notice that the oblong will now glow with the red hue we saw before, giving you an indication that the line can be attached to this shape.

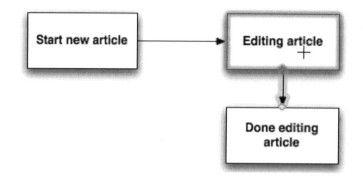

# Step 6: Moving a shape

We suddenly notice that we need to move the **Done editing article** shape to the right.

Before we move the shape, let's make sure that the **Smart Alignment Guides**, and the **Smart Distance Guides** are turned on. These are found in the **Arrange | Guides** menu:

Turning on these two guides will give use some nice visual hints along the way, making sure our diagram will turn out visually great.

Earlier in this chapter you learned that the canvas is WYSIWYG. Simply click on the **Done editing article**, and drag it to the right of the other two shapes.

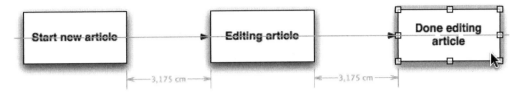

You will notice two things as you move the **Done editing article** shape to the right of the two other shapes:

- First, is the thin blue line going through all three shapes. This is a visual cue that the three shapes are aligned vertically centered to each other.
  What you see here, is the *Smart Alignment Guides* in action.
  When you align two or more shapes, the Smart Alignment Guide kicks into action and shows you that the shape you are now moving around is aligned with other shapes.

- Secondly, between the shapes we see some distance indicators. This is a visual cue that the distance between shape number 1 and shape number 2, is equal to the distance between shape number 2 and shape number 3.
  What you see here, is the *Smart Distance Guides* in action.

- While alignment and distance guides may seem minors feature at present, in time, their power (if you elect to use them) will become apparent.

You can temporarily enable or disable guides by holding down the *command* key (⌥) after you have started to drag your selected shape around.

> When moving a shape, correctly connected connection lines will stay connected to their corresponding shapes.
>
> When moving a connection line, the line may lose its connection—the connected shape will **not** move. The reason for this is that shapes are conceptually more important than lines (this is true for most diagrams).

# Step 7: Adding the editor check

The next step in the workflow is adding the logic around the editorial step. This is where the editor decides if the article is worth publishing.

We start by replicating Step 5. Click on the **Done editing article** and its corresponding arrow, then press the ⌘+D keyboard shortcut combination to duplicate the shape and the arrow. Move the newly created shapes below the current diagram:

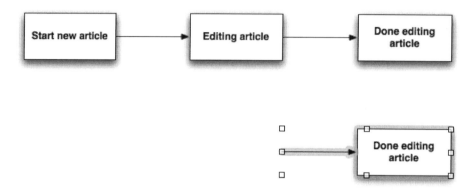

Now, click on the new **Done editing article** shape.

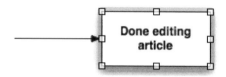

We are now going to change this shape into a "decision" shape. Traditionally, such decision shapes have had the diamond form.

If you take a look in the **Style inspector**, you'll notice that the bottom half has changed from when we added the arrowhead to our connecting line. This area is called the **Shape Collection**.

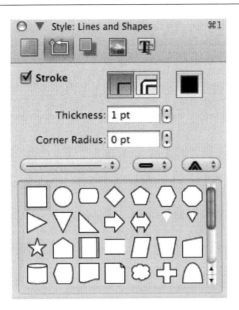

More precisely we are looking at the section with a lot of small shapes—and this is where you select the diamond shape:

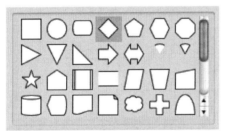

Your oblong shape is now a diamond! Pretty neat!

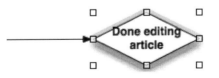

We need to do two things to be done with this step. Firstly, we need to amend the **Done editing article** text inside the diamond to **Publish article**. Secondly, we need to connect the arrow to our other diagram.

To change the text, double-click inside the diamond and type in the new the text. You will find the details of how to perform this in Step 3 (found earlier in this chapter).

To connect the arrow to the other diagram, click on the arrow. Then drag the end with the red circle to the **Done editing** shape. Notice how the shape is glowing red when you put your cursor on the shape.

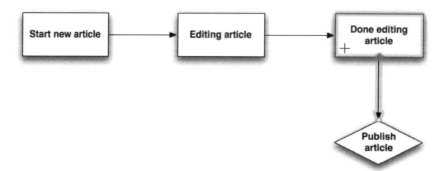

We now have the decision step in place, but without logical outcomes. There are two logical outcomes of this step. The article is either ready for publication — or if the article is to be published on the front page, we need to add another logical step — the step where the *Director of Communication decides if this article is worthy of the front page of our website.*

Let's end this step in the workflow by adding the notion that an article will not be published until the content has been reworked.

In practise, we want to connect the **Publish article** diamond with the **Editing article** oblong.

To achieve this, click on the **Line Tool** in the tool-selector on the canvas toolbar. You will notice a blue circle with the number 1 inside. This is an indication that the tool has been selected to perform its task once.

Now place the cursor on the **Publish article** diamond (it should now become glowing red) — then click. Now move the cursor to the **Editing article** oblong (this shape will also become glowing red), and click.

We now have a connection between these two shapes:

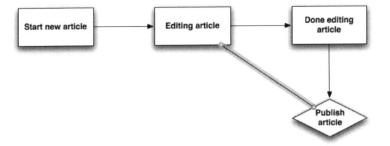

This does not look very good. We need to add an arrow to the line, and we need to add a corner to the line.

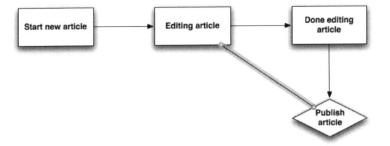

To add an arrow to a line, you need to use the Style inspector. If the style palette is not visible, press the ⌘+1 keyboard shortcut combination. The style palette is now visible. Click on the **Line and Shapes** style and you have access to the line properties.

As you notice with this inspector, there are several properties you can use to alter the appearance of a line.

In fact, you can alter certain properties on all drawn shapes (lines, circles, oblongs, and so on).

What is important for us is the following part of the line and shape inspector:

The left selector controls the appearance of the start of the line.

The right selector controls the appearance of line ending.

The middle selector is what kind of line you want to have.

Change the right selector to an arrowhead:

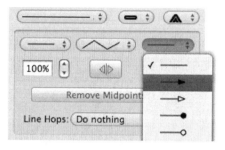

Then change the middle selector to **Orthogonal**.

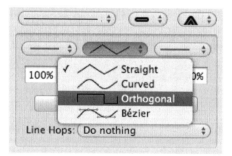

Your diagram should now look like this:

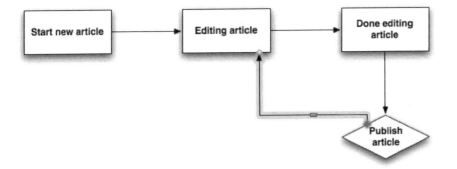

We are very close now. What we really want is to have the line between the **Editing article** oblong and the **Publish article** diamond, start at the left tip of the diamond.

To achieve this we need to add **Magnets** to the shapes. A magnet is a fixed point on a shape where the connection lines will attach themselves. The connection lines will automatically take the shortest path between two shapes that have no magnets—magnets will give you full control of where connection lines will attach to shapes. You will learn more about magnets in Chapters 3 and 4.

First select both the **Editing article** and the **Publish article** shapes:

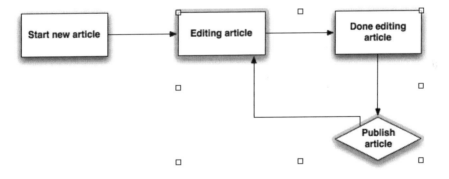

Then open up the **Connections property inspector**.

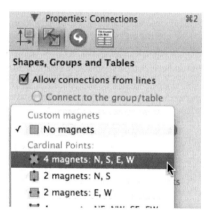

Click on the drop-down list saying **No magnets**, and select **4 magnets: N, S, E, W**.

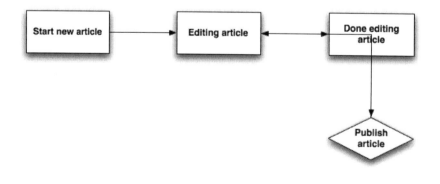

Unfortunately, now your drawing looks even worse than before.

To fix this, click on the arrowhead on the right of the **Editing article** oblong.

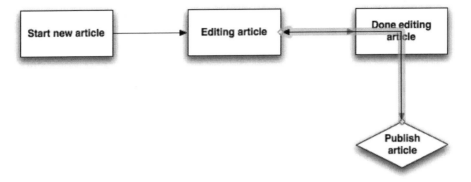

Remember earlier when you learned that the start of a line (or an arrow) has a small red circle and the ending point of the line has a small green circle.

All you have to do now is to drag the small red circle (it should be at the top of the **Publish article** diamond) to the left point of the diamond. Notice how we now have four small pink circles at each point of the diamond—these are the magnets we added earlier.

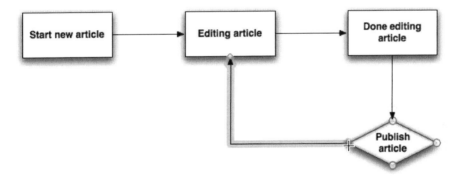

We need to add a text label to the line between the **Publish article** diamond, and the **Editing article** oblong.

To achieve this, click on the **Text Tool** in the tool-selector on the canvas toolbar. You will notice a blue circle with the number 1 inside. This indicates that the tool has been selected to perform its task once.

Notice how the cursor has changed its appearance (Ⓘ) to indicate that we are now working with the text shape.

Next you move the new cursor over the line—notice how the line will slightly glow to indicate that it is possible to associate the text with the line.

Click on the line and notice how OmniGraffle asks you for a **Line Label**—another visual cue that we are attaching a label to a line.

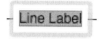

Enter **Not ready** in the text box, and your diagram should look like this:

Now the workflow states, that if the article is not ready for publication, it's back to the **Editing article** workflow step.

# Step 8: Workflow step—publish on the front page

This is another logic-based step much like the one in the previous step. We will thus copy the **Publish article** diamond, and amend the text associated with this shape to **Front page worthy**.

Highlight the **Publish article** diamond, and press the ⌘+*D* keyboard shortcut combination. As always this will duplicate the shape. This is the ideal way to continue, compared to adding a shape from the bottom up. The main reason is that we want to save the time it takes to set up the magnets again.

[ When duplicating any shape, including lines, every aspect such
as magnets, color, size, and fonts of the shape will be duplicated. ]

After duplicating the **Publish article** diamond, move the copy below the original.
The **Smart Alignment Guides** and the **Smart Distance Guides** will aid you in the
placement of the shape.

Notice that the thin blue line is going through the center of the **Done editing article**
oblong, the original **Publish article** diamond, and our copy of said diamond.

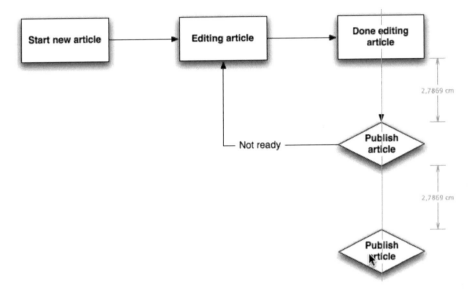

Let's change the text in our new diamond to **Front page worthy** by double-clicking
on the **Publish article** text. You will now have a brand new diamond with the correct
text – and the valuable magnets intact.

Now you need to connect an arrow between the **Publish article** diamond and the
**Front page worthy** diamond. You can either copy an existing arrow or you can create
the arrow from the ground up like you learned in Step 4.

Let's copy the arrow between the **Start new article** and the **Editing article** oblongs. Click on the arrow *once* to mark it, then hit the ⌘+*D* keyboard shortcut combination. You will now have a copy of the original arrow – the copy has the usual red and green circles on each end. Drag the green circle (which coincidently is the arrow head) to the top of the **Front page worthy** diamond – now notice how the pink colored magnets spring to life. Attach the arrowhead to the top of the diamond:

Now attach the end of the arrow (where you see the red circle) to the bottom of the **Publish article** diamond. The resulting diagram should look like this:

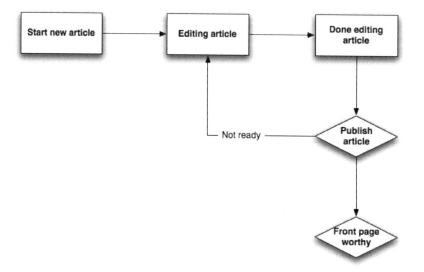

To complete this step in the workflow, we need to add a line label on the arrow connecting the two diamonds.

Click on the **Text Tool** in the tool-selector on the canvas toolbar. Notice the usual blue circle with the 1 inside indicating that this tool will perform its task once.

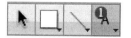

Also, notice how the cursor has changed its appearance () to indicate that we are now working with the text shape.

Next you move the new cursor over the line between the two diamonds. The line will slightly glow to indicate that it is possible to associate the text with the line.

Click on the line and notice how OmniGraffle asks you for a **Line Label** — another visual cue that we are attaching a label to a line. If you compare this line label, to the label you added in step 6 you will see that the label is always horizontal — no matter if the line is horizontal, vertical, or even oblique.

Change the label text into **Yes**. Your diagram should resemble the following one:

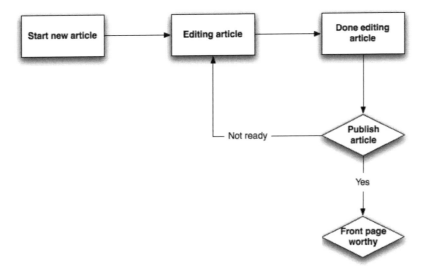

# Step 9: Workflow step—publish on the front page

This workflow step does in fact consist of three diagram elements. One element will indicate that the *Director of Communication* needs to be notified, one logical element which will show if the article is to be published on the front page, and one last element that says **Published on front page**.

Let's start with the notification of the Director. This is an oblong saying **Notify DoC**. Place this oblong to the left of the **Front page worthy** diamond.

To save you some time, not only duplicate an existing oblong, but also remember to duplicate an arrow in the same operation. Mark the **Start new article** along with its associated arrow and press the ⌘+*D* keyboard shortcut combination to duplicate these two elements. Also move them in line with the **Front page worthy** diamond.

**Copy as much as you can in each step**

As you build up your diagram, you will quickly see that a lot of the elements you use can be re-used elsewhere in your diagram. Copy and paste elements until your heart's content – or use the ⌘+*D* key combination to duplicate elements.

Change the text in the oblong to **Notify DoC**.

You will now end up with an oblong and an arrow pointing the wrong way.

Do not despair—this is easy to fix!

What you now want is to switch the direction of the arrowhead.

To change the direction of the arrowhead, you need to use the **Lines and Shapes property inspector**. If the style palette is not shown, use the ⌘+1 keyboard combination.

First you need to click on the line with the arrowhead you want to change the direction of. In your case, it's the arrow pointing away from the **Notify DoC** oblong.

Now click on the 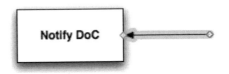 symbol in the **Lines and Shapes palette**. Presto! The arrow is now pointing the correct way.

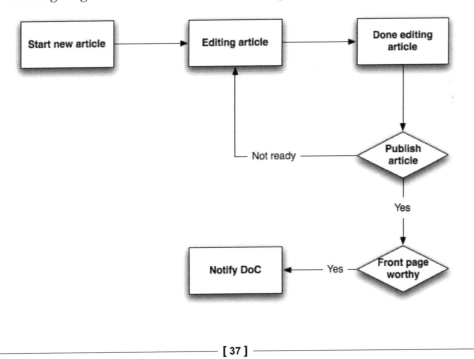

Now connect the red circle to the **Front page worthy** diamond; with the help of the Smart Alignment, and the Smart Distance Guides you can now align the **Notify DoC** oblong to both the **Editing article** oblong, and the **Front page worthy** diamond. These smart guides work in both directions at the same time.

Also, make sure to enter **Yes** on the line label – after all, the article is deemed to be worthy of publishing to the front page of the company website!

The resulting diagram should now look something like this:

gen.

The next part of the workflow is the logical step: The Director of Communication's decision if the article is of the quality for publishing on the front page or not. If the quality is not adequate, the author must amend and change the article some more. What we need is yet another diamond with an arrow pointing back to the **Editing article** oblong, and of course an arrow from the **Notify DoC** oblong.

Place this diamond to the left of the **Notify DoC** oblong.

You should now have come so far into your OmniGraffle education that you do not need the step-by-step handholding. If you are unsure about how to proceed, you could always take a peek at Step 6.

A hot tip is to copy both the **Publish** article diamond and its corresponding line going back to the **Editing article** oblong.

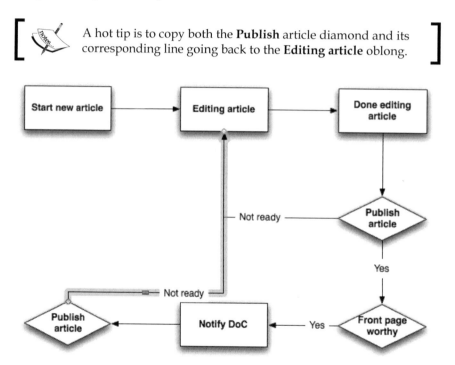

This does not look very pretty as it now stands.

There are two things you can do to fix this and make a "better look". First you can click on the little blue box next to the newly created line going from the newly created **Publish article** diamond. Now drag this upwards to align with the line from the other **Publish article** diamond:

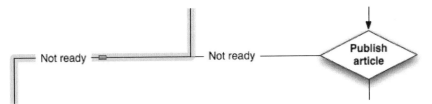

The second operation that you can do, is to move the **Not ready** line labels as close to their respective diamonds as possible.

> **How close should a line label be to a shape?**
>
> There are really no fixed rules on this. However, the whole point about creating a diagram is to ease the understanding of the reader. It is quite important to place the labels accordingly.
>
> A best practise regarding labels corresponding to diamonds in the kind of diagrams you are working with in this chapter is to have the label text as close as possible to the diamond – but always leave just enough line between the diamond and the line label so a reader can see the connection between the label and the diamond.

The resulting diagram is now only two steps until completion—so let's continue.

# Step 10: Publishing!

The workflow states that an article can either be published on the front page after the approval of the Director of Communication—or it can be published elsewhere on the web page.

So you'll need two oblongs—one under the Director of Communication's **Publish article** diamond, and one under the **Front page worthy** diamond.

Given the "magic" of the Smart guides, it will make sense to start with the non-front page publication part of the workflow. Duplicate any of the existing oblongs with the ⌘+D keyboard shortcut combination; change its content to read **Published on the company web**.

Now move it under the **Front page worthy** diamond, and see how the Smart Guides will not only help you align it correctly, but also space it out evenly!

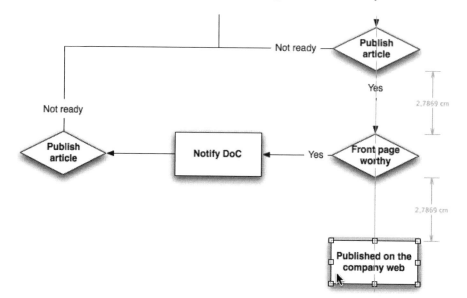

Now add an arrow from the **Front page worthy** diamond to the **Published on the company web** oblong. Add a line label saying **No**. Don't forget that the question is if the article was worth publishing on the front page or not. It still is published even if it's not front page material.

Now repeat the step from the diamond associated with the **Notify DoC** oblong. The only difference is that the text in the published oblong is **Published on the front page**, and the line label between the diamond and the oblong is **Yes**.

While performing this operation notice how the Smart Alignment Guides springs into life, assisting you in the optimal placement of this shape:

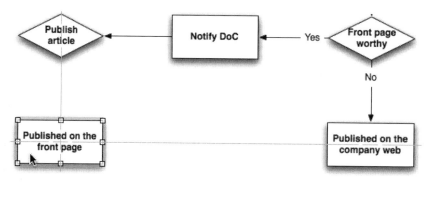

Congratulations! You have now finished your first OmniGraffle diagram. Good work. If you have followed all the steps, you'll now have a diagram resembling this:

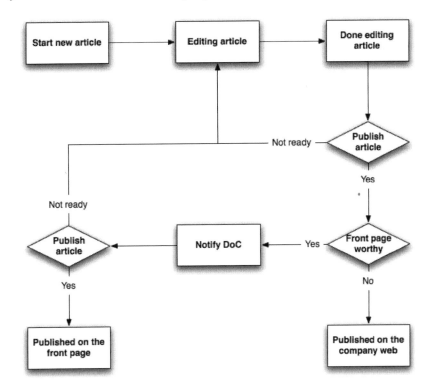

# Step 11: The icing on the cake—making your diagram spring into color

Seen from a design perspective, the lines are on the thin side. Also, only the boxes and the diamonds have shadows.

We can also enhance the diagram with color.

Why use color to enhance a diagram? One reason is to clearly extrude which parts of the workflow belong to the author, the editor, and finally the Director of Communication.

Let's first make all the lines a bit thicker. In the diagram portrayed in the book all lines are 1 point thick. This is a bit flimsy for the kind of diagram we have made here. Let's make all lines 2 points thick.

The easiest way to have all shapes 2 points thick is to select all the shapes, lines, and text. You can either do this with your mouse or simply use the ⌘+A keyboard combination. This keyboard shortcut command will select all shapes in your diagram.

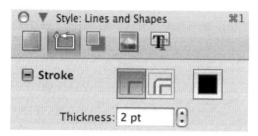

After you have selected all the shapes, go to the **Lines and Shapes property inspector** and then change **Thickness** to **2** pt. All your lines and shapes should now be a tad thicker than before.

Now you will add shadows to the lines.

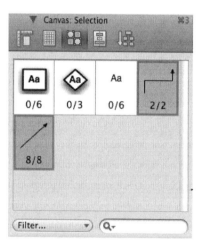

You do not want to simply mark the whole diagram again and add shadows. Let's do it using the very handy **Selection property inspector**. If the inspector is not visible, just use the ⌘+3 keyboard shortcut combination, or use the **Inspectors** program menu.

This inspector shows you all the various shapes that are present in the current canvas. The numbers under each shape tells you the total number of a given shape, and the number of currently selected shapes of the same type.

Hold down your *Shift* key while selecting the two arrow-lines present.

Now use the **Shadow property inspector** and enable the checkbox.

All your lines now have a shadow.

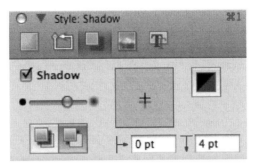

**A word of caution**

Not every shape in a diagram will look good with a shadow. If you believe that your diagram is best without shadows altogether, then remove all shadows. One important point about diagrams is to make information and ideas easier to understand for the reader. If shadows add to the understanding, then everything is good. The exception is of course if you just want to make a nice looking diagram with all the bells and whistles on.

Let's move on to putting some color into the diagram. We'll need three colors, one for each stakeholder in the process. The colors will indicate which part of the workflow belongs to which stakeholder.

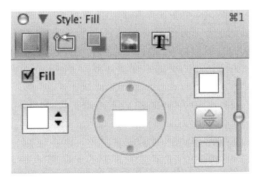

Start with selecting the **Start new article** oblong. Next, use the **Fill property inspector**. This is the inspector that governs how shapes are to be filled. On the right hand side of the inspector there are two squares. Click on the topmost square and the color-picker will appear.

If you have used other programs on the Macintosh where you could select colors, you'll notice that this may look and behave much like what you are used to from other Macintosh software titles.

There are several ways to choose a color, and what you see here is the **Crayons** color selection. Compared to the other modes of choosing colors, the crayons are quite limited with regard to the actual number of colors available.

However, for a lot of diagrams, like the one you now are working on, only a few colors are needed. As a general rule *less is more* when coming to use colors in diagrams. Try not to fall into the trap of using too many colors.

Now, choose the lightest green color you can find on the palette. It's crayon number 2 from the left on the bottom row.

Your oblong will now be in a lime green color.

Let's color the rest of the author's task with the same color.

You can of course repeat the process two more times for the **Editing article** and the **Done editing article** oblongs. However, OmniGraffle has a more efficient way to copy the whole look and feel of a shape onto another shape. The shapes do not even need to be of the same type.

# The Canvas Style Tray

Select the green **Start new article** shape and look at the bottom left of the canvas. You will notice a set of small icons. This is called the **Canvas Style Tray**.

The Style tray contains style properties or attributes for a selected object. You'll see a collection of small squares. In OmniGraffle "speak", each of these small squares is called a **style chit**. The left-most chit is a collection of all style properties for the currently selected object – this chit is the **Complete Style Chit**.

The other chits are, in succession, the fill style, the line stroke style, the image style, the shadow style, the actual shape, the font for the same, and finally the text placement.

Now you can drag the complete style chit over the **Editing article** and then the **Done editing article** oblongs to replicate all styling aspects of the **Start new article** oblong. Notice how the shape starts to glow when you hover over the oblongs while dragging the chit. This is a visual cue that you can drop the complete style chit onto the shape.

It is also possible to drag any of the chits onto the **Selection property inspector**.

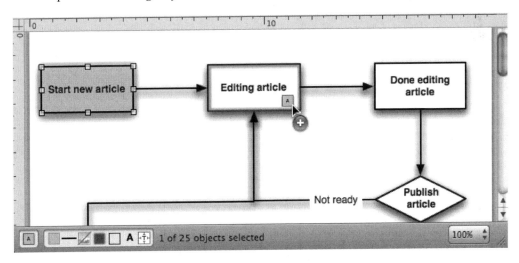

Let's say you want to have the various labels using the same font type, size and color as our oblongs – then you just drag the font chit (number two from the right) onto the line labels. If you really want to save some headaches – just drag the font chit onto the **Canvas: Selection Aa** object.

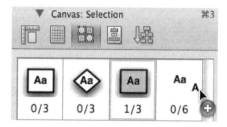

**Use of fonts – do not get carried away**

When people first got access to graphical computer user interfaces in the early 90s and a word processor that was able to display more than one font – people went on a "font rampage". This syndrome was known as Desktop Publishing Sickness.

Even if your diagramming software can "do anything" – do not become either fontblind or colorblind.

General rule of thumb: If you use more than two different kinds of fonts – rethink your design.

Now you need to color the tasks belonging to the editor. These are the two decision diamonds along with the oblong on the right-hand side of the diagram. For this task, you should really use the *color style chit*, and not the *complete style chit*. The reason is that if you use the complete style chit, and drop this over the **Published on the company web** oblong, the oblong will become a diamond – and this is **not** what you want.

We suggest that you use the mauve color, this is the fourth crayon from the right, on the bottom row.

Finally, the last step: Color the resulting two oblongs and diamond, which belong to the Director of Communication. The color we would love to use here a light orange one – you will find this as the first crayon on the bottom row.

You may notice that when the diagram is done in flying colors, the shadow under the arrows does **not add clarity** to the diagram. In fact, the shadows under the arrows make the diagram look murky. If you remove these shadows, you should have a diagram that looks like the one below.

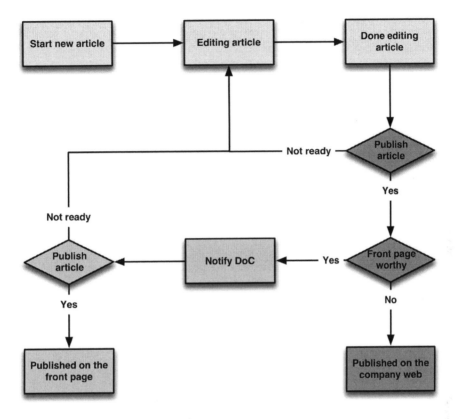

If you want to see the finished diagram in full color—please open the file named your first diagram.png found in the Chapter 1 folder in the download bundle.

# More on moving shapes around the canvas

So far, you have used your mouse to move a shape by selecting the shape, holding down the mouse key and then dragging the shape to its new location.

You can also select more than one shape and move all shapes at the same time.

When you move a shape, any correctly connected connection lines will be glued to the shape so you do not have to reattach these.

If you hold down the *Shift* key while you try to move a selected shape – you are restricted to movement in the horizontal or vertical plane. This is great if you need to move your shape either horizontally or vertically. Holding down the shift key will also prevent the shape skewing out in the other direction.

If you quickly need to rotate a shape, you can hold down the *command* key (⌘) while the mouse pointer is placed on top of a shapes selection handle. You can now click and drag the shape into its new angle.

Start by creating a new canvas and place a rectangle on the canvas.

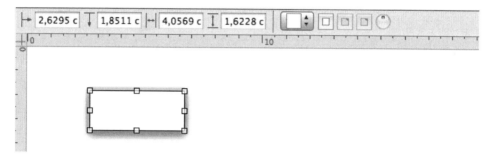

Hold down the command key and watch the mouse pointer change from an arrow to semi-circled double arrow (↻).

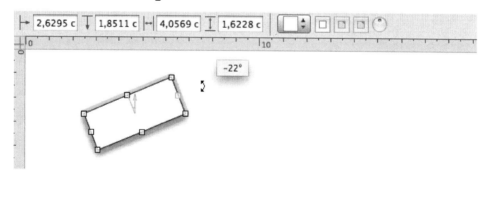

You can now rotate the shape into its new angle. To add more control, you can also hold down the *Shift* key to limit the rotation to incremental steps of 15°.

A more controlled, very precise rotation is achieved by using the Geometry property inspector, which you'll learn about in Chapter 3.

Even if you are going to use your mouse to move shapes most of the time, there are a few other more precise ways to move a shape (or a collection of shapes). Just use your arrow keys to move a selected shape one pixel at a time. Holding down the *Shift* or option key will increase the number of pixels moved to 9.

# Saving diagrams

You save a diagram by either using the **File | Save** or **File | Save As** menu commands, or you can use the ⌘+S or ⌘+⇧+S keyboard shortcut combinations. The save or save as dialog is the standard Macintosh one, thus you should feel quite at home.

Confusingly, on the Macintosh a file might really be a folder. A good example of this behavior is the Application folder. The "applications" (like OmniGraffle) are really a folder on their own with a special file structure. In these folders you will find a lot of supporting files and directories.

This collection of files is called a **bundle**. For applications we have Application bundles—and data saved by an application is called a **file bundle**.

OmniGraffle *might* store your diagram in a file bundle. If you let OmniGraffle store your diagram in a file bundle, you cannot send this as an attachment as it is really a directory.

If you want to send your OmniGraffle diagram in an email, you have two choices: You can either create an archive of the file, or you can force OmniGraffle to save your diagram as a single file.

If you want to choose to save the diagram as a single file, or a file bundle, you will have to use the Document: **Document property inspector**. If the inspector is not visible, just use the ⌘+4 keyboard combination, or use the **Inspectors** program menu.

In this property inspector you have a drop-down menu called **File format options**. In in this drop-down menu, choose **Save as flat file** if you need to e-mail your diagram.

You might ask if there is a drawback to saving diagrams as flat files, compared to creating an archive of the file bundle. Without going into too many details, the answer is that saving your diagram might take up more space when being sent by email, compared to creating an archive of the file bundle.

An alternative is to check the **Compress on disk** option in the **Document property inspector**.

Without compression, the diagram you created in this chapter will take up approximately 128 kilobytes of space. With compression, the document will only take 52 kilobytes. If your diagram becomes a bit elaborate, the size can become quite big. It is not unknown for diagrams to become several megabytes in size. Sending documents of such size can be cumbersome.

# Exporting diagrams

If your co-workers, friends or family have not installed OmniGraffle or perhaps even don't use a Macintosh (such a shame!) you can still share your diagrams by exporting your diagram. To access the export dialog, use the **File | Export** command, or by using the ⌥+⌘+*E* keyboard shortcut combination.

There are several unique OmniGraffle options in this dialog that you should familiarize yourself with (however, it's a bit out of the scope for us to go into the details of the common options like navigating your files, creating new folders, and so on).

The first thing you must decide is the **Format** of your export file. OmniGraffle supports several well-known formats—but for common, inter-office use you should either use **PNG bitmap image** or **JPEG bitmap image**. If your exported diagram is to be used in another Macintosh application, it might be more suitable to use **PDF** or **EPS vector image**.

If you decide to use JPEG bitmap, a tailored dialog box for JPEGs will be shown instructing you to choose the amount of compression. Always choose the best quality possible unless your drawing is really enormous.

In fact, most of the various formats will add their own tailored dialog box.

The **Export area** is a drop-down menu where you can export either just selected shapes, a specific region, the current canvas, or the whole document. If you just want to export your diagram without any white space around your diagram – select all the shapes (that is, select the whole diagram by using the mouse or the ⌘+S keyboard combination), then choose the **Current selection** from the dropdown.

The **Scaling** should be set as appropriate. The value in this dialog really depends on what you are going to use your exported drawing for. If it's only for showing a draft of the drawing to a co-worker, then 100% is more than good enough. If you want to use your drawing in printed matter like a brochure, then 150% or even 300% is needed, depending on the size of your printed matter. You will have to ask your printer about this.

The **Bitmap resolution** is also dependent on where your exported image is going to be used. For printed matter, 150 or 300 **dots per inch** is adequate. If your diagram is going to be used in a Powerpoint or Keynote presentation, 92 dots per inch is enough.

# Handy tips regarding inspectors

So far you've have only selected an inspector palette by clicking on the corresponding icon.

More than once you had to switch between the various palettes within the same selector.

If you want to have an inspector palette always activated, you can double-click on the corresponding icon.

As you can see in the screenshot there are small padlock icons on top of the Fill property inspector, the Lines and Shapes property inspector, and the Shadow property inspector.

This is a visual indication that these inspectors are always visible when using the Style selector.

To achieve this, just double-click on one of the property inspector icons to toggle the sticky activation on or off.

Those inspectors which contain input fields, can do simple arithmetic operations such as add, subtract, mutiply and divide. Some of the fields even take on the % sign, so entering 25% will effectively divide the current number by four.

Just enter the numbers you want to add, delete, and so on, exit the input field, and the new value appears. This is suitable if you want to halve or extend the length of a line or the size of a shape.

Let's say the current corner radius is set to **36** points.

Entering **/ 2** behind the **36** and hitting the *Enter* key (↵), or just exiting the input field, will not only change the content of the field to 18, but it will of course also amend the shape.

Even if your OmniGraffle document is set up in one particular measurement unit (that is, cm, inches, and so on), entering another unit in the input box will make OmniGraffle automatically calculate what you entered into the chosen measurement unit for the document.

# Tips and pitfalls—tips on how to make great visual diagrams

As information is becoming more and more complex, people like to have some visual help with understanding the information provided. This is where diagramming comes to the rescue. However, if your diagrams are not visually appealing and easily digestible, your carefully crafted diagram won't communicate your information in the way you like.

Diagramming is really communication. There is a substantial field of study out there, which only deals with the psychology of communication. It is outside the scope of this book to go into the theoretical background on the best way of visually presenting an idea (consider, as an example, some of the works of Edward Tufte). What you will learn in this section are a few handy tips that you may or may not follow. If you decide to follow these tips, your visual diagramming will not go wrong.

However, do not follow these tips as "rules". Obey them if they make sense and disobey them when they get in your way. Most importantly, don't lose sight of, or forget what you want to communicate with your diagram.

If you are well versed in graphical design — you can skip these steps.

# Tip 1: Do some planning before you start

OmniGraffle may be the best diagramming tool on the Macintosh. Complex diagrams are still a lot of (hard) work to get right, even with the aid of a computer. OmniGraffle is still just a diagramming tool — it will not do your thinking processes for you.

For small and simple diagrams where you have full knowledge of what you want to communicate, you can start working directly in OmniGraffle. However, for bigger and more complex diagrams, it may be easier to start your thought process using a white board, or some paper and a pencil.

If you still insist on using a computer for organizing your thought processes, you should take a look at OmniOutliner from the same people that make OmniGraffle. The cool thing about using OmniOutliner is that you can import your outliner documents into OmniGraffle and then OmniGraffle will create a diagram for you.

If outlining is too simple, and you are more used to mind mapping — there are some simple mind mapping stencils at Graffletopia. However, you may be better off using a specialty tool like MindManager from MindJet Corporation (http://www.mindjet.com/).

> A very good example of planning ahead is traffic signs. Designing traffic signs takes into account the driver's needs and requirements (that is, easy to understand pictograms going by in 120 km/h on the highway). These signs may seem simple to create – but a lot of work has been put into them to make them this simple. Even if you have not seen a given sign before, there is a good chance that you will understand it's meaning without further explanation.
>
> A good diagram should be like a well designed traffic sign.

# Tip 2: Colorize gently

The old adage that "less is more" really applies to diagramming at large.

Use light colors whenever possible when filling shapes. Try not to mix strong and light colors on the same diagram.

If want to use text in colored shapes – take into account the contrast of the background color and the text. Light colors should have black text, and strong colors should have white text. Stick to either black or white text.

Use as few colors as possible – never use *yet-another-color* just because you can.

If you need ideas on which colors *may* match each other you should investigate the software tools found on the ColorJack website (`http://www.colorjack.com/`). The ColorSphere and the swatches are a good starting point.

Another interesting website to get some ideas on good color combinations is the *Kuler* community. In this community users are both sharing their own color swatches, and can vote on the best-looking color swatches in the community. You find *Kuler* community at `http://kuler.adobe.com/`.

If you need to use colored text on a colored background – and really care about the readability (contrast) of your message (which you should), then you should try the *Colour Contrast Check* tool from `snook.ca` – go to `http://www.snook.ca/ technical/colour_contrast/colour.html` and experiment with foreground and background colors.

# Tip 3: Use few fonts

The rule of thumb to use on any publication with regards to font use: Never use more than two fonts.

Unless for the title of your diagram, avoid using serif fonts. Serif fonts have small details on the end of each stroke making up a letter. A very good example of a serif font is Times Roman.

The text you are reading right now is set in a serif font. The various headings found throughout this book are without serifs. These fonts without serifs are also known as *sans serif fonts*.

Good diagramming fonts are Helvetica, Futura, Optima, and Lucida Grande. All these fonts are sans serif fonts, and readily available from the *Fonts stencil* found in the Common stencil directory. This said, if your main document is not using any of these fonts—try to match your diagram fonts with your main document.

Though one of the "rules of thumb" regarding fonts and types is not to use ALL CAPS, there may be times when it is appropriate for your diagram. The same also is true regarding starting a word with an upper case letter. It *may* look better to start a word using lower case.

# Tip 4: Consider your output media

If your diagram is going to appear in a printed report, thin lines may be better than thicker lines.

If your diagram is going to appear on a wall poster—thicker lines will probably be better than thinner lines as the reader is reading the poster from a distance.

If your diagram is going to appear only on screen, thicker lines may be better than thinner lines, but try not to go beyond 2 points thickness.

A thin line is a 1 point thick line—a thicker line is 2 points or more.

# Tip 5: Symmetry is better than asymmetry

By nature, our brains tend to seek symmetry. Symmetry helps your diagram look balanced. Balance makes your diagram look more professional.

There is a caveat regarding visual symmetry: Visual symmetry does not equal mathematical symmetry. A good example of mathematical symmetry is the income diagram you will create in the next chapter. The cylinders below the blue arrows are mathematically correct but if you study the diagram you might get a nagging feeling that there is something not quite right. However, you cannot really put your finger on what the problem is. This is probably due to the lack of visual symmetry.

Any educated graphics designer (architect, photographer, illustrator, and so on) will tell you that you should favor visual symmetry rather than mathematical. If you are unsure about how to do this—just create diagrams that "feel and look right". If this fails, go down the mathematical symmetry route.

# Tip 6: Have one, and only one, focus point

The focus point is the most important part of your diagram.

Creating diagrams means that you will have several elements in your diagram. If you are not careful, your readers will not "get" your diagram without spending a lot of time studying the details. It is really important to have as few focus points as possible. If you can get away with only one focus point – this is excellent. If your number of focus points increases beyond five, your diagram runs the risk of becoming *everything and the kitchen sink* – as such, you should really go back to your planning stage!

If your diagram is conveying more than one message, try to make more than one diagram. Even if your audience is versed in the subject it will often pay to either divide the diagram – or create separate ones.

# Tip 7: Apply the Golden Ratio to stand alone diagrams

If your diagram is not part of an accompanying and explanatory text, you should apply the so-called Golden Ratio. Another name for the Golden Ratio, is the Rule of Thirds. In practise you divide your page into thirds, both horizontally and vertically. You will now have a grid of nine boxes. However, it's where the horizontal and vertical lines cross each other that you should concentrate. This is the part of your diagram where you should place the most important elements.

# Tip 8: Use titles, figure captions, and legends

Stand-alone diagrams must always have a title telling the reader what the diagram is about.

If your diagram is part of a book or a report, you may want to include figure captions – at least if you reference your diagram at more than one place in the text. Instead of addressing the diagrams as "*In the second diagram from the bottom on page 34, we see that ...*" – put a figure caption below the diagram, and you can now address the diagram in the text as "*In fig. 12, we see that ...*".

If your diagram contains elements that may not be intuitive for the reader, then add a legend to your drawing. If the lines between elements have different colors — then you absolutely need a legend to explain the difference between the red and the green lines.

It may be an excellent idea to place the legend inside a box a bit away from the diagram with a readable heading stating: *Diagram legend*.

# Tip 9: Be liberal with white space

Use space around your elements. Do not cramp them together, as this will make your diagram look messy and dirty.

It's better to use a whole extra page in *landscape* mode in a report for an important diagram, rather to compress the diagram to fit within the text.

In the planning stage of your diagram, take white space into account – and you may end up with a different layout that is more fitting for your report than your original plan.

A lot of times your diagram will end up in a report or on a web page. Most of these places adhere to portrait-based layouts. It may be a good thing trying to make your diagram fit a portrait-based layout – rather than sticking to using landscape out of habit.

# Tip 10: Be consistent

Never use two different shapes for the same kind of element.

Never use two different colors on shapes or lines to convey the same meaning.

Never use different fonts, and font sizes, within the same types of shapes.

Let's say you need to have a diagram involving animals in the general sense. If you can't find a drawing or a picture of a group of animals – use the same animal concisely. Also, use a shape/picture/drawing (animal) that people recognize.

# Summary

This first chapter has given you the means to understanding the basics of creating diagrams in OmniGraffle and then exporting your diagram for other users.

You have also learned to:

- Create various shapes like oblongs and diamonds
- Connect two or more shapes with lines
- Add arrow-heads to lines
- Add text both to shapes and labels to lines
- Create basic styles for shapes
- Copy partial or complete styles from one shape to another

In the next chapter, you will learn everything there is about stencils. A stencil is a collection of ready-made shapes. OmniGraffle has very good support for stencils and using these will save you a heap of time and frustration.

# 2
# Stencils

The previous chapter taught you how to build diagrams from the ground up, using only the built-in shape tool. This chapter will extend your OmniGraffle proficiency by showing you that Stencils are great time savers.

If a picture is worth a thousand words, then a good diagram is worth tenfold. We'll go through a few simple, easy to remember rules, that will make your diagram stand out from the crowd.

In this chapter, you are going to get an introduction to **Stencils** and the **Stencils Library** (pictured next). The chapter will continue extending your knowledge into managing and creating your own Stencils.

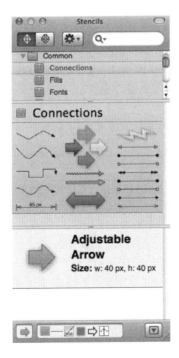

A very good reason for creating your own stencils is to select the most common shapes you use in your day-to-day diagramming and put this into a *favorite shapes stencil*.

OmniGraffle does have a **Favorite Stencils** collection available. You'll later learn how to manage this. However, the name *favorite shape stencil* does not indicate that such a function is built into OmniGraffle. Even if it's not built in, this is easy to do on your own.

In this chapter, we will take a close look at the following topics:

- Your first stencil based diagram — teaching your kids how to save $0.50
- Using the stencils palette
- An introduction to the built-in OmniGraffle stencils
- Sources for finding and importing external stencils
- Creating your own stencil and importing third party graphics
- Exporting and sharing your stencils with other users
- Successfully importing Microsoft Visio templates

# Defining a stencil

In *Chapter 1, Getting Started with OmniGraffle* you learned that **Stencils** are a collection of ready-made shapes. The shapes can be anything from simple shapes such as a line or a circle, to a group of shapes, and even more complex shapes such as imported graphics objects from external sources.

A stencil often has a name that connotes its meaning or theme; this is especially true of third party stencils dealing with a given subject. A good example is the author's stencil named Rounded Numbers. This stencil has not only a lot of rounded numbers for annotation purposes but also rounded letters.

# The stencil library

There are several ways of opening the **stencil library**. If you cannot see the stencil palette shown in the beginning of this chapter, you can either use the ⌘+ 0 keyboard shortcut, or you can click on the stencil symbol (⊞) on the canvas toolbar. As a last resort you can use the **Window | Stencils** menu command.

The stencils library has several elements that we will explore in the following section.

The second part of this chapter deals with creating and managing your stencils.

# Overview of the Stencils palette

Each section will be covered in detail later in this chapter.

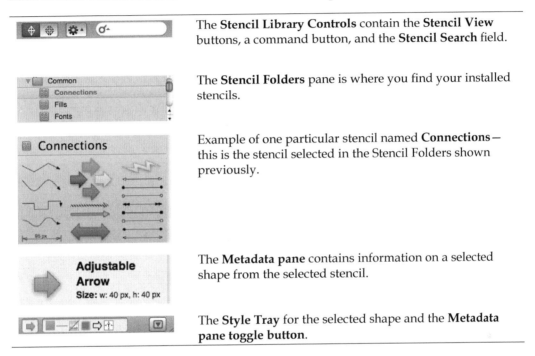

The **Stencil Library Controls** contain the **Stencil View** buttons, a command button, and the **Stencil Search** field.

The **Stencil Folders** pane is where you find your installed stencils.

Example of one particular stencil named **Connections** — this is the stencil selected in the Stencil Folders shown previously.

The **Metadata pane** contains information on a selected shape from the selected stencil.

The **Style Tray** for the selected shape and the **Metadata pane toggle button**.

# Built-in stencils

OmniGraffle comes installed with 30 stencils. These range from common shapes — much the like one you worked with in your first diagram — to complex shapes for space planning.

The built-in stencils are grouped in various folders or collections — **stencil folders**. Later in this chapter, you'll learn to add stencils from external sources.

# Common stencils

The seven stencils in this group are a collection of ready-made connections, color, and texture fills, font examples, and various shapes.

- The connection stencils contain various arrow configurations that can be used to connect shapes. Using these stencils is a time saver compared to creating the various shapes manually. This stencil has both straight, curved, orthogonal, and Bézier enabled arrow lines.

- You have two basic diagramming stencils, which cover some shapes – with or without magnets. When you created your first diagram, you could have used the shapes with the magnets instead of making your own magnets.

- The fill stencil has several ready-made color combinations along with a few textures (textures are only available in OmniGraffle Professional). Use the Style Tray found in the bottom of the stencil library to apply the color combination to your existing shapes.

- The fonts stencil contains a font very suitable for diagramming.

- OmniGraffle contains a collection of dynamic information called **variables**. These variables can be found in the **Edit | Insert variable** menu. To save you some time, there is a built-in stencil with these variables readily available. Variables are covered in great detail in *Chapter 7, Property Inspectors*.

# Maps stencils

This folder contains seven stencils covering the following regions of the earth: Africa, Antarctica, Asia, Pacific, Russia, Middle East, Europe, North America, South America, and USA.

Some of these maps, like Asia, Pacific, Russia, and Middle East are all grouped into one stencil. Also in this stencil you will find parts of Europe. This may seems a bit confusing at first, but you'll quickly notice which maps have the best representation of the country you need to use.

# Organization charts stencils

There are three built-in stencils dealing with organizational charts. These range from very "serious" and plain looking, to chart elements with nice color combinations, and to elements where you can insert pictures of the people in your organization.

# Science stencils

In the science folder we find stencils for Boolean gate construction, basic shapes for Circuit engineering, and a periodic table.

# Software stencils

One of the places where diagramming software is used today is in software engineering. There are a few schools of diagramming in this area. OmniGraffle can both accommodate the traditional Flow chart style — and the modern **Unified Modeling Language** (**UML**) style.

For you **Information Architects** (**IA**) out there — you will find the Garret IA symbols. For more information on the Garret IA symbols, please see `http://www.jjg.net/ia/visvocab/`.

No software project is complete without a database model, and no documentation of a database model is complete without an entity-relationship (ER) diagram. OmniGraffle does of course support ER diagrams out of the box.

# Space planning stencils

OmniGraffle may not be the best software for your architectural endeavors, but if all you want to do is create a layout model of your kitchen restoration project — or show your spouse how you would love the new bathroom — then OmniGraffle is for you.

Beware that the stencils in this stencil folder are geared towards the use of imperial measuring units. This is great news if you live in the USA, Burma, or Liberia — the only countries in the world still using imperial units.

# Your first stencil-based diagram

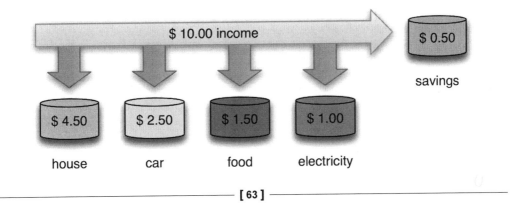

Let's create a very simple flow type of diagram by using the stencils library. The diagram will explain how your income should be used.

These kinds of diagrams may be ideal to use when trying to explain to your kid that a financial goal is to save money.

Start with a blank canvas—either using the **File | New** menu command, or simply using the ⌘+N keyboard shortcut combination.

# A helping guide

Before you start, you'll need to make sure that your canvas has **rulers** enabled. Use the menu command **View | Rulers** to enable canvas rulers. You should now see both a horizontal and a vertical ruler on the top, and to the left, of your canvas.

The reason why you need these rulers, is that they will enable you to easily add some visual guides to your canvas.

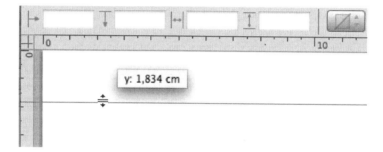

You can add guides by using the **Arrange | Guides | Add Horizontal/Vertical Guide**, and then moving the guide around.

Place your guide in the middle of the canvas.

You can also use the **Arrange | Guides | Clear Manual Guides** menu command.

If you are using OmniGraffle Professional, you can just place your mouse cursor over either the horizontal or the vertical ruler, then click the mouse button and drag a lilac colored guide to the canvas. To remove a guide, just click-and-drag the guide back to the ruler you got it from. Horizontal guides are to be dragged to the top ruler, and vertical ones to the left ruler.

# The incoming cash flow

The first thing you'll need is a filled horizontal arrow. Navigate to the **Common** style folder, and open the **Connections** stencil. Find the yellow adjustable arrow, and drag this onto your blank canvas.

You will need to extend the length of the arrow. At the head of the arrow, you'll notice a small green square. Now click on this square and drag the arrow horizontally to the right. You might find it hard to not slope the arrow upwards or downwards. To solve this issue about keeping your arrow horizontal, you could place it on top of the guide, and then click-and-drag the arrow.

However, there is a very simple way to achieve a very straight horizontal arrow: Just hold down the *Shift* key (⇧) while clicking and dragging. In fact, holding down the *Shift* key while extending a shape in either the horizontal or vertical direction will **always** keep things straight. Remember to release the mouse button **before** releasing the *Shift* key — if you do not, your arrow may end up sloped.

The text on the arrow should be **$ 10.00 income**. Kids may have trouble with big numbers, so using just 10 dollars may make them understand the reality of economics better. If you do not use dollar as your currency, feel free to use Euro, Kroner, Bath – or even seashells if you so prefer.

Notice the lilac horizontal guide on the very top of the arrow.

**Straight is really a multiple of 45°**

Holding down the *Shift* key will let you draw perfectly in a horizontal or vertical direction. However, you can also use this technique to draw in a perfect 45° angled slope.

Holding down the *Shift* key is really limiting your shape's slope to increments of 45°.

# Adding expense buckets

Now drag the blue adjustable arrows from the same stencil on to your canvas.

We are now going to rotate the arrow 90° to the left – making it point downwards.

Select the blue arrow, and locate the **Geometry property inspector** (covered in detail in chapter). On the right hand side of the inspector, you'll see a field saying **0°** along with a rotation control. Enter 90° into this field. When you click outside of the field, you'll see that the blue arrow now points downwards.

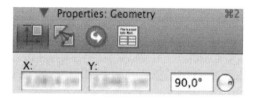

Place the blue arrow in such a way that its tail is just touching the yellow arrow.

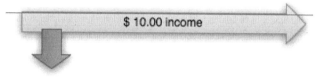

Next we need a bucket. There is no dedicated bucket symbol built into OmniGraffle—so we will have to use our imagination.

If you are familiar with information technology diagrams, you may have noticed the cylinder symbol used for databases. This may in fact look like a bucket, so let's use that. This symbol is not readily available – so you will have to adjust another shape into the cylinder form.

First you need an oblong.

Navigate to the **Common | Shapes** stencil in the stencils library—there you will find an oblong, drag this oblong under the blue arrow. Use the **Smart Alignment Guide** to help you place the oblong under the blue arrow.

Secondly, you will now convert the oblong into another shape. The shape we are looking for is the cylinder shape. This shape is often used as a conceptual hard drive or database shape.

Select the newly created oblong, if it's not selected already. Then you activate the **Line and Shapes property inspector** found in the Style selector. As you learned in Chapter 1, if you have selected a shape – you can easily change your selected shape into another shape. When you created your first diagram, you changed an oblong into a diamond shape. Now you just have to change your oblong into a cylinder shape.

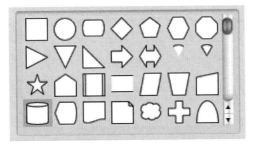

Now, fill the cylinder with a light gray color. Next, you see a part of the color picker, which is in fact the same palette as you saw in Chapter 1. Instead of using the "crayon box" palette ( ), you now select the third palette from the right – the Color palette ( ), as it's named.

You'll also see a **Palette:** dropdown – select **Classic Crayons** from this dropdown.

Now choose **Soapstone** as the color for the cylinder shape.

The main reason why you should use the list of colors, instead of the crayons you used in chapter one is that it's easier to remember a color name – than a position in the "crayon box".

Double-click on the cylinder shape and enter $ 4.50.

We will need to name this first bucket. Given that we're talking about 45% of our ten dollars – this is probably our mortgage. Mortgage is a very difficult word for a young person to deal with—so use the word "*house*" instead. To achieve this, you will need to put stand alone text under the cylinder shape.

Click on the **Text Tool** in the canvas toolbar, and then click somewhere under the cylinder and enter the text **house**. When done, use the Smart Alignment Guide to center the text correctly.

Your diagram should now look more or less like this:

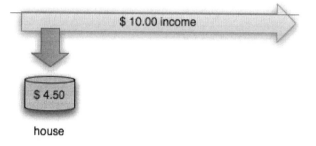

Now select the blue arrow, the gray cylinder, and the corresponding text and duplicate them using the ⌘+D keyboard combination. Instead of using ⌘+D you can also use the copy and paste from the **Edit** menu – or the ⌘+C followed by ⌘+V keyboard shortcut combinations.

Add three more buckets, named **car** ($ 2.50), **food** ($ 1.50), and **electricity** ($ 1.00). Change the colors or these new buckets to **banana** (for the car), **violet dusk** (for the food), and **fire** (for the electricity).

You may need to extend the length of the income arrow to accommodate the three extra cylinders.

At the end of the yellow income arrow, add a cylinder called **savings** ($ 0.50). Change this cylinder to a green color (a good suggestion is the color named *Ocean green*).

To put the icing on the cake, you should make the yellow income arrow overlap the blue vertical arrow. This is quite easy—all you have to do is select the yellow arrow and use the **Arrange | Bring to Front** menu command. If you feel more comfortable with keyboard shortcuts, then ⇧+⌘+F it is. However, the quickest way is to use the **Bring to Front** command (⊞) on the canvas toolbar.

You can now remove the guide by using the **Arrange | Guides | Clear Manual Guides** menu command.

You should now have a diagram that resembles the one shown next:

If you want to see the finished diagram in full color — please open the file named `your second diagram.png` found in the `Chapter 2` folder in the download bundle.

# External stencils

If you feel that the stencils that come with OmniGraffle are not adequate for your use, there are a few sources where you can get more stencils.

# Omni Group downloads

On the Omni Group website you will find a few selected stencils you can download. There are also some links to external stencil makers. Check out `http://www.omnigroup.com/products/omnigraffle/extras/`.

# Graffletopia

Graffletopia is the premier website for OmniGraffle stencils.

Graffletopia is a community effort open to anyone who has created a stencil. These stencils need not be very advanced (i.e. there is a stencil with just a mouse pointer), but a lot of the stencils available from the website can be quite complex.

As of writing this book, there are more than 400 different stencils, grouped in 12 categories. New stencils are added every week.

The good people at Omni Group (the makers of OmniGraffle) have recognized this valuable source – making it possible to search and import stencils from Graffletopia directly into OmniGraffle. You'll learn how to make the best of Graffletopia in the next section.

You should now take a break from reading this book and just head over to `http://www.graffletopia.com/` and browse the collection of stencils available.

# Commercial stencil sources

The stencils found on Graffletopia are free for everyone to download and use. However, not everyone wants to put his or her stencils on that website. There is at least one supplier of stencils that sells part of its stencil collection. We'll investigate this source later in the book.

# Importing MS Visio stencils and templates

It is also possible to import certain Microsoft Visio stencils. We are going to look at this in detail later in this chapter..

# Searching and importing stencils from Graffletopia

There are two methods of importing stencils into OmniGraffle: A manual method and an automatic method. You use the manual method if the stencils you are importing are not found on Graffletopia. Such stencils may be company-internal stencils, or even commercial ones.

# The manual method of importing any stencils

This method works with any stencils, not only the ones found at Graffletopia, but for the sake of explanation we'll use Graffletopia as an example.

Lets say you need to annotate your diagram, but adding a lot of lines and text will clutter up the diagram. A common way to annotate a diagram is to use numbers or letters surrounded by a circle. In the accompanying text you can then explain in length about each annotated point.

You start by creating small circles with numbers inside. You find this extremely tiresome after a while, and ask yourself if there is a ready-made stencil available.

You go to the Graffletopia home page and enter **numbers** in the search box on the website. You are now presented with the search result and one of the returned answers looks to be what you are looking for.

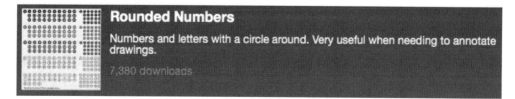

You click on the preview, and are presented with a close-up of the stencil. You decide that this is exactly what you need.

You click on the download link—and the file ends up as a ZIP file in your **Download** folder. After double-clicking on the ZIP file—a file with the `.gstencil` suffix is extracted into the folder. This file needs to be moved to your personal `Library/Application Support/OmniGraffle/Stencils/` folder.

**Finding your Library folder**

You can find your personal Library folder using the following steps:
1. Locate your hard disk icon on your desktop.
2. Click on the **Users** folder.
3. Click on your user name.
4. Click on the **Library** folder.
5. Continue clicking on the **Application Support** folder, then the **OmniGraffle** folder and finally the **Stencils** folder.

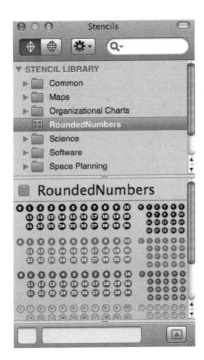

After you have moved the file, the stencil will automatically appear in your Stencil library as you can see in the preceding diagram. Compared to other software titles, you do not need to restart OmniGraffle to use the stencil—it's there and ready to be used.

The method of downloading and extracting a stencil from a ZIP file, and then moving the `.gstencil` file into your `Library/Application Support/OmniGraffle/Stencils/` folder is the only way to manually import stencils from third party suppliers who are not present at the Graffletopia website.

# The automatic method of importing stencils from Graffletopia

You learned a few pages ago that Graffletopia is integrated into OmniGraffle 5. If you are using OmniGraffle version 4 or earlier, you have no choice other than manually installing the stencil as outlined previously.

Instead of going to the Graffletopia website, you can search the website from within OmniGraffle. In the search box of the stencil library, you can click on the magnifying glass and be presented with a context sensitive menu. This menu will let you switch between local searches and searching on Graffletopia.

Select Graffletopia and enter *numbers*, and hit the enter key. You will now be presented with the search result that also includes the preview you saw on the Graffletopia website.

You may also extend the Stencils window to get a better view of the stencils preview.

When you have found the right stencil, click on the **Download** button. The stencil will be downloaded and you'll have a full view of the stencil.

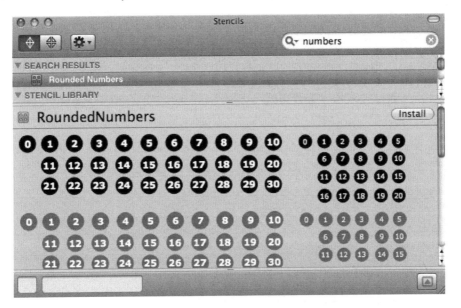

Even if you see the stencil in its full glory, it is still just a detailed preview. If you decide that this stencil is exactly, or very close to, what you are looking for, then press the **Install** button. The stencil is now installed into OmniGraffle, and will appear in the stencil library along with all your other stencils.

If you decide that this stencil is not for you, then you do not have to do anything, just continue working with OmniGraffle.

As your local stencil library grows, you will want to organize your stencils into folders, this is covered later.

**Annotations are not only for diagrams**

You can also use annotations for images. If you ever need to address various parts of a image, you can use OmniGraffle to achieve this. OmniGraffle can import several graphical formats or you can simply paste an image into the canvas. It is also possible to drag an image file from the finder onto the canvas. You then add the annotations and export the image with annotations as a JPG or a PNG file.

# Amending your income flow diagram

The diagram you created earlier in this chapter is a bit boring for a young person to understand. Adults may be happy with cylinders, but they are not very childish. Your job is to amend this diagram into a more childish design.

Let's start with the aim of the diagram: Saving $ 0.50. Why not use a piggy bank for this part of the diagram? If you search Graffletopia using the word **piggy bank**, you should find a stencil called **Cash Flow** which does have a piggy bank symbol. Install this and amend your diagram using the piggy bank instead of the cylinder.

Given that the symbol of the piggy bank is well known in the western world as a savings symbol, you may even remove the word **saving** below the symbol.

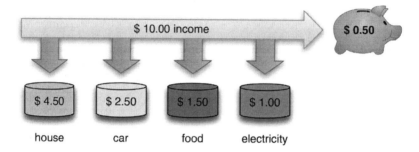

You can now continue amending your diagram with various symbols and shapes from existing stencils on Graffletopia. For instance, you could use the cash register from the **Cash Flow** stencil to replace the **food** cylinder.

A word of caution before you go completely crazy with various symbols in your diagrams: Unless all the symbols you want to use have the same look and feel, your diagram may suddenly look less than professional. This word of caution brings you to your next topic.

# The details of the Stencils palette

## Overview of the palette sections

Each section will be covered in detail later in this chapter.

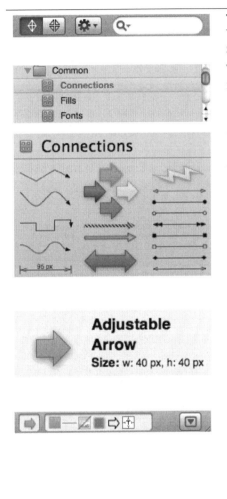

The **Stencil Library Controls** contain the **Stencil View buttons**, a command button, and the **Stencil Search field**.

The **Stencil Folders pane** is where you find your installed stencils.

Example of one particular stencil named **Connections**—this is the stencil selected in the Stencil Folders above.

If you click on a whole folder in the Stencil Folders pane, all the stencils found within the folder will be consecutively displayed. If you have a folder with very large stencils, it may feel that OmniGraffle is going completely bananas. If this happens you can either wait it out or force-quit the application. Remember that if you force-quit the application any unsaved work will be lost.

The **Metadata pane** contains information on a selected shape from the selected stencil.

The metadata contains the name of the shape and the size. For most shapes, the size you see in this pane does not limit the resizing capabilities a given shape has.

The **Style Tray** for the selected shape and the **Metadata pane toggle button**.

The Style Tray works just like the Style Tray in the canvas. See Chapter 1 for more information on the canvas Style Tray.

The **Metadata pane toggle** button hides or shows the Metadata pane. If you hide the pane, you will have more screen real estate for displaying the stencil. This can be crucial if one of your stencils is very big, or you have clicked on a folder in the Stencil Folders pane.

# The Stencil Library Controls

The Stencil Library has a few controls that are worth looking into as they will make your life a tad easier when working with a big stencil library. From left to right you see the two Stencil View Mode buttons which control how a stencil is displayed; An action button which let you do all sorts of stencil library control; Lastly the search field letting you look for stencils that are stored both locally and in an on-line stencil repository.

# The Stencil View Mode buttons

The **Stencil View Mode buttons** control whether shapes will be shown as the stencil author decided (left button), or if the shapes should be shown on a grid (right button).

The main difference between these two modes is that when using the grid all shapes become the same size.

In the following picture, the left version of the stencil is displayed how the stencil author wanted. The version to the right shows the stencil after the right **Grid View Mode button** has been enabled (that is, grid mode).

This stencil is named **USA** and is found in the **Maps stencil** folder.

On the left you see the map with all the various states in their correct positions. In the grid version you'll notice that there is really no order to the chaos, except that each state is in a well-defined space making things easier to find.

In this map example, this may not make much sense to you, but consider the following example. This is taken from a stencil with *often used shapes* that the author uses on at least a weekly basis. The shapes are collected from at least ten different stencils.

The stencil is quite big and contains lots of shapes, is not very organized, and the preview makes some of these shapes unreadable. Using the grid functionality makes a messy stencil organized with just one simple click.

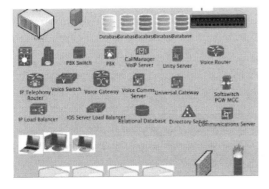 

# The Stencil Action button

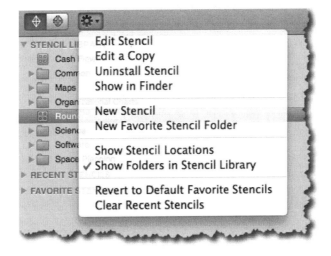

The **Stencil Action button** gives you access to useful functions.

| Function | Description |
| --- | --- |
| Edit stencil | If you have selected a stencil in the library and this stencil is not one of the stencils that came with OmniGraffle, you can edit the stencil. |
| | It's also possible to right-click on a selected stencil to get access to this function. |
| Edit a Copy | If you want to create a new stencil based on an existing one, you can use the Edit a Copy function to do this. |
| | It's also possible to right-click on a selected stencil to get access to this function. |
| Uninstall Stencil | If you are done using a stencil, you can uninstall it. Unless you are one hundred percent sure you are never going to use a stencil, there is no need to remove it from your system. It is better to spend a few minutes organizing your stencils gradually as your collection grows. |
| | It's also possible to right-click on a selected stencil to get access to this function. |
| Show in Finder | Except for the stencils that came with OmniGraffle you can quickly get access to the folder where the selected stencil resides. |
| | There are two common usage scenarios for doing this. One is to export the stencil to other users. Scenario number two is when you need to organize your stencil collection. Both scenarios will be covered later in this chapter. |
| | It's also possible to right-click on a selected stencil to get access to this function. |
| New Stencil | Use this function to create a new blank stencil. |
| | This function is also available from the **New \| New Resource \| New Stencil** OmniGraffle menu command. |
| New Favorite Stencil Folder | You can group your stencils in logical folders called Favorite Stencil Folders. |
| | This topic is covered later in this chapter. |
| Show Stencil Location | You can toggle this menu option so that each stencil in the Stencil Folder pane is also showing its location on the disk. |

| Function | Description |
|---|---|
| Show Folders in Stencil Library | Depending on if you activate this option, your stencil will be put into its respective folder.<br><br>If you de-activate this option, all your stencils will be sorted alphabetically. |
| Revert to Default Favorite Stencils | If you use the Favorite Stencils function a lot you will end up with a lot of favorite stencils. Instead of deleting each favorite stencil folder and single favorite stencils, using this function will revert the favorite section of the Stencil Folder pane back to its default setup. |
| Clear Recent Stencils | As you will learn in the section about the Stencil Folders pane, you will notice there is a **Recent Stencils** section.<br><br>Using this function will clear up the section. |
| Delete | This function is only available if you have selected one of the Favorite Stencil Folders. |
| Remove from Favorite Stencil Folder | This function removes a selected stencil from within a Favorite Stencil Folder. |

# The Stencil Search function

By using the **Stencil Search function**, you can search for stencils installed locally or you can search for stencils from the Graffletopia.com website.

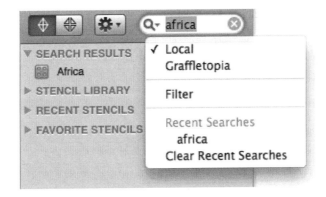

No matter how you search (locally or on Graffletopia) your search result will appear as a **SEARCH RESULTS** section in the **Stencils Folders** pane.

You can enter any search text criteria you want to look for in the **Search Field**. In the previous example, you'll notice that we have entered **africa** in the search field, and OmniGraffle displays the **Africa** stencil. Searching is case insensitive, and will not only search against the stencil name, but also any text belonging to shapes, notes, and other custom data that you have saved in your stencil.

When you click on the small triangle in the search field, you access the **Search Field popup** revealing a menu that controls how searches are performed.

You can select between searching locally or on Graffletopia. Earlier in Chapter 2, you learned how to search and install stencils from this online resource.

The **Filter** command found in the stencil search field, toggles what to display when clicking on a stencil in the **SEARCH RESULT** section of the **Stencil Folders** pane. If this menu command is enabled, shapes with text not matching your search criteria will be grayed out. This option makes it easy and quick to find your shape in a stencil.

The **Search Field** popup will also show your latest searches — very handy when you use the search function to switch between stencils in your stencil library.

# The Stencil Folders pane

The **Stencil Folders pane** is divided into several sections:

- The **STENCIL LIBRARY** section
- The **RECENT STENCILS** section
- The **FAVORITE STENCILS** section

If you have performed a search using the Search Field, you'll also see a section called **SEARCH RESULTS**.

---

Depending on whether the Show Folders in Stencil Library is enabled or not, your stencils may either be alphabetically sorted from A to Z or your stencils may be grouped into folders (this is the default behavior).

## The Stencil Library

The stencil library contains all installed stencils, both third party stencils and the ones that came with OmniGraffle. You have the choice to organize your stencils as you see fit. You will learn how to do this later in this chapter.

Third party stencils are installed in your `Library/Application Support/OmniGraffle/Stencils` folder. OmniGraffle has no provisions for using stencils found on a shared drive or a common folder on your computer — making sharing stencils for a small workgroup of people tiresome: Each user must install all the stencils the group has decided to use in their work.

The only way to install stencils for all users on the same computer is to use the `OmniGraffle.app` application directory. However, this should be avoided as you may inadvertently mess around with internal application settings, rendering OmniGraffle unusable.

## The Recent Stencils section

This section contains the last five stencils you selected. This also includes stencils which are not installed but only previewed from GraffleTopia website.

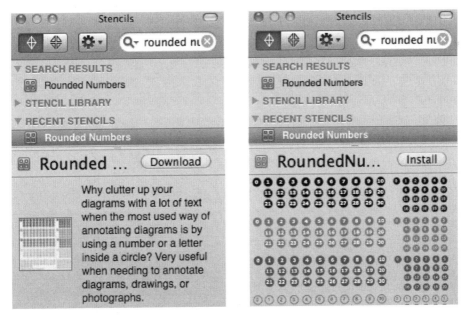

If you search for a stencil on GraffleTopia and click on the name in the **SEARCH RESULT** section, it will also appear in the **RECENT STENCILS** section.

Even if you clear your search so that the stencil is no longer found among the search results – you can still click on the Download and then the Install buttons when clicking on the stencil name in the **RECENT STENCILS** section.

## The Favorite Stencil section

By default the **Favorite Stencil section** contains the three stencil folders that were installed with OmniGraffle.

However, you may manage this section exactly as you want. You can delete the existing folders, you can add new folders, and you can drag and drop existing stencils into this section.

Deleting a stencil in this section does not remove the physical stencil from your hard drive. The stencil is not stored in the Favorite Stencil section, it's still stored in the library and only a pointer is stored in the **Favorite Stencil** section.

You can either right-click on a selected stencil or folder and choose **Delete** to delete. You can also use the **Stencil Action** button to achieve the same result.

To create a new folder within this section, right-click on any folder or stencil and use the New Favorite Stencil Folder menu action. As you also learned earlier in this chapter, the same function is also available from the **Stencil Action** button.

To add an existing stencil as a favorite, just drag the stencil from the **STENCIL LIBRARY** section into this section.

When all this is said, you may feel more comfortable organizing the stencils in the **STENCIL LIBRARY** section than adding stencils to the **FAVORITE STENCIL** section.

# The selected shapes Style Tray

The selected shapes Style Tray is found in the bottom of the **Stencils Palette**, and becomes active as soon as you select a shape in the stencil library. The Style Tray operates and behaves exactly the same as the **Canvas Style Tray** that you learned all about in Chapter 1.

As with the Canvas Style Tray, not all shapes will display all options.

If you are unsure about how the Style Tray works, please consult the relevant section in Chapter 1.

# Creating your own stencil

Making your own OmniGraffle stencil is nothing more than creating any other diagram.

Start by either using the **File | New Resource | New Stencil** menu command, or using the **Action** button found in the Stencil palette and execute the **New Stencil** command.

This will give you a new blank canvas. Notice that the title of the canvas contains the word **Stencil**.

Let's drag and drop shapes from other stencils so that we have our own *Favorite Shapes stencil*. This can be used to keep your often-used shapes.

Take the happy looking piggy bank from the **Cash Flow** stencil we used earlier, a few of the shapes in the **Connection stencil** (found in the Commons folder), add a few clouds and color these in various colors.

Save your stencils using the **File | Save** menu command (or use the ⌘+S keyboard shortcut command) as you would save any other OmniGraffle documents.

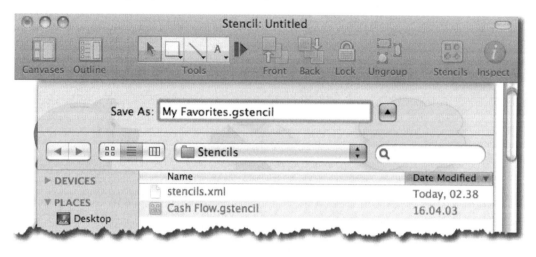

OmniGraffle will open the file-save dialog directly in the program's stencil disk folder.

After you have saved your new stencil, it will appear in the stencil palette automatically.

In Chapter 4 and Chapter 5, you will learn how to create your own shapes. These shapes can of course be put in your stencil.

# Creating stencils with cool graphics

You may have already noticed that some of the stencils contain some pretty cool graphics, or clip-arts. The happy piggy bank from the Cash Flow stencil is a very good example. In fact, the whole Cash Flow stencil is a collection of fancy clip-art made into a stencil.

Before you go ahead and collect lots of nice looking graphics from all kinds of sources there are two things you must have in mind:

- OmniGraffle is a vector-based diagramming application.
- The legal side of using other peoples' graphical works.

## The vector side of things

Drawings in OmniGraffle are vector based. For all practical purposes, this means that a diagram you create should look equally good if you print it out on your laser printer or if you let a special print shop create a 20 x 20 feet banner of your diagram to hang on your wall.

You can of course use a JPG or a GIF, but if you try enlarging these kinds of pictures, you may quickly see that certain details do not look quite right.

When you see these two pictures side by side it is not easy to see which one is a JPG file and which one is a vector graphics file.

Now, let's enlarge the heads of the horses by some 500%.

Now it's pretty clear that the horse on the right is a vector graphic file, it is still 100% clear and sharp, while the horse on the left has become quite jagged.

The moral is to use vector graphics as often as you can or use very large JPG or GIF files. However, with large JPG or GIF files you will be penalized with big file sizes.

# The legal side of using third party graphic files

If you intend to use third party graphics files you should always seek permission from the owner of these files. Even if you download a file from a website on the Internet, it does not mean that you can use it for whatever you want.

There are a lot of websites which claim to have large collection of "free" or "public domain" clip-art you can use – but most, if not all, of these sites come with a disclaimer in the realm of:

> *... this website does not claim ownership of the graphics in this archive and any use of them is at your own risk.*

The only exception we can fully endorse is the Open Clipart Library project found at `http://www.openclipart.org/`. There are two reasons why we can endorse this website. The primary reason is that all of their clip art is in a vector format (SVG), and secondly the content can be traced back to the various contributors. Traceability is very important with respect to the legal side of using third party graphics.

If you are really in doubt, the only sane solution is to buy clip-art from well-known sources like `http://iStockphoto.com/` or `http://www.graphicsfactory.com/`. Both websites supply vector-based illustrations. However, Graphics Factory will for most of their images supply you with an EPS version. This vector format can easily be imported into OmniGraffle. One last piece of advice, even if you buy clip-art from safe sources, you cannot probably distribute stencils to third parties (distribution of your finished diagram is probably OK).

## Creating a stencil with fancy graphics

Unfortunately, OmniGraffle does not understand how to import too many vector file formats. The program has no problem exporting to a whole slew of vector file formats, like the most common one found on the Internet, the SVG format – cannot be imported.

If you want to import SVG based clip-art (which is what you really want instead of importing JPG, PNG or GIF files), you'll need to convert the SVG file to a format which OmniGraffle understands, that is, PDF or its sister format EPS.

Converting from a SVG based file format to PDF or EPS can be done using third party applications like Adobe Illustrator. Unfortunately, for most people, Adobe Illustrator is quite expensive and a bit complex to use for the casual user.

A hefty contender to Adobe Illustrator is a free and open source program called InkScape (http://www.inkscape.org/) – which without problem can convert from SVG to the EPS format. Be aware that InkScape can be very daunting to work with, even for seasoned computer users. However, for converting from SVG to EPS, you really do not need a lot of knowledge of InkScape. Installing InkScape can be a bit cumbersome if you are not very technically inclined. The reason for this is that the Macintosh version of InkScape will only run under a system called X11. X11 must be installed prior to using InkScape, and it is out of scope for this book to guide you through the installation of X11. You can read about installing X11 and InkScape on the Macintosh from the InkScape Wiki at http://wiki.inkscape.org/wiki/index.php/Installing_Inkscape.

Another third party application which is not only free to download and use, but also very easy to use is svg Detective from gandreas software. Download the program from http://projects.gandreas.com/svgdetective/. svg Detective does a very reasonable job when converting from SVG to PDF. The Read Me file that comes with the documentation will outline the programs limits. In general, Inkscape and Adobe Illustrator will do a better job in converting SVG to PDF or EPS than svg Detective.

**Use the right tool for the job**

Even if in general *InkScape* and *Adobe Illustrator* will do a better job in converting SVG to PDF or EPS than *svg Detective*, it does not mean that this program is a bad one. In fact, it's extremely easy to use. Another point in favor of using these programs is that they do not require you to install X11, or have you to pay a lot of money for commercial software.

If you are only going to casually convert SVG files for use with OmniGraffle, stick to *svg Detective*.
If you are going to convert a lot of SVG files, then you should use one of the other two software packages.

However, depending on your diagram usage you may be quite happy using a JPG or a PNG file instead of using a vector format.

Let's create a stencil with a nice looking strawberry.

Start by issuing the **File | New Resource | New Stencil** menu command.

Now, point your web browser to the Open Clip Art Library website
`http://www.openclipart.org/`.

In the search box, enter **strawberry** and perform the search. If you do not like
strawberries, search for any other fruit. It does not matter as the work flow is
identical no matter what you choose.

You'll now get an overview of all the strawberries available.

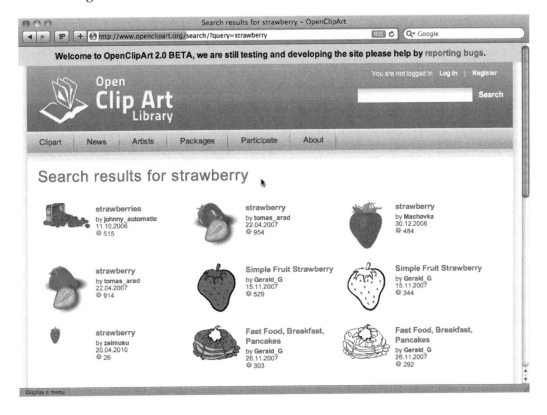

Click on the glossiest strawberry you can find.

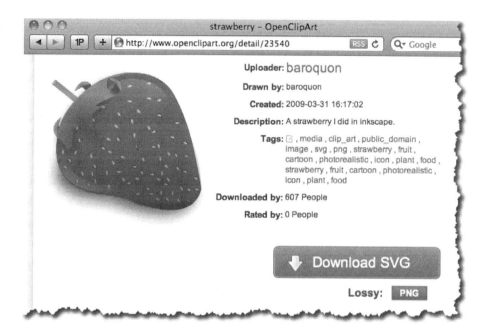

Notice the two buttons on the bottom left: **Download SVG** and **Lossy: PNG**. Clicking on the PNG.

If you click on the PNG button, you'll get a very big version of the strawberry shown on your screen.

You can now right-click on the image and issue the **Copy Image** menu command.

Switch back to the OmniGraffle software and use the **Edit | Paste** (⌘+C) menu command.

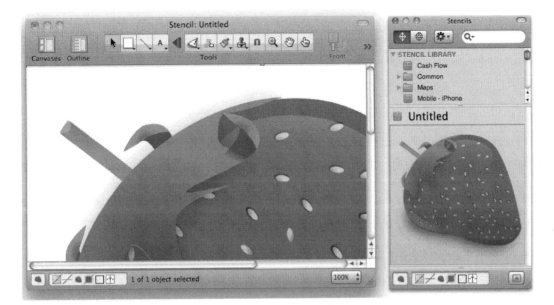

Congratulations! You have now imported a strawberry to your new stencil. Given the size of the berry, you may think that this would suffice for most diagramming uses. This may be true if you are only going to use only a few berries in your diagram. However, if you plan to use more than a few berries, fruits or any other objects, the size of your diagram might quickly grow to an unmanageable size.

Let's use the SVG version file instead but as OmniGraffle does not read SVG files natively, you will have to convert the SVG file to a format (PDF or EPS) that OmniGraffle understands.

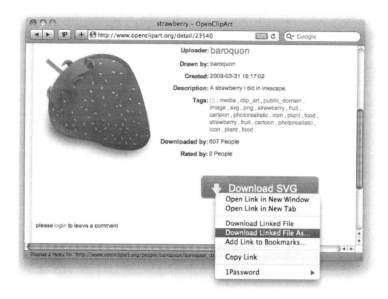

If you just click on the **Download SVG** button, the file may just be shown in your browser. It is best to download and save the file in a folder on your computer.

Before you can proceed, you will need to download and install the *svg Detective* software, or the *InkScape* program.

For illustrative purposes, we show you both programs and our downloaded strawberry in the same folder.

# Using svg Detective to convert the SVG file

Before you start doing this exercise, you will have to download and extract the program.

Start *svg Detective* and use the **File | Open** command to open the downloaded SVG file. If the software is able to open the SVG file, you'll get a preview of the file in a separate window. Be aware that not all SVG files will open correctly in *svg Detective*.

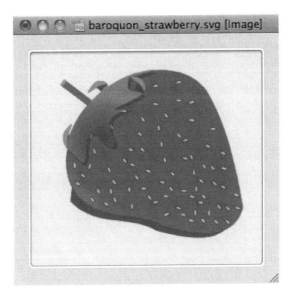

As in the previous screenshot, you see that the shadow of the berry does not look like the shadow on the Open Clip Art Library website. The berry itself is also a little less glossy than the original portrayed on the website. What you see here are examples of limitations mentioned in the Read Me file that comes with *svg Detective*.

From within *svg Detective,* use the **File | Export PDF** menu command and save the PDF file in a designated folder.

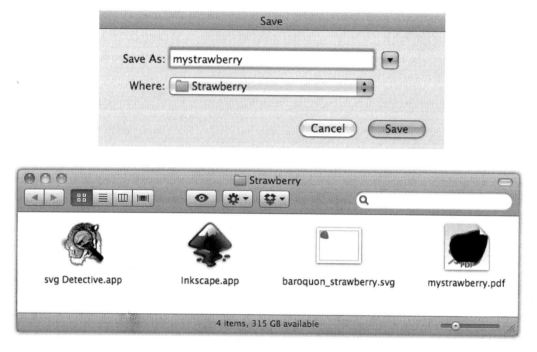

The preview icon of the converted file does not look quite right, but let's try to import it into OmniGraffle.

Switch to OmniGraffle and use the **File | Place Image...** menu command, locate and select the file.

You could also have dragged the file directly into OmniGraffle.

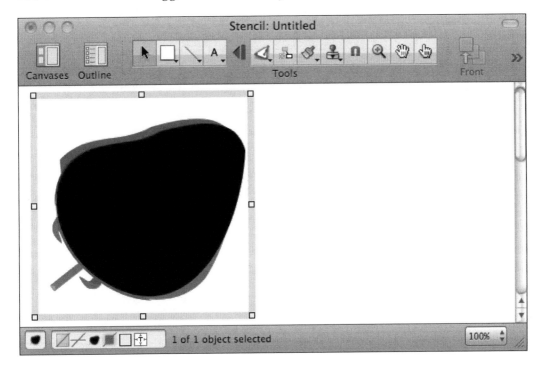

The resulting import is not usable at all.

This is not really the fault of *svg Detective*. Most SVG files found on the Open Clip Art Library website will convert to PDF without any problems at all. The horse we used earlier in this chapter is a file we converted to PDF using *svg Detective*.

The reason why this conversion failed was probably due to the glossiness and the shadow of the strawberry.

The next section will show you how to achieve greater success with converting SVG files to a format that can be imported into OmniGraffle.

# Using InkScape to convert the SVG file

Download and install InkScape before continuing.

Start *InkScape* and use the **File | Open** dialog, locate and open the downloaded SVG file. This file dialog does not resemble what you are used to when running pure Macintosh software, the reason is you are now running the software from within X11.

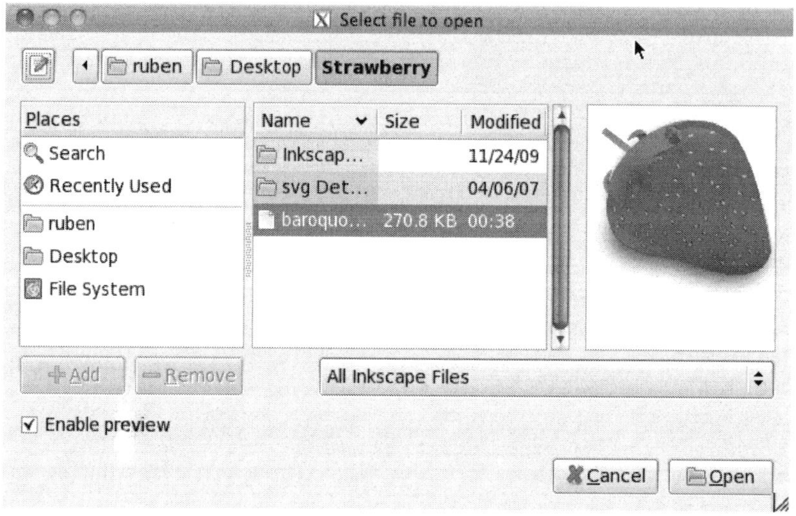

After opening the file, the strawberry is placed on a canvas not unlike the one you are used to with OmniGraffle.

As InkScape's internal file format is in fact SVG, this program understands this file format extremely well.

If you compare the strawberry in the following screenshot, with the one you found on the Open Clip Art Library website, they are exactly 100% the same.

If your version of InkScape does not look exactly like the following one, do not despair. You are **not** going to learn InkScape in any detail. You are just going to learn enough to convert your SVG file to an EPS file.

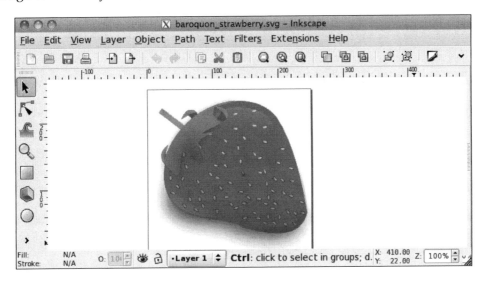

To convert and export your strawberry into an EPS file, use the **File | Save As** menu command.

You will have to enter the filename you wish to save the file as, and also select **Encapsulated PostScript (*.eps)** in the file type drop-down.

Continue by clicking on the **Save** button.

If any other dialog appears, just click on the **OK** button and let the default parameters be.

Compared to when using *svg Detective*, the preview icon looks quite right.

Let's import the EPS file.

Switch to OmniGraffle and use the **File | Place Image...** menu command, locate and select the file.

You could also have dragged the file directly into OmniGraffle.

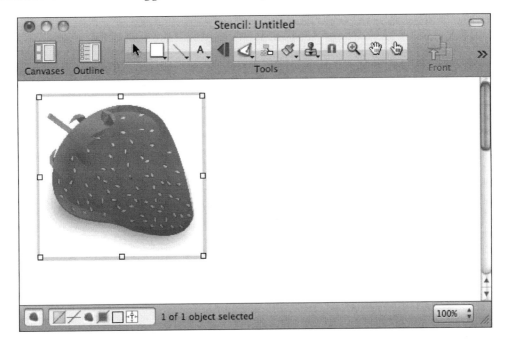

A perfect vectorized strawberry!

# Exporting your stencil

If you want to export your stencil for sharing with other OmniGraffle users, this is quite easy to do.

Right-click on your newly created stencil, and select the **Show in Finder** menu command. This command is also found in the **Action button** menu.

Each stencil's filename will be have a .gstencil file suffix.

| Name | Date Modified | Size | Kind |
|---|---|---|---|
| Cash Flow.gstencil | 16.04.03 01.44 | 1,4 MB | Omni... Stencil |
| My Favorites.gstencil | Today, 02.43 | 143 KB | Omni... Stencil |
| stencils.xml | Today, 02.43 | 4 KB | Text document |

Select your stencil file in the Finder window, and use the **File | Compress** *"your-stencils-filename"* menu command to create an archive.

| Name | Date Modified | Size | Kind |
|---|---|---|---|
| Cash Flow.gstencil | 16.04.03 01.44 | 1,4 MB | Omni... Stencil |
| My Favorites.gstencil | Today, 02.43 | 143 KB | Omni... Stencil |
| My Favorites.gstencil.zip | Today, 02.57 | 106 KB | ZIP archive |
| stencils.xml | Today, 02.43 | 4 KB | Text document |

Now you can take this zip-file and send it your colleagues – or you can put it up on the GraffleTopia website if your stencil is for general consumption.

# Importing Microsoft Visio Templates

Given the sheer number of Windows based computers out there, you will also find that Microsoft Visio Templates are readily available.

There are several reasons why you want to use these templates. One very valid reason is that you cannot find an equivalent OmniGraffle template. Another reason is that your company has standardized MS Visio Templates for certain diagrams and since you are using Macintosh and OmniGraffle, you should thus be able to stick to "company policy".

 A quick word of warning when converting a MS Visio Template to a OmniGraffle Stencil: Even if you successfully convert the Visio Template to a Stencil you may not legally re-distribute your OmniGraffle Stencil to other OmniGraffle users.
You must always seek permission from the owner of the Visio Template to re-distribute any derived work.

Converting a MS Visio Template is, in a lot of cases, no more difficult than opening the Visio file.

For this exercise you are going to download a template from the VisioCafe — http://www.visiocafe.com/. VisioCafe contains a lot of official stencils from several hardware vendors. Another good thing is that very few of the stencils found at VisioCafe come as a Windows .EXE or .CAB installers. They come as ZIP files which your Macintosh understands perfectly.

Another site with links to all kinds of Visio Templates is the VisioMVP download section `http://visio.mvps.org/3rdparty.htm`.

Let's say you need to create a stencil for your boss showing him how your server infrastructure is put together. You have bought all your servers from Dell and you will thus need a couple of Dell stencils to make things look good.

On the left-hand side on the VisioCafe website you'll find a list of brand names, and IBM should be among these. Click on the Dell brand name and you'll be presented with a list of available stencils—including a collection of **every** IBM stencil available. Locate and download the stencil named **3D Isometric Topology shapes for IBM Products**.

In your download folder, you can click on the ZIP file and a folder will appear. In this folder, you'll find two documents; a `.vss` file—this is the Visio Template—and a `readme.txt` file containing the license text of a given template. Read the license document carefully before proceeding.

| Name | Kind | Date Modified | Size |
| --- | --- | --- | --- |
| IBM-3D.zip | ZIP archive | Today, 00.12 | 971 KB |
| IBM-3D | Folder | Today, 00.12 | -- |
| readme.txt | Smult...ument | 12. mai 2008 01.30 | 4 KB |
| IBM-3D.vss | Visio® stencil | 3. mai 2009 21.41 | 1,1 MB |

The document may or may not even tell you if you are allowed to distribute your OmniGraffle stencil within your company, or to the public. Some licenses would even suggest, or demand, that you cannot use these in OmniGraffle. This may not be stated directly with respect to OmniGraffle, but you may encounter wording like "... you may not ... decompile ... reverse engineer ... disassemble ... these downloaded files". We can only give you one piece of advice: If you are in doubt, consult a lawyer.

Of course, not every Visio Template will have a accompanying readme file.

Now, all you have to do is double-click on the `.vss` file and if everything is set up correctly, you will be importing the Visio Template into OmniGraffle.

You can also use the **File | Open** menu command to import the template into OmniGraffle.

From time to time, you may encounter an error message like the following one. Depending on the error message, you may import only a few of the shapes originally found in the Visio Template.

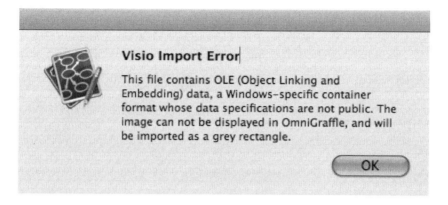

After importing the VSS file, it will appear in the **RECENT STENCILS** pane (seen in the left picture given next). After clicking on the **Install** button, the stencil will be installed in the **STENCIL LIBRARY** pane (as seen in the following middle picture). Most Visio Templates you'll import will be very messy, and the easiest way to view each shape is to use the **Stencil Grid View button** (as seen on the right).

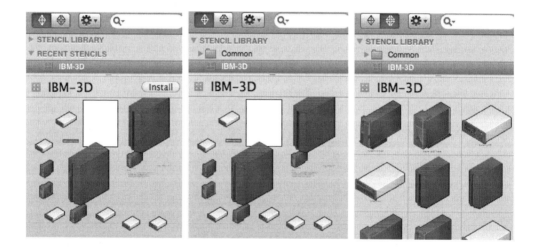

To show you how cluttered imported Visio Templates can become, there is a telecommunication related template that the book's author uses in his daily work. The stencil contains around 200 shapes— so the only sane way to view the stencil is to use the Grid View.

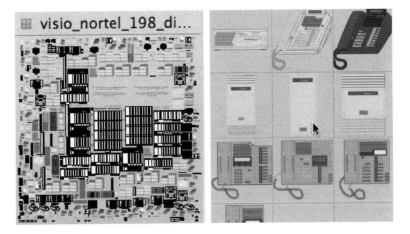

Drag any of the server shapes onto your canvas.

You'll notice one particular thing: The area around the shape is not very tight, and it's difficult to read the shapes caption.

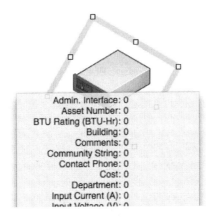

If you are using OmniGraffle Professional, your **Note Property inspector** palette will be full of various data labels. You may want to keep some of these or you may want to delete them all. The reason why all these data labels are present is that certain versions of Visio may automatically fill out the corresponding values. OmniGraffle version 5 cannot do this.

To remedy the larger sized rectangle around the shape – use the **Arrange | Ungroup** menu command (or use the ⇧+⌘+*U* keyboard shortcut command).

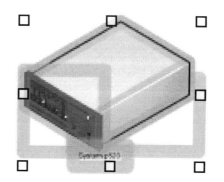

You could also use the **Ungroup command** (⊟) in the Canvas toolbar.

You may want to either remove the caption text for the shape or amend the current caption with larger text. In the following diagram, we have kept the shape caption in place but increased the font size from 4,5 points to 12 points.

To keep the shape together, you need to create a shape group. Use the **Arrange | Ungroup** menu command, or use the ⇧+⌘+ *G* keyboard shortcut.

You could also use the Group symbol (⊟) in the Canvas toolbar.

The result is a grouped shape without any of the previous surplus around it.

In theory, you could now use this amended shape in your own *IBM 3D Stencil*. However, the usage license for the very stencil may prevent you from doing this. If that's the case, then you'll need to take these steps every time you use a shape from an imported Visio Template.

# Organizing stencils

After you have imported alot of stencils, your **STENCIL LIBRARY** will become a mess.

For illustrative purposes, we have put a screen capture sideways, showing a third of the **STENCIL LIBRARY** after approximately six months of using OmniGraffle for an ordinary user.

This is quite messy but very easy to fix.

Right-click on any of the stencils and select the **Show In Finder** menu command:

All you have to do now is create appropriate folders and move corresponding stencils into those folders.

If you create folders with the same name as the built-in folders in OmniGraffle both your imported or created stencils and the built-in stencils will be available in those folders.

In the screenshot shown next you see the **Stencils** folder after the re-organization and on the right the **STENCILS FOLDER** in OmniGraffle.

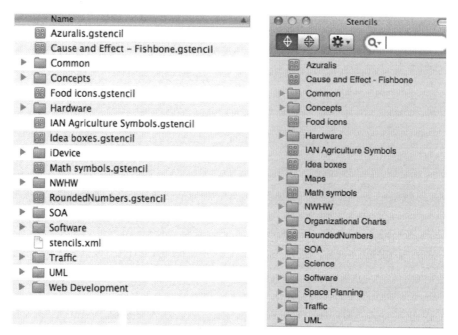

# Summary

This chapter taught you everything you need to know about stencils in OmniGraffle.

You learned to use stencils that come pre-installed with OmniGraffle. You also learned to take a look at stencils from other sources like GraffleTopia and import these kinds of stencils into OmniGraffle.

You created your own stencil using third party clip-art which introduced a couple of auxiliary tools for converting from one vector format (SVG) to formats understood by OmniGraffle (PDF and EPS).

You learned about the organization of the Stencil Palette and its different sections.

You saw that you could search for stencils not only your in local stencil repository, but also the online GraffleTopia repository. A pretty cool thing about this function is that you can in fact download and install stencils directly from GraffleTopia from within OmniGraffle.

We also dealt with the two viewing options for stencils where the Grid View may come very handy in several situations.

You also learned to import Microsoft Visio Templates, and saw that this was not necessarily in a very straightforward road.

Lastly, organizing stencils is nothing worse than organizing your files.

The next chapter will teach you everything you ever need to know about shapes. Shapes are the building blocks for your diagrams and this means that the next chapter may be the most important one in the book.

# 3
# Shapes, Building Blocks for Diagrams

Shapes in OmniGraffle comes in many forms.

You have rectangles, circles, squashed rectangles, diamonds, hexagons, octagons, triangles, arrows, double arrows, wedges that looks like PacMan stars, houses, puzzle pieces, cylinders, clouds, speech bubbles, lightning bolts, patches, hearts, and so on. These shapes are called compound shapes.

The American Heritage ® Dictionary of the English language, fourth edition defines a compound to be a combination of two or more elements or parts. We are missing one type of shape, and that is the line. Line shapes are called singular shapes.

The second shape type missing is the text shape. We'll deal with this shape later in this chapter.

Shapes are the basic building blocks of diagrams. In the very first diagram you made in *Chapter 1, Getting Started with OmniGraffle* you used three different shapes: The rectangle in the form of an oblong, the diamond, and the line. You gave the shapes different characteristics like color, line weight, shape labels, and so on.

You can also connect shapes to each other using connectors. A connector is really a line.

This chapter will continue to expand your knowledge about the shapes in OmniGraffle.

This chapter will teach you:

- That compound shapes are the shapes you will probably use the most
- That singular shapes are called lines
- That text is nothing special—text is just shapes
- How to operate on shapes, such as changing behavior and appearance
- That line endings (and starts) do not have to be arrow points
- How OmniGraffle lets you have favourite styles on shapes – and even favourite shapes easily available
- Everything you ever wanted, or needed, to know about line labels
- Filling shapes (including text shapes, but not line shapes) with color, text, and images
- How to add text to your diagrams
- The importance of having the correct order of shapes
- How grouping and ungrouping shapes makes your life easy
- That the only way to connect shapes is by using magnets and how to operate the various magnet options

# Differences from other software

Some literature on other diagramming tools quite often calls lines *one dimensional* shapes, and compound shapes *two dimensional* shapes. Some books even operate with a *third dimension* (for the cylinders you used in the income flow diagram in *Chapter 2, Stencils*). On top of the dimensions, you can have open and closed shapes. It might sound very impressive or important to have these distinctions but in the end your result will be a diagram.

Even if OmniGraffle does not complicate its jargon by using dimensions or open or closed shapes, the results are often more stunning to look at compared to other diagramming software.

 If you have been using Microsoft Visio on a Windows platform, you should know that none of the shapes in OmniGraffle (version 5) are, at the time of writing this book, *intelligent shapes* the way Visio defines this.

# Compound shapes

**Compound shapes** consist of more than one element. An element in this case is a simple line (there is an exception to this, which we will cover later).

A compound shape can have the following style properties:

- Shape type
- Shape stroke and color
- Fill color and fill type
- Stroke corner radius
- Shadow type, color, and size
- Text type (font), color, size, and rotation
- Connection points

Except for the Shape type, most of the other style properties are common for both the singular shape (lines) and the text shape; these will be covered later in this chapter.

# Shape types

There are quite a few basic shape types that come with OmniGraffle. All these basic shapes are found in the **Lines and Shapes property inspector**. You can change between these types of shapes easily by selecting a shape on the canvas, and then clicking on the shape type in the inspector.

Let's say you need to have a star shape in your diagram.

In the tool-selector on the canvas, click on the **Shape Tool**. You will see a blue circle with the number 1 inside, on top of the shape tool. The circle with the number 1 inside is a visual cue that this tool will perform once and then revert back to the **Selection Tool** ( ). If you click twice on the shape tool, it will become sticky. This means that you can now draw more than one shape *of this type*.

If you hold down the *Shift* key on your keyboard while drawing on the canvas, you'll get a perfect square or a perfect circle shape.

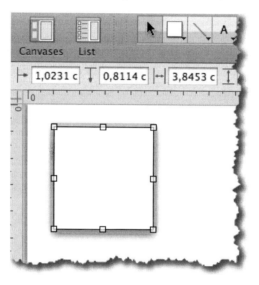

Now click on the star shape symbol in the Lines and Shapes property inspector.

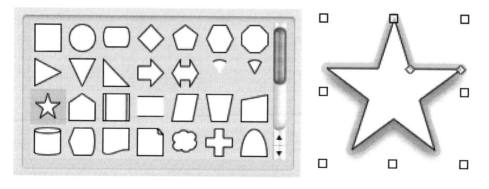

Notice the two small blue diamonds on the right side of the star shape. The inner diamond controls the length of the lines, while the outer controls the number of points in the star.

Without too much work, you can then create a more "splashy" star shape:

Not all compound shapes have this ability to change their geometric properties. The shapes that you can adjust this way are the Adjustable arrow (⇨), the Adjustable double arrow (⇔), the Adjustable arc ( ), the Adjustable wedge (▽), and finally the Adjustable star (☆).

In the arrows, you can change the thickness of the base along with the size of the arrow. In the arc and the wedge, you can change the angle of the shape. You already have experience with what you can amend in the star shape.

# Adding a text caption to a shape

If you want to add text to a shape, just double-click on the shape and write your text. If you want to change the font type, size, or color of the text, just use the **Text style** inspector. This inspector is covered in detail in the *Text shapes* section.

# Drawing a copy of an existing shape

If you need to draw another star or any other shapes that you have already drawn previously in your OmniGraffle document, you can duplicate it like you did in Chapter 1 or copy/paste the shape. However, OmniGraffle will let you select a previously drawn shape in your current document and let you redraw this shape.

If you have a document with two shapes, a star, and a cloud, clicking and holding down the mouse button on the Shape Tool will give you a context sensitive menu which also contains a list of your previously drawn shapes in your current document.

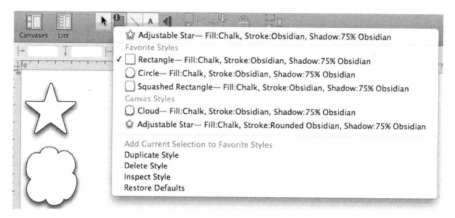

Selecting any of these shapes will now change the icon in the Shape Tool.

Congratulations! You have now changed the default shape to draw.

# Favorite shapes and styles

Favorite shapes and styles are only available in the professional version of OmniGraffle. You might want to skip this section if you are using the standard version of the program.

If you want your shape to be available in other OmniGraffle documents, you can select one or more shapes on your canvas, and then use the **Add Current Selection to Favorite Styles** menu command in the context sensitive menu below. Of course, you can also right-click on a shape and add it as a favorite shape style.

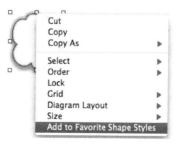

Also notice the wording style. It's not only the shape that you put into your favorite shape list — it's the whole enchilada: Fill colors, line types and thickness, shadows, and so on. If you like to have your base shape in a pink color, OmniGraffle lets you do this.

To remove a favorite shape style, just select the shape from the context sensitive shape menu and delete the shape.

If you want to change the properties of a shape, you can click on the **Inspect Style** menu command. You will now be able to change the various style parameters (fill color, and the color of the line, the line thickness and the radius of its corners, shadowing and so on) of the chosen shape.

The various styles will be covered later in this chapter since they are common between the compound, line, and text shapes.

# Singular shapes – lines

As you've learned in Chapter 1, a line can have an arrowhead. It is also possible to assign an arrow tail to a line. It would thus not make much sense calling this shape a one-dimensional shape.

When working with the diagrams so far in the book, you may have noticed that the line shape works a bit differently from the compound shapes. Compared to other shapes, you can drag and drop the size of the shape in both the horizontal and the vertical direction to change how the shape looks.

A good example is if you start with a perfect square (or a rectangle as the proper name really is), you can extend this shape into an oblong. With a line shape you cannot make this into a rectangle. You can only change the length of the line by dragging and dropping; you cannot extend its thickness without resorting to using the **Line and Shape** style palette.

A line shape can have the following properties:

- Shape stroke and color
- Stroke corner radius
- Shadow type, color, and size
- Connection points

These style properties are the same for both the singular shape (lines) and the text shape (these will be covered later in this chapter).

Specific to the line shape, you have the opportunity to adjust the following parameters:

- Line type
- Line tail arrow type and arrow start type
- Midpoints
- Line hoops
- Line captions

You draw a line by clicking on the **Line Tool** in the canvas toolbar. Notice that this tool works exactly the same way as the shape tool: You have a blue circle with the number 1 inside to indicate that you can draw one line before reverting back to the **Selection Tool** ( ).

To draw a line, click on the starting point of the canvas, then move the mouse cursor to the ending point on canvas and double-click. If you do not double-click, you effectively place a *line midpoint*. We'll cover the details regarding midpoints on lines in a few paragraphs.

If you hold the *Shift* key down while drawing your line, you will get a 100% straight horizontal or vertical line.

Actually if you drag your mouse pointer up, down, to the left, or to the right while you hold down the *Shift* key and draw your line, you may notice that not only does the direction of the line change from horizontal to vertical but also a 45° intermediate slope is also introduced.

Next you see two lines. The first line is a line without any midpoints. The second line has one midpoint indicated with a blue circle in the middle of the line.

The starting point of a line is indicated with a small red circle, and the ending point with a small green circle. Even though the following lines both start from the left, you will often start lines from arbitrary places on your diagram.

In the section named *Reversing a line*, you'll learn how to change the direction of lines.

# The Line Style inspector

The Line Style property inspector is used for managing lines. We will cover the various controls in detail further on.

# Midpoints on lines

**Midpoints** may seems a to be a misnomer. A midpoint can be placed anywhere on a line—not just the middle of the line.

You can place a midpoint during the creation of the line by clicking once, and then continue drawing your line. If you already have drawn a line, double-clicking on the line will add a midpoint where you double-clicked.

If your line has a midpoint, you can now drag and drop this midpoint wherever you need.

Let's draw a line here. Hold down the *Shift* key while drawing. Do not release the Shift key before you have double-clicked on the ending point. Your line will now be as straight as can be.

Now double-click on the line – approximately one third from the left and then one third from the right.

Notice that the line is not straight any more.

Next, drag the left midpoint upward, and the right midpoint downward.

You could achieve the same result by drawing the line in the same jagged pattern and by single-clicking on the points where you wanted to have the midpoints. Some OmniGraffle users prefer this alternate method.

Double-clicking on a line segment normally adds a midpoint to an existing line segment. However, if you have set up OmniGraffle to add *Line Labels* when you double-click on a line, you will instead have to right-click on the line and select the **Add Midpoint** menu command to add a midpoint.

So far you have only moved one midpoint at one time. If you hold down the *Shift* key while clicking on one or more midpoints (or even end points), you can then move that particular segment of your line as you please. If you take hold of the line and try to move it around—the whole line will move—you need to drag just one of the midpoints.

If the midpoint is hidden behind a selection handle (which will happen if your line inhabits symmetric features), just use the *option-command*-click (⌥+⌘) to get to the midpoint.

The following picture shows that both midpoints have been *Shift* clicked and the middle segment has been moved to a new position.

To delete a single midpoint, all you have to do is to select the midpoint and press the *Delete* key (⌫) or use the **Edit Delete** menu command.

You can remove all your midpoints by clicking on the **Remove midpoints** ( Remove Midpoints ) button on the style inspector for lines. Midpoints can also be removed by right-clicking on a line and selecting the **Remove midpoints** menu command.

# Line types

OmniGraffle supports four kinds of lines: Straight, Curved, Orthogonal, and Bézier. Let's take a look at each of the four types. You change the line type by marking the line and then using the **Set line type** drop-down menu in the **Lines and Shapes** inspector. This is the middle drop-down button in the inspector, also known as the **line type selector**.

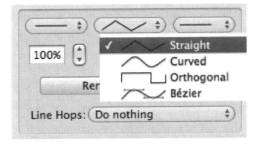

You could also use the **stroke style** button (⊟) from the **inspector bar**.

| Line type | Example | Description |
|---|---|---|
| Straight | | Straight lines have the shortest possible path between endpoints or between midpoints. |
| Curved | | Curved lines will turn smoothly through each midpoint it passes. Also notice the subtle curvature close to each endpoint. |
| Orthogonal | | Orthogonal lines travel through each midpoint either horizontally or vertically. |
| Bézier | | Bézier lines travel through each point on the line in a smooth way much like the curved lines. However, you can adjust the curvature on each point on the line with the small red colored handles.<br><br>The length and the angle of these lines will control the line segment's curvature. |

Depending on what kind of diagrams you are going to create, there is no set rule for which kind of line you will use. For most office types of diagramming, you will probably be using the orthogonal or the straight lines.

The Bézier curves are very powerful tools worth mastering; with patience, you could use these curves as the basis for your sketches. The sketch of an eye (seen next) is created by using only the tools available in OmniGraffle. It might not look perfect, but it gives you an idea of the power of the Bézier curve within OmniGraffle. If you do have artistic skills, you might use OmniGraffle to create some pretty neat illustrations.

If you want to see the finished diagram in full color, please open the file named `The eye.graffle` which is found in the `Chapter 3` folder in the download bundle.

# Bézier lines in detail

Bézier lines have midpoints at each vertex (that is, corner) along with the control points at each of the line endpoints. On each midpoint there are two handles, these handles controls the curvature of the point (**curvature handles**).

You add a midpoint to a Bézier line as you would with ordinary lines — right-click and select **Add Midpoint** (depending on how you have set up OmniGraffle, double-clicking on a line segment should normally also add a midpoint).

Newly added midpoints on Bézier lines do not have curvature handles. To convert a midpoint to a point with these handles, just hold down the *command* key (⌘) while dragging away from the midpoint.

To manage the curvature handles, just select the midpoint by clicking. When the midpoint becomes active, the handles will appear. As with other lines, if the midpoint is hidden behind a selection handle (which will happen if your line inhabits symmetric features) — just use the *option-command* click (⌥+⌘) to get to the midpoint.

Normally, when you drag one of the curvature handles, the other handle will also move in the opposite direction. You can avoid this by holding down the *option* key (⌥) while dragging a handle — this will only move the handle you are currently working on.

By moving a handle very close to the midpoint, the handle will disappear completely. To get the handle back, use the *command* key modifier while dragging away from a selected midpoint.

Without holding down any of the modifier keys, you can drag and rotate the curvature handles to any arbitrary point of degree you choose. However, if you want to have more control over the rotation, hold down the *Shift* key (⇧) and you'll only rotate the handles in increments of 45°.

To delete a single midpoint on a Bézier line, all you have to do is to select the midpoint and press the *Delete* key (⌫). You can also use the **Edit | Delete** menu command.

# Line endings—tails and (arrow) heads

A very nifty property regarding lines is the ability for the line to have a head and a tail. The most common use is probably to create arrows, like you did in your first diagram. However, there are quite a few line endings that you can use, from arrows and circles, to squares and crowfeet.

On the left and right-hand side of the **line type selector** you will find two groups of controls. The topmost selectors are the type of beginning or ending of a line, and below is a percentage gauge indicating the size of the line endings.

The sizes of the line endings are relative to the thickness of the line. In the following picture, you'll see two arrows.

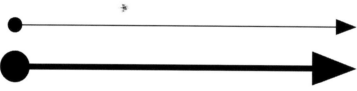

Both have their size set to 200%, but the thickness of the lines are 1 and 5 points, respectively.

OmniGraffle does not care what you put on the end of lines. You can have an arrowhead both on the end and the beginning of a line. In fact, the symbols are the same both for the beginning and the end of lines:

| ↑ ↑ ♦ ↑ ♀ ↑ ♣ ↑ ↑ ↑ ◇ ↑ ↑ ↑ ↑ ↑ ↑ ↑ ↑ ↑ ♈ ↑ ♈ ↑ ↓ ♈ ♈ ♈ ♈ ♀ ↑ ↑ ↑ ♀ ● ♈ * |

Notice the symbol on the very left—it does not have any distinctive line ending. If you want to remove a line ending, this is the symbol you must use.

# Reversing a line

A short recap on lines: The beginning of a line is indicated with a small red ring, the end of a line is indicated with a small green ring.

To reverse the direction of a line, just click on the line you want to reverse and then click on the **Reverse the line's connection** button ( ) found below the **Line type** selector.

The thick line below has a small green circle on its arrowhead to visually indicate that this is the end of the drawn line.

After clicking on the **Reverse the line's connection** button, the line is in fact reversed though the green circle is still on its arrowhead. However, the line as you can see, is now the mirror opposite of what it was before.

The thicker of the two lines may now look like it has been moved to the right, but this is an optical illusion. The line still has the same length between its end points, however, the line-ending makes the line look longer than it actually is.

# Line Hops

The **Line Hops** drop-down menu indicates how lines crossing each other should behave.

Line Hops: Do nothing

If you choose to **Do nothing**, lines will just cross each other. If the lines have different colors, this may make sense.

You can also choose to hop over or under lines that are above or beneath your current line. In the following picture, the black line is set to **Round hops under**, and the gray line to **Round hops over**.

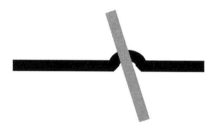

OmniGraffle will choose the "best" viewing method of these lines. If you do not agree with how the program is displaying your line hops, you can manually override the default settings.

If you choose to **Ignore this line** in the **Line Hops** drop-down menu, this will override any line hops settings crossing lines may have. In the picture below, the black line hop is set to **Ignore this line**, and the gray line is still set to **Round hops over**. The gray line now is just crossing the black line – without any hops.

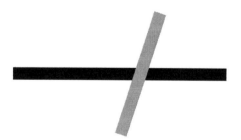

Line hops are well suited for electrical circuit diagramming. Notice the two line hops in the following diagram:

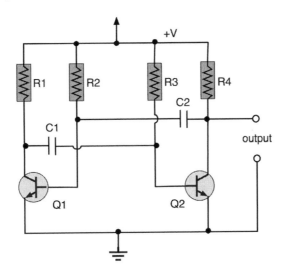

Using the **Circuit Engineering** stencil that comes with OmniGraffle we were able to create the schematic. The schematic is of a design called a stable multivibrator or free-running square-wave oscillator.

If you want to see the finished diagram in full color, please open the file named `Multivibrator.graffle` found in the appropriate folder in the download bundle.

# Favorite line styles

Favorite line styles are only available in the professional version of OmniGraffle. You might want to skip this section if you are using the standard version of the program.

If you need to have your well-crafted lines (i.e. arrows) available in other OmniGraffle documents, but you do not want to create a stencil just for a few line types (see Chapter 2 for more information on creating your own stencils) – you could add your line to the favorite line style list.

Select the line type you want to make a favorite from your canvas, then click and hold the line tool in the canvas toolbar and choose the **Add Current Selection to Favorite Styles** menu command. It is also possible to right-click on the line and then **Add to Favorite Line Styles**.

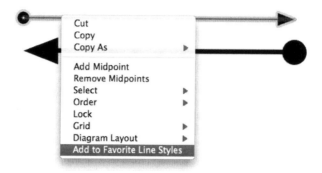

To use a favorite style, just click and hold the line icon in the canvas toolbar and the line should appear ready for use:

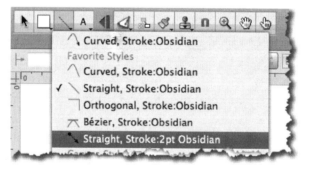

To remove a favorite line style, you will first have to select the line from the line tool menu on the canvas toolbar, and then select the **Delete Style**.

If you want to change the properties of a line (that is, color, thickness of the line, start and ending points, and so on) – click on the **Inspect Style** menu and then use the style inspector for lines to amend its properties. The next time you use the favorite line style to draw a line the new properties will be used.

# Line labels revisited

In Chapter 1, you added a few line labels to your lines. You did this by first selecting the **Text Tool** in the canvas toolbar and then clicking on the line you wanted to have a label on.

This is a quick and efficient way of adding line labels.

You can also set your OmniGraffle preferences so that double-clicking on a line will add a line label instead of adding a midpoint. Use the **OmniGraffle | Preferences** menu command and click on the **Drawing Tools** icon. A super-quick way to get to the **Preference** menu is to press the ⌘, keyboard shortcut command.

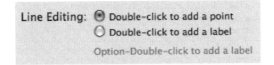

On the right-hand side of this **Preference** dialog box you set up what will happen if you double click on a line. Notice how ⌥-**Double-click** changes to **add a label** or **add a point**—depending on your selection.

So what is a line label then?

A line label is nothing more special than a text shape filled with a white background and having both the Side and Top/Bottom margins set to 5 pixels.

Start by drawing a straight line. Next, add a line label by either double-clicking on the line or by option-double-clicking on a line (depending on your set preferences). Enter the text **Default line label** as the label text.

Now, click on the **Text Tool** and add a text shape above the line stating **Line label wannabe**.

When you drag the wannabe label down to the line, you will notice that the text shape will automatically "glue" itself to the line.

While leaving the wannabe label selected, use the Text property inspector and enter **5** in the **Side Margin** and the **Top/Bottom Margin** fields.

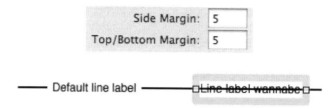

The last thing you need to do is to enable the **Fill** checkbox in the Fill property inspector.

As you can see, the wannabe label is exactly the same as the default label. This new line label will behave exactly as any other line labels added the usual ways. If you have a Bézier curved line, your new line label will follow the curves as expected. You can of course control a few aspects of the placement of the line label using the **Geometry property inspector** (see *Chapter 7, Property Inspectors* for more information regarding this inspector).

As a bonus, you can try to drag the **Default line label** below the line.

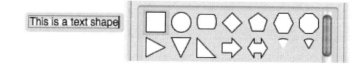

The **Default line label** is not a line label anymore, but a mere text shape—which you'll learn everything there is to know about in the next section.

# Text shapes

A text shape has a behavior that is the same as a special configured compound shape. Notice that the rectangle is selected when you type your text – this clearly shows that your text shape is really a compound shape. In fact, the default text style is surrounded by a oblong which has no fill color, no shadows and no line strokes.

This also means that it is possible to start with a text shape, and then convert this into a compound shape. This is not something you normally would do, but working through the steps teaches you the *how's and why's* of the text shape.

1.  Click on the **Text Tool** in the tool-selector on the **Canvas** toolbar. The same principle about clicking once to execute the tool action once, applies to this tool in the same way as the **Line Tool** and the **Shape Tool**.

2.  Click on your canvas and enter the text: **This is a text shape**.

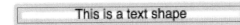

3.  Most of the work you are going to perform is in the **Text style** inspector palette. Click on this palette before you continue.

    The first thing you need to do is to enter **5** as the **Side Margin** and the **Top/Bottom Margin**.

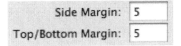

    Notice how the margins around the text have changed.

4.  Now you may try to extend the text box and you'll experience that you can only extend the text box horizontally. You have only two **drag points** — one to the left and one to the right of your shape.

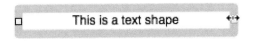

The reason for this is that the **Resize to Fit** in the **Text** palette is selected.

5.  Click the left of the three **text fitting** buttons—the name of the button is **Overflow**. This means that the text within the shape may overflow the shape boundaries. You also will have the normal eight drag points available and you can thus resize the shape as you want.

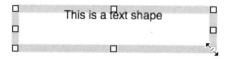

6.  You may have noticed from the previous diagrams you created while reading this book that the text is centered both horizontally and vertically. In the previous picture the text is centered horizontally but not vertically. To center the text horizontally, click on the **Align Middle** button.

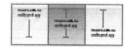

Your text-only shape is now a bit closer to an ordinary shape:

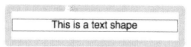

7.  We're missing three things: Some white filling, a line, and a shadow. Click on the **Fill** inspector palette and enable the **Fill** checkbox (☑ Fill). Next, click on the **Line and Shapes** inspector and enable the **Stroke** checkbox (☑ Stroke). Lastly, click on the **Shadow inspector** and enable the **Shadow** checkbox (☑ Shadow).

After you have performed these tasks, your shape should look like the one on the left—the shape on the right is a compound shape where the text has been entered after the shape was drawn.

This is a text shape

This is a shape with text

Unless you know, you cannot tell the difference. To put some icing on the cake, you can even change the text shape into a cloud and add some filling color.

The style properties for the actual text (shapes) are the same as the text properties within a compound shape. We have also demonstrated that this is the same for line labels as well. The style properties will be covered later in this chapter.

# Favorite text styles

Favorite text styles are only available in OmniGraffle Professional. You might want to skip this section if you are using the standard version of the program.

If you need to have your well-crafted text styles available in other OmniGraffle documents, but you do not want to create a stencil just for a few text types (Chapter 2 taught you about creating your own stencils) — then you could add your text to the favorite text style list.

If your text shape has a line stroke and a fill color, you cannot add the text shape to your list of favorite text shapes. However, if you remove the checkboxes for the fill color and the line stroke, you will be able to add the shape to the favorite text tool menu.

Select the text type you want to make a favorite from your canvas, then click and hold the line tool in the canvas toolbar and choose the **Add Current Selection to Favorite Styles** menu command. It is also possible to right-click on the line and then select **Add to Favorite Text Styles**.

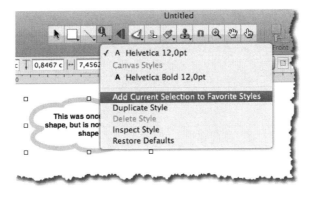

To use a favorite style, just click and hold the line icon in the canvas toolbar and the text shape should appear ready for use. If you choose this text shape, and add some text to the canvas you'll get the following results:

□**This is a new text shape**□

This may not be what you expected—in fact you are back to square one, except for the fact that you now have a cloud surrounding the text, and not a oblong.

To remove a favorite text style, you will first have to select the line from the line tool menu on the canvas toolbar, and then select the **Delete Style**.

If you want to change the properties of a text style (i.e. color, size, font type, etc) click on the **Inspect Style** menu and then use the text style inspector to amend its properties. The next time you use the favorite text style to write a text on your canvas, the new text properties will be used.

# Shape style properties

Some of the style properties and parameters are shared by compound shapes, line shapes and text shapes. Specific shape properties are covered in the respective sections on shapes.

# Shape stroke inspector and the color of a stroke

The common dialog of the **Lines and Shapes property inspector** is all you need to control the look and feel of a stroke. It does not matter what kind of shape the stroke belongs to. The shape can be a compound shape, a line shape, or a text shape.

The following table lists out some of the controls in the Lines and Shapes property inspector:

| | |
|---|---|
| ☑ **Stroke** | The **Stroke** checkbox toggles whether a shape will have a line or not.<br><br>If you have selected a line shape, this element is disabled as a line will always have a line stroke. |
| (Single Stroke / Double Stroke buttons) | These two elements are called the **Single Stroke** and the **Double Stroke** buttons. These two buttons control the number of strokes a shape can have. A shape may be drawn with a single stroke or a double stroke.<br><br>If you have clicked on the **Double Stroke** button and are using either a round corner or a bevel corner, it's only the outlying stroke that will be affected. |
| (Color button) | The **Color** button lets you choose the color of the line. Clicking on this button will activate the color picker and let you select your preferred color. |
| Thickness: 1 pt | The **Thickness** field determines the thickness of a stroke.<br><br>If you have clicked on the **Double stroke** button, both the outlying and the inner stroke will be affected.<br><br>The maximum thickness a stroke can have is 1,000 points. |
| Corner Radius: 0 pt | The **Corner Radius** field determines the roundness of a shape's corner.<br><br>If you have enabled the Double stroke button, this will affect both the inward and the outward stroke.<br><br>The maxium roundness possible is 50 points. |
| (Stroke Pattern dropdown) | The **Stroke Pattern** drop-down menu has a list of 25 different patterns. The default pattern is a solid line.<br><br>Clicking on this dropdown will yield a preview of all the patterns along with a letter (a – y) when inside the drop-down menu, you may directly press any of these letters on your keyboard to select the stroke pattern. Unfortunately, these shortcut keys are not available outside this control. |

The **Stroke end** drop-down menu lets you select how the ending of a line will look. If you use a head or a tail symbol on a line, this will hide whatever you have chosen using this drop-down menu.

You have three choices: **Butt** option, **Round** option, and **Square** option.

The Butt option will cut the line at the very end of the line endpoint, while the Round and Square options will increase the length of the line past the endpoint.

For very thin lines, this does not matter, but if you have a thick line, this may matter as we will see next.

The **Corner Control** drop-down menu lets you set the behavior of corners of a shape.

You have three choices: **Miter** option, **Round** option, or **Bevel** option.

The Miter option will give your corner the sharpest look.

The Round option gives your corner a rounded look.

The Bevel option cuts off your corners.

Let's try out some of these parameters.

Draw an oblong, and set the thickness of this rectangle to 13 points.

Duplicate the oblong and place the duplicate to the right of the original.

You should now have two oblongs with the exact same widths and heights.

If you mark the right-hand oblong, and then click on the **Double Stroke** button you may think that the oblong on the right is much bigger. The truth is that it's only the thickness that has changed. The thickness is now 52 points instead of 13. Why 52 points you may ask? The reason is that 4 times 13 equals 52.

If your left oblong had a 10 points thickness, the resulting double stroke would yield a thickness of 40.

To prove that these two oblongs have the same height—the following screenshot shows each of the oblongs marked with a guide going through their horizontal **drag points**.

What you see here is that the upper and lower borders of each oblong are exactly the same.

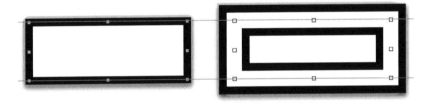

Now mark both oblongs, and then set the **Corner Control** drop-down menu to the **Round** option.

Notice the innermost line of the double line oblong—the corners are not rounded.

The reason for much heavier rounding of the double line oblong is that its outer stroke is farther from the oblong's actual border.

While you still have both oblongs marked, change the **Corner Control** drop-down menu to the **Bevel** option. The Bevel option will not alter the inner stroke.

The last thing you should try is to increase the **Corner Radius** of both oblongs. Notice how the bevel disappeared as soon as you increased the corner radius beyond 0.

If you increase the corner radius all the way (the maximum of 50 points), you will realize that this will also influence the inner stroke on the double stroke oblong.

If you want to see the finished diagram in full color – please open the file named `Oblong experiments.graffle`. As always, the file is found in `Chapter 3` folder in the download bundle.

You may also experiment with the stroke endings – below is how the various stroke endings affect the end points. For demonstration purposes, our strokes have a thickness of 20 points. Observe how the **Butt**, **Rounded**, and **Square** options influence the oblong.

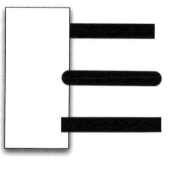

# Fill color and fill type

The **Fill property inspector** located in the Style selector is what you use to fill a shape. There are five kinds of fills available: Solid, Linear Blend, Radial Blend, Double Linear Blend, and Double Radial Blend.

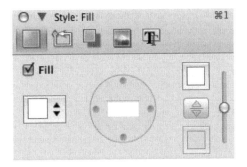

You can only fill a shape with a surface; this means a compound or a text shape. A line shape may be very thick, but it does not really have a surface.

| | |
|---|---|
| **☑ Fill** | The **Fill** checkbox toggles whether a shape will have a line or not. |
| | For the line shape, this checkbox disabled—that is, you cannot have a line that is filled. |
| | For compound and text shapes—if you leave this box unchecked—the shape becomes transparent. |
| [box] | The **Fill Style** drop-down menu lets you choose between the five fill styles. |
| | A **Solid** fill will render the shape with the chosen color. |
| | The **Linear Blend** fill will render the shape gradually from one color on one side of the shape, to a second color on the opposite side of the shape. You can control the direction with the Blend Direction wheel. |
| | The **Radial Blend** fill renders the shape from a particular point and outwards. You can control the center of the blend with the Blend Center control. |
| | The **Double Linear Blend** works much the same way as the Linear Blend, except it utilizes three colors instead of just two. |
| | The **Double Radial Blend** works the same as the Radial Blend, except it also utilizes three colors instead of just two. |

The **Blend Direction wheel** appears if the Linear Blend or the Double Linear Blend has been selected in the Fill Style drop-down menu.

The wheel controls in which direction the blend is flowing.

You can enter a number in the input box of the wheel—or you can take one of the four handles and use your mouse to drag the blend to the correct grade.

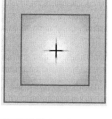

The **Blend Position** controls where the center of a Radial Blend or a Double Radial Blend will start.

The **Double Color Wells** appear if you have selected the Solid, Linear, or Radial blends in the Fill Style drop-down.

If you chose the Solid fill color—only the upper color well will be activated. Clicking on this button will activate the color picker and let you select your preferred color.

If you choose the Linear or Radial blends—all four elements of the control will be active. The upper color well selects the first blend color, while the bottom well selects the second blend color. The swap button will swap the first and second blend colors—while the **bias slider** on the right controls the shift between the two blend colors.

The **Triple Color Wells** are displayed if any of the Double Linear or Double Radial blends are activated with the Fill Style dropdown.

The three color wells behave the same as the Double Color Wells – you can choose the starting, the middle and the ending color of your blend.

There is unfortunately no swap-button available – but the bias slider will control the amount of starting and ending color.

Let's try out some blends.

Start by creating five shapes. The shapes do not need to be of the same kind. Then fill each shape with a different blend.

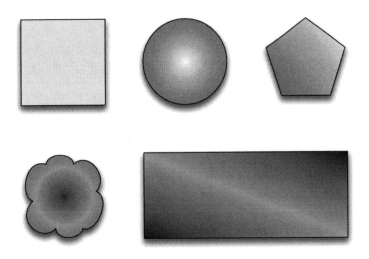

The rectangle shape is just filled with the Mercury color from the Crayons color palette.

The circle shape has a Radial Blend fill with the colors Snow and Tungsten (in the Crayons color palette).

By using the same colors as the circle, but using the Linear Blend with a 140° twist, the pentagon shape is not dull anymore.

The cloud has been filled using the Double Radial Blend—our selected colors are Lead, Aluminum, and Tungsten.

Lastly, the oblong is filled using the Double Linear Blend, with the start and ending color of Licorice—and the middle color of Tungsten.

**Blend well**

Look back in the *Tips and Pitfalls* section found in Chapter 1. The second tip was to colorize gently—this is important with simple two-color blends, but critical with triple-color blends. As a rule of thumb, never colorize with colors not complementing each other.

If you want to see the finished diagram in full color—please open the file named `Fill experiments.graffle`. The file is found in the `Chapter 3` folder in the download bundle.

In the beginning of this section you learned that if the Fill checkbox was not checked—the shape would become transparent. On the left you see two rectangles on top of each other. Both rectangles have been filled with different colors. On the right you see the same two rectangles, but now the topmost rectangle does not have a fill color.

Notice how the topmost rectangle still casts a shadow from its stroke.

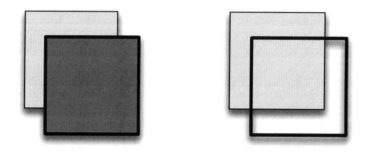

# Shadow type, color, and size

The **Shadow property inspector** is used when you want to add a shadow to a shape—or remove the shadow. Not all parts of your diagram will look good with shadows. Using shadows is a double-edged sword—it can make or break your diagram. If you shadow the wrong shapes, your diagram will not look true to life (that is, the way a shape interrupts a light source, creating a shadow). Like a fine illustrator, if you shadow the right shapes, your diagram becomes stunning, engaging the viewer more effectively.

If you recap the diagram you created in Chapter 1—you removed the shadow from the connection lines.

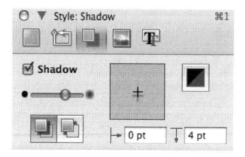

The following table lists out some of the controls from the Shadow property inspector:

| | |
|---|---|
|  | The **Shadow** checkbox toggles whether a shape will have a shadow or not.<br><br>You can shadow any shape irrespective of the shape, as long as it's a compound shape, a line shape or a text shape. |
|  | The **Shadow Fuzziness** slider let you choose how blurry your shadow will be. |
| 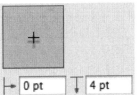 | The **Shadow Casting** buttons will control how the shadow of a shape will behave with respect to underlying shapes on the same layer.<br><br>To have a shadow situated on the shape below your current shape, you click on the **Shadow Beneath this Shape** button (the left button). Exercise caution about the order of your shapes—you might need to reorder your shapes when creating your diagram, for your shapes to be true to life.<br><br>If you want to have shadows from all shapes appear at the bottom of the stack of shapes, you use the **Shadow Behind all Shapes** button (the right button). |
|  | The **Shadow Offset** controls enable you to control the distance between the shape and its shadow. You can either use the **Shadow Offset Crosshair** or the **Shadow Offset Fields**. The Shadow Offset Fields have input for both vertical and horizontal placement.<br><br>The greater the offset, the further from the background your shape will look.<br><br>Do not make these numbers too big—if they are too big compared to the shape, then your diagram will look blurry and lackluster. |
|  | The **Shadow Color** well let you select which color the object shadow should have.<br><br>A good color for shadow use is black with an opacity of 75% - which incidentally is the default color of the OmniGraffle shadow palette. |

Let's do some experimentation with shadows.

The first thing you should do is to create a square and then a perfect circle. Place the circle on the square, letting the circle cover part of the square.

The square should have its shadow enabled, and the circle should not.

The result probably does not look quite right.

You will now mess this up even more by adding a shadow on the circle. After you have enabled the shadow on the circle, click on the **Shadow Beneath this Shape** button, and finalize your creative venture by entering **3 pt** in the **Horizontal Shadow Offset** field, and **5 pt** in the **Vertical Shadow Offset** field.

You should now have shadow from the circle on top of the square.

Not pretty, but that's the whole point of this exercise.

To make this diagram more effective, select the circle shape and click on the **Shadow Behind all Shapes** button. Notice how the shadows from the circle and the square are integrating into each other flawlessly.

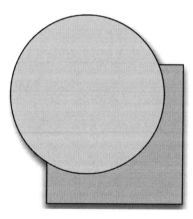

# Text type (font), color, and size

You use the **Text property inspector** every time you deal with text. Text is either a stand-alone text object, text within a compound shape, or as a line label.

The **Horizontal alignment** buttons change the text justification. You can justify your text four different ways:

- Align the text to the left within a shape
- Center the text within a shape
- Align the text to the right within a shape
- Justify the text within the set margin of a shape

The OmniGraffle default is *Center text within a shape*.

The **Vertical alignment** buttons control whether the text aligns to the top, middle, or bottom of a shape.

If you chose to align the text to the top of a shape, the text will start at the top and flow downwards.

If you choose to align the text to the middle of the shape, the text will start vertically centered and flow up and downwards.

If you chose to align the text to the bottom of the shape, the text will float from the bottom and upwards.

The OmniGraffle default is to *align the text to the middle of the shape*.

The **Text containment** buttons let you control what happens when there is more text that a given shape has room for. These controls give you three choices.

The left button controls if the text should **Overflow** the shape. If this button is activated, the text will flow above, below, or both above and below, depending on the **Vertical alignment** buttons. The text will be kept between the right and the left hand side of the shape, and not overflow horizontally.

The middle button controls if the text should be **Clipped**. When the text is clipped, the text will be cut off dependent on which of the **Vertical alignment** buttons is active. The text will be kept within the right and the left hand side of the shape, and no horizontal clipping will occur.

The right button vertically resizes the shape to fit the text. OmniGraffle will not on its own adjust the size horizontally — this is something you'll have to do by yourself.

The OmniGraffle default behavior is to *Overflow* the text of the shape.

The **Font** button brings up the standard Macintosh OS X font dialog where you can select the font family (Times, Courier, Helvetica, and so on), font type (normal, *italics*, bold, and so on), and size.

The **Color** well lets you choose which color your chosen font will have. Clicking on this button brings up the standard Macintosh OS X color chooser.

The **Kerning** checkbox automatically controls the spacing between the characters making your text look its best. For most text, this is the best choice.

When the **Kerning** checkbox is enabled, the **Tracking** cannot be set.

Tracking is the manual version of Kerning—that is, you can have 100% control of the spacing between characters.

**Leading** is a very fancy word for the space between each line of text. When you choose a font size, OmniGraffle will perform some internal calculation on the best possible space between lines based on typographic best practises.

You can use the Leading dialog when you need to override whatever is designated by OmniGraffle.

| | |
|---|---|
| Side Margin: 0 <br> Top/Bottom Margin: 0 | The **Margin** controls set the margins between the text and the shape edge. |

If you have the OmniGraffle Professional version, there are also a few extra options to control text behavior:

| | |
|---|---|
| ☑ Wrap to Shape | Tick the **Wrap to Shape** checkbox if the width of the text within a shape will be based on the *Text Offset* settings. Untick, if not. |
| Text Offset: <br> X: Y: <br> 0% 0% <br> Width: Height: <br> 100% 100% <br> ☐ Use default offsets | The **Text Offset** dialog box controls how the text is to be placed in relation to the corresponding shape. <br><br> By manipulating the **X%**, **Y%**, **Width**, and **Height**, you can create a bounding box for the text within your shape. <br><br> The **X**% and **Y**% controls where the bounding box is going to start. <br><br> The **Width** and **Height** control behave in proportion to the shapes *Margin*. |
| Text Rotation: <br> ⦿ Relative <br> ○ Absolute <br> 0° ○ | The **Text Rotation** lets you choose the rotation of the text. <br><br> The text can be rotated either to the relative rotation of the shape, or absolutely compared to the canvas. <br><br> The rotational value can be entered in a field, or you can rotate the rotation wheel to adjust. |

Now it's time to experiment with the various text settings.

The first thing you need is a shape—a rectangle shape is a good starting point.

This is a plain vanilla oblong with shadows and a 1 point line stroke.

You'll also need some text. In this example, we have used a passage from *Pride and Prejudice* by Jane Austen. The text is taken from the excellent Project Gutenberg free-eBook repository. You can find the project home page at `http://www.gutenberg.org/` and the full text of *Pride and Prejudice* at `http://www.gutenberg.org/etext/1342`.

We'll use a passage from *Chapter 20*, and if you have seen the blockbuster movie with Keira Knightley, you may remember this to be one of the most enjoyable parts of the film.

If you want to use the same text as found in our example, you can open the file named `Text experiments.graffle` from the download bundle. The file is found in the `Chapter 3` folder in the download bundle

After pasting the text, things do not look quite right, due to the default settings of OmniGraffle.

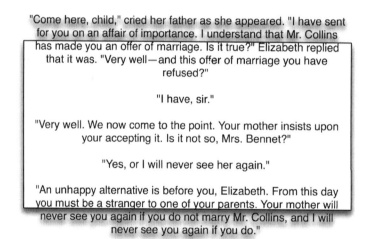

Notice how the text inherits the shadow from the oblong. Actually, the whole text has a shadow, but since the oblong is filled with the white color, this will override the text shadow within the oblong.

Before we fix the text and the shape, let's make detour by clicking on the Clip text containment button (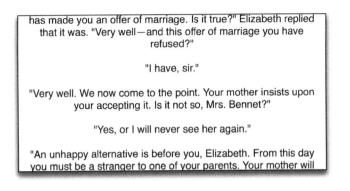). A lot of interesting text is now gone.

has made you an offer of marriage. Is it true?" Elizabeth replied that it was. "Very well—and this offer of marriage you have refused?"

"I have, sir."

"Very well. We now come to the point. Your mother insists upon your accepting it. Is it not so, Mrs. Bennet?"

"Yes, or I will never see her again."

"An unhappy alternative is before you, Elizabeth. From this day you must be a stranger to one of your parents. Your mother will

Now, let's fix this once and for all and have the shape fit the text. You could of course manually extend the shape in whichever direction you want or you could click on the **Resize to Fit** text containment button (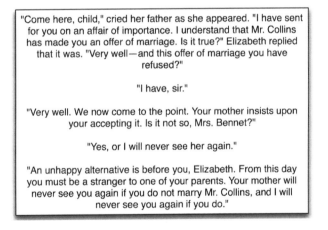), to transform it into nicely enclosed text.

"Come here, child," cried her father as she appeared. "I have sent for you on an affair of importance. I understand that Mr. Collins has made you an offer of marriage. Is it true?" Elizabeth replied that it was. "Very well—and this offer of marriage you have refused?"

"I have, sir."

"Very well. We now come to the point. Your mother insists upon your accepting it. Is it not so, Mrs. Bennet?"

"Yes, or I will never see her again."

"An unhappy alternative is before you, Elizabeth. From this day you must be a stranger to one of your parents. Your mother will never see you again if you do not marry Mr. Collins, and I will never see you again if you do."

Another solution would of course be to change the size of the font—with the standard OmniGraffle shape font (Helvetica) changing the size from the default 12 point to 10 point would also solve the problem.

Unless you, and the rest of the world, are very comfortable with reading centered text passages, this makes for less than Elysian diagrams. Centered text is good for key words and smaller sentences. By clicking on the left justification button ( ) you should have a pretty good-looking text passage. The only thing missing is a tad wider margin. Enter the value of **15** into the **Side** and **Top/Bottom** margin dialog boxes—notice how the shape will adjust the height on its own.

> "Come here, child," cried her father as she appeared. "I have sent for you on an affair of importance. I understand that Mr. Collins has made you an offer of marriage. Is it true?" Elizabeth replied that it was. "Very well—and this offer of marriage you have refused?"
>
> "I have, sir."
>
> "Very well. We now come to the point. Your mother insists upon your accepting it. Is it not so, Mrs. Bennet?"
>
> "Yes, or I will never see her again."
>
> "An unhappy alternative is before you, Elizabeth. From this day you must be a stranger to one of your parents. Your mother will never see you again if you do not marry Mr. Collins, and I will never see you again if you do."

# Placing images inside shapes

You use the **Image property inspector** when you need to use an image as the background of a compound shape (this also includes text shapes). You cannot add a image background to a line shape as lines do not have an "area" to speak of.

It is unfortunately not possible to copy and paste an image directly into a shape as you can do with text, but as you will learn next—it is possible to paste an image using the Image style palette.

If you copy and paste an image into OmniGraffle without first selecting a shape, this image will in fact become a new oblong or square shape without shadows, line strokes, etc.

However, even if you cannot paste an image directly into a shape, you can drag an image from another application like Photo Booth and iPhoto and drop it onto the shape.

| Image ▼ | The **Image** drop-down menu is used to add an image to a shape or to remove an already set image for a shape. |

The **Image** drop-down menu is used to add an image to a shape or to remove an already set image for a shape.

When clicking on the dropdown and choosing the **Set Image...** option, you'll notice a pretty standard Macintosh OS X file dialog box, except for two extra options at the bottom of the dialog box:

- Include image in document
- Link to image file

If you include the image in the document, you'll be safe if you need to share your OmniGraffle document with others—the image will be embedded into the OmniGraffle document.

If you link to the image file, the image may be lost if you try to open the document on another computer or if the image file is moved or deleted.

When you have linked an image instead of embedding the image – the Image drop-down menu will have three extra choices:

- Open in the Preview program
- Reveal in finder so you easily can locate the file
- Embed the linked file into the document

The **Image well** contains a preview of the image, but with respect to the shape's bounding box.

In the empty image well on the left you can see the shape's bounding box.

In the image well on the right, you'll notice an image of a sparrow not extending all through the boundaries of the shape.

A very cool thing you can also do with the Image well is to paste an image into the Image well. Copying an image from the Image well also works as expected.

You can also use the Image well to position the image — just drag the image around the Image well. Notice that this can only be done if the natural aspect ratio is selected, use the **Aspect Ratio** buttons. When moving the image around, the values in the **Positioning Offsets** will also change.

You can also click on the Image well, and then press the *Delete* button on your keyboard to delete the image from the shape.

The **Aspect Ratio** buttons control the associated images aspect ratio.

The left button toggles the natural aspect ratio of the image. You can then use the **Image size** slider and the positioning control to correctly place your image.

The middle button stretches the image to the boundaries of the shape. If this button is toggled, you cannot use the **Image size** slider to control its size.

The right button tiles up the image to fill the shape. Be aware that this button will not make tiled images automatically align to a shape's borders. If you need to align the image to a shape's border, you'll have to adjust its size with the **Image size** slider. Even adjusting its size will not guarantee a perfect fit unless the aspect ratio of the shape is the same as the image.

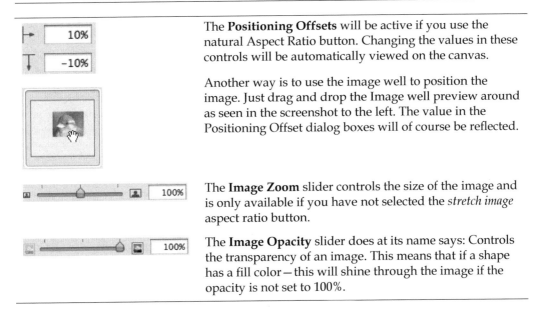

The **Positioning Offsets** will be active if you use the natural Aspect Ratio button. Changing the values in these controls will be automatically viewed on the canvas.

Another way is to use the image well to position the image. Just drag and drop the Image well preview around as seen in the screenshot to the left. The value in the Positioning Offset dialog boxes will of course be reflected.

The **Image Zoom** slider controls the size of the image and is only available if you have not selected the *stretch image* aspect ratio button.

The **Image Opacity** slider does at its name says: Controls the transparency of an image. This means that if a shape has a fill color—this will shine through the image if the opacity is not set to 100%.

Let's play around with a few images found in the `Image` folder in the download bundle.

First thing you need is a shape—a nice big rectangle will do.

Now click on the **Image** drop-down menu ( Image ▼ ) and click on the **Set image...** option. Navigate to the `Image` directory in the download bundle. Click on the `Sparrow head.jpg` and embed the image into your OmniGraffle document.

In this folder, there are a few images, which you can experiment and play around with.

> If you did not click on the shape before you clicked on the image drop-down menu, your image will be set as the canvas' background image. This is also how you associate an image with a canvas background.

If you click on the various aspect ratio buttons, you'll notice how the image is either stretched or tiled:

Now you should fill your shape with a color—any color will do. In the following picture we have used the **Silver** color from the Crayons palette.

If you now play with the opacity slider, you'll notice that the background color will shine through your picture—this is especially true if you use a very bright color instead of the Silver color we have chosen for this example.

Instead of the sparrow's head, let's use the image named `sparrow.jpg`. This is a much bigger image, which includes the whole sparrow and some background scenery.

On the right you see the corresponding screen capture from the *Image well*. Notice how the size of the image goes beyond the boundaries of the shape.

As it stands now, the picture is badly cropped—the poor bird has its feet and tail cut off! Just drag the image around in the Image well to position the sparrow better. You may also have to use the *Image resize slider* if your shape was smaller than the one portrayed in this example.

With some work, your final diagram should look like the following one. To the right is the Image style palette as it appears with this very diagram.

# Ordering shapes

To get your diagram to look exactly as you want, you may need to reorder your shapes. One way to do the reordering is via the canvas layers. This will become very tedious if you have a big diagram, also best practises regarding canvas layers are to stick conceptually equal shapes on the same layer.

This section will teach you to reorder shapes within the same layer.

Start with three shapes drawn in the following sequence: Square, Circle, and Cloud. Let the Circle overlap the Square and let the Cloud partly cover both the Square and the Circle. Inside the square, write **1**, inside the Circle write **2**, and inside the Cloud write **3**. These numbers indicate in which sequence the shapes where created.

What you have done here is for each new shape you draw, the shape will be put on top of the other shapes. If you never draw overlapping shapes, you may not have noticed this at all.

If you try to drag the circle in and out of the group of shapes, it will still be sandwiched between the square and the cloud. The same applies to the square—it will always be at the bottom of the stack.

What if you needed to move the square to the top of the stack of shapes?

There are a couple of ways to achieve this—you can click on the shape you want to reorder, and use the **Arrange | Bring to Front** menu command. The keyboard shortcut is ⇧+⌘+*F*. Using any of these two methods will bring the square to the front of the shape stack.

To put it back at the bottom of the stack, use the **Arrange | Send to Back** menu command, or the corresponding ⇧+⌘+*B* keyboard shortcut command.

On the standard Canvas Toolbar, you will also find commands to bring shapes to the back or front of the shape stack:

What if you need to just move your shape up or down one position in the shape stack? You can reorder shapes by right-clicking on a shape and then using the **Arrange** context menu. This will not only bring up the **Bring To Front / Send To Back** actions, but also **Bring Forward** and **Send Backward**.

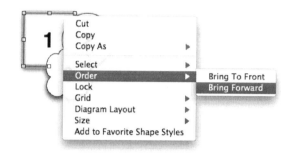

Executing **Bring Forward** will result in the following diagram. Because this is a context sensitive menu, only menu commands that can be executed will be activated.

# Grouping shapes

When working with diagrams, you will often encounter the possibility that several shapes belong together as a group and that you would like to work on these shapes like they were one complex shape. This is possible with OmniGraffle; you can group shapes together to become a single shape.

If you have used corresponding group functionality from other software titles, you may have become annoyed that you must ungroup your shape groups—change one shape—and then regroup your shapes again. With OmniGraffle you do not need to be annoyed anymore. In fact, you can change just one shape in a group of shapes. This is pretty cool and a great time saver.

You can also apply style formatting like color fill, thickness of strokes, font formatting, and so on to the whole group. When you do this, every shape in the group will inherit this new style.

# Creating a group of shapes

A group of shapes must have two or more shapes. These shapes can be placed anywhere on the canvas. The shapes can even be on separate layers, but when you group them together they will be moved to the topmost layer of the grouped shapes.

Grouping shapes is done by selecting the shapes you want to have in a group and using the **Arrange | Group** menu command, or use the ⇧+⌘+*G* keyboard shortcut command. You can also right-click on the selected shapes and operate the **Group** context menu command. Depending on how you are working with OmniGraffle, clicking the group tool on the Canvas Toolbar may be more efficient than keyboard shortcuts or navigating menus. The Canvas Toolbar group tool icon is seen previously.

Now, let's group some objects.

First, create three shapes: An oblong, a perfect circle that goes inside the oblong, and then a triangle to the right of the oblong.

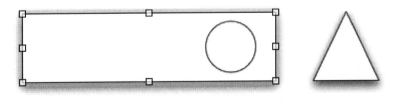

The next thing you do is mark the oblong and the circle, and then group these shapes by using one of the group commands.

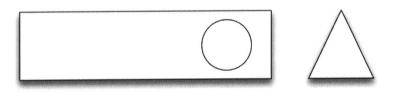

Notice how the circle and the oblong now are one object. Also observe how the **Group** command on the Canvas Toolbar is actually a toggle, and it now displays **Ungroup**. This is the visual cue that you are dealing with a group of shapes.

You can now proceed to select both the group containing the oblong and the circle— and then the triangle – and group these together. What you now have is a **nested** group. This may not be what you want to do, and having nested groups can be potentially confusing when working with these complex objects.

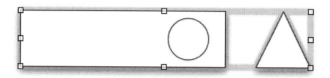

# Ungrouping a group of shapes

When clicking on a group of objects, the grouping symbol on the Canvas Toolbar will state that you are now working with a group of objects. Clicking on this tool will ungroup your shapes. If you have a nested group, the last objects grouped will be ungrouped. You can of course also use the ⇧+⌘+U keyboard shortcut command. You will also have access to the **Arrange | Ungroup** menu command, and the **Ungroup** command in the context menu when you right-click on the group of shapes.

Now, you can right-click on the grouped shape, and then execute the **Ungroup** command.

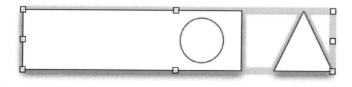

The result after this ungroup operation is now two shapes . . . your first group of shapes (oblong and circle) and the triangle:

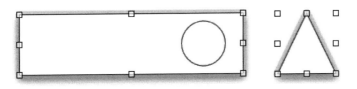

# Resizing shape groups

You can resize a group of shapes, but you can also resize individual shapes within a group.

Add your triangle to the existing shape group. You will now have the new group marked the same way as if you were to click on the group once.

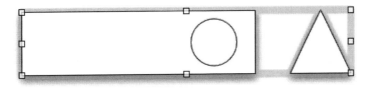

Let's resize and move the triangle next to the circle.

To do this, click once more on the rectangle. You will now see that the rectangle shows all of its eight drag points—this means that you can resize the triangle, but also move it around—like it was never part of the group at all.

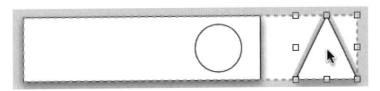

You can even restyle the triangle if you like. Fill the triangle with some color and add a shadow immediately beneath the shape.

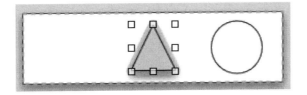

If you need to resize the whole group, just click on one of the groups and use one of the drag points as you would on any other shape. Extend the length of your group.

The first thing you should see is that the circle is not a circle anymore, but an oval.

If you really wanted to keep the circle round, you would first have to select the oblong element within the group and extend this as far as you needed. Then you would have to move all the other elements in the shape group to their correct places. This can become very elaborate and very often it's faster to ungroup all shapes; move and resize whatever elements you need to move and resize; and then finally regroup your shapes.

# Adjusting shapes with the Geometry property inspector

The **Geometry property inspector,** as the name implies, helps you control the geometry of a shape. These properties are the X and Y positions on the canvas, the width and height of the shape, and the shape's rotation.

You have also access to functions for flipping (that is, mirroring) your shape both vertically and horizontally.

Finally, you can adjust how the *Line Label* should be placed in relation to its line.

Let's examine the various options available in this inspector.

| X: | Y: |
| --- | --- |
| 4 cm | 10 cm |

The **Shapes Coordinate** fields control the shape's placement on the canvas. The placement is shown based on the current document *measurement type* (cm, inches, pixels, and so on).

You can enter any legal values in these fields. The measurement type can also be entered, and OmniGraffle will automatically convert the value into your document's chosen unit.

You can also enter offset values (that is, 50%), and OmniGraffle will automatically compute the new value, and move the shape(s) to the new position.

The values represent the upper-left corner of a shape's selection box. If your shape is rotated, it might not be very obvious that these values are correct—you'll investigate this later on.

The value in these fields is in relationship to the canvas' origin. The canvas' origin (where both the value of the X and Y is zero) is normally in the upper-left corner.

If you select more than one shape – you may notice a double dash (--) in one or both fields. This is a indication that at least one shape has different values from the others.

| Width: | Height: |
|--------|---------|
| 6 cm | 3 cm |

☑ Maintain aspect ratio

The **Shapes Size** fields control a shape's size. The width and height shown is based on the current document measurement type (cm, inches, pixels, and so on).

You can enter any legal values in these fields. The measurement type can also be entered, and OmniGraffle will automatically convert the value into your document's chosen unit.

You can also enter offset values (that is, 50%), and OmniGraffle will automatically compute the new size value, and resize the shape automatically.

The **Maintain aspect ratio** checkbox will change the width or height based on the value you enter in the opposite box (that is, entering a new value in the width field, will automatically change the height field with the appropriate proportional value and vice-versa).

If you select more than one shape, you may notice a double dash (--) in one or both fields. This is a indication that at least one shape has different values from the others.

The **Shapes Rotation** wheel controls a shape's rotation.

You can either enter a number in the field, or you can drag (clockwise or counter clockwise) the rotation wheel.

As with all input boxes in the property inspectors, this field will also compute new values, and perform rotation based on offset values.

The **Flip** buttons, or the **Mirror** buttons as they are also named, will flip a shape 180° either horizontally or vertically.

Beware that clicking any of these buttons **will not** impact the value in the rotation field above.

Label Location:      Label Offset:

Horizontal

✓ Horizontal
Vertical
Parallel
Perpendicular
Independent

The **Line Label** controls manage how a line label is placed in relation to its line.

You can control how far from the beginning or end of the line a label should be using the **Label Location** slider.

You control how far below or above a line the label should be placed using the **Label Offset** slider.

The **Label Orientation** drop-down menu controls a label's rotation in lieu of its line.

Let's perform a few experiments with the basic controls before venturing into the more complex Line Label controls.

Start with a new OmniGraffle document. Add a Right Triangle at the position **X = 1 cm**, **Y = 1 cm**, **Width = 10 cm**, and **Height = 4 cm**.

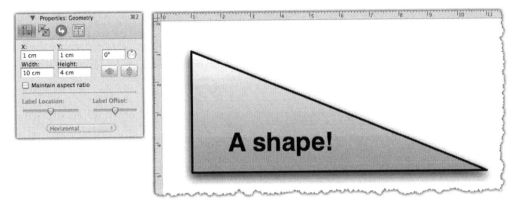

Click on the Horizontal Flip button.

The text and the Linear Blend fill are still intact.

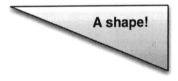

Now, enable the Vertical Flip button.

The text and the linear blend are still intact.

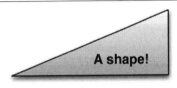

Release both the Flip buttons, and rotate the shape 180°.

Everything is now turned upside down.

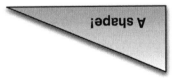

Enable both Flip buttons.

You now have the original shape, but with the text and the Linear Blend filling upside down.

This small experiment shows how easy it is to change the look of a shape just by manipulating the geometric properties.

You could achieve the same result through a lot more work were it not for these controls.

# Line Label controls

The Line Label controls may at first sight be quite a challenge. However, it's really easy to get a grasp of these.

In the following table, we have four lines—one horizontal, one vertical, one horizontal line rotated 45°, and lastly a sloped line. You can find these lines in the file name Line Label experiments.graffle, which can be found in the download bundle, under the Chapter 3 folder. The download bundle contains most of the diagrams found in this book, and can be downloaded from http://www.packtpub.com/.

This is the default placement of the Line Labels.

Nothing fancy here, but the labels still look quite good.

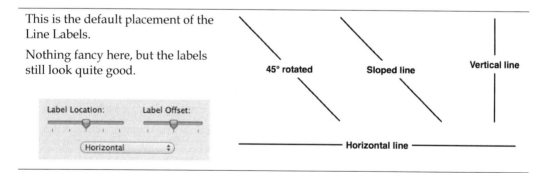

Setting the orientation drop-down menu to **Vertical** is really the same as rotating the label 270°.

This really does not look very good.

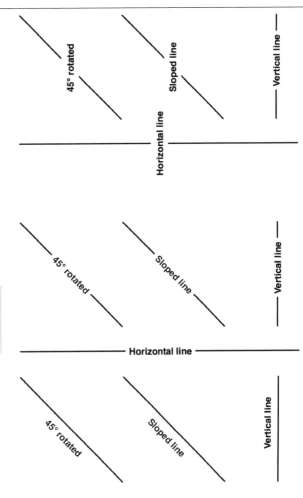

The basic **Parallel** orientation is good to use if you have a lot of sloped (or rotated) lines.

The orientation is still set to **Parallel**.

However, we have adjusted the **Label Offset** a little to the left.

The result of moving the offset to the left is that the labels will be placed either to the left or under the corresponding line.

If the offset were to be moved to the right of the center, the labels would be placed over, or to the right of the line.

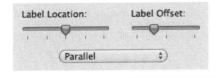

The **Perpendicular** orientation might be good for a vertical line—and even acceptable for a rotated or a sloped line—but for a horizontal line this does not look too good!

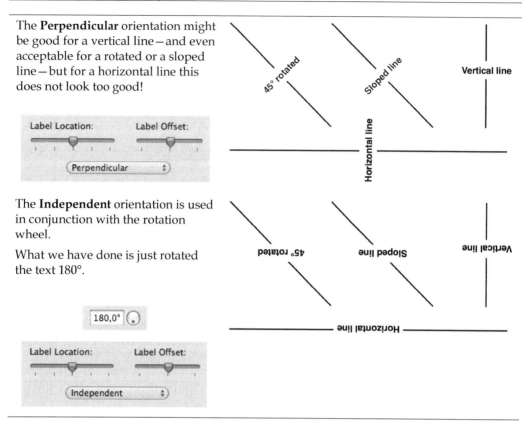

The **Independent** orientation is used in conjunction with the rotation wheel.

What we have done is just rotated the text 180°.

You have now learned how to get perfect placement for your Line Labels.

For most day-to-day uses, the **Horizontal** or default orientation will be more than sufficient. If this does not give you what you want, try to use the **Parallel** setting and adjust the **Label Offset** appropriately.

If this also fails to give you the desired results, then you should first try out the **Independent** orientation before any of the remaining orientations.

# The Rulers and Inspector Bar

The **Inspector Bar** comes in two editions. The first bar shown here, is visible if you have selected a shape, the second version is visible if you are editing text.

Below the Inspector Bar are the canvas rulers.

Using the **View | Rulers** you can turn on and off the visibility of the inspector bar and the rulers. You can also use the ⌘+R keyboard shortcut command. We'll deal with the ruler later on.

# The Shape Inspector Bar

The really nifty thing about the **Shape Inspector Bar** is that it gives you quick access to geometry settings from the *Geometry property inspector*, color fillings from the *Fill property inspector*, line controls from the *Line and Shapes property inspector*, shadow control from the *Shadow property inspector*, and finally the connection toggle from the *Connection property inspector*.

Instead of opening and closing all these inspectors for a lot of common tasks, you can use the *Shape Inspector Bar* instead.

Granted, what you get from the *Shape Inspector Bar* is a subset of available functions. However, the functions provided by this bar are those that you will probably be using all the time.

| | |
|---|---|
| ⊢ 3 cm   ↨ 4 cm   ↔ 10 cm   ↕ 6 cm | These controls are the same as you will find in the *Geometry property inspector*. |
| | From left to right we have the X and Y position of the shape. |
| | The last two control the width and the height of the selected shape. |
| [fill controls] | These controls are the simplified version of the *Fill property inspector*. |
| | You can choose the fill type (No Fill, Solid Color, and the various blends available). |
| | You have access to the same three color wells that you normally find in the inspector. The wells will be enabled based on the fill type you have chosen. |
| | If you have chosen one of the linear blends – the blend direction wheel is then enabled. |
| [line controls] 1 pt | The simplified version of the *Line and Shapes property inspector* affects only the line property (i.e. you cannot change the shape type). |
| | The dropdown gives you access to the stroke style and corner styles. You also get access to the line type (straight, curved, orthogonal and Bézier), and you can even choose the line endings. |
| | The color well let's you choose the color of the line. |
| | The control to the very right is the thickness of the line. |

This button turns shadowing on or off for the selected shape.

This button enables or disables line connections to and from other shapes on the selected shape.

# The Text Inspector Bar

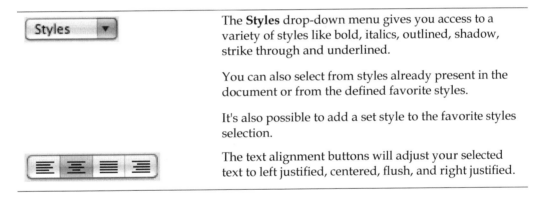

The Text Inspector Bar appears as soon as you begin to edit text. The text can be a pure text shape, or text within a shape.

While active, you'll see a whole lot of small black triangles on the canvas ruler – these triangles are the various tab stops defined for your selected text.

The **Styles** drop-down menu gives you access to a variety of styles like bold, italics, outlined, shadow, strike through and underlined.

You can also select from styles already present in the document or from the defined favorite styles.

It's also possible to add a set style to the favorite styles selection.

The text alignment buttons will adjust your selected text to left justified, centered, flush, and right justified.

**Spacing** ▼

The Spacing drop-down menu controls the spacing between the selected text lines. You have three choices: **Single**, **Double**, and **Other...**

Selecting the **Other...** option reveals a dialog box which lets you fine tune the line spacing.

| | | | |
|---|---|---|---|
| Line height multiple | 1,0 | | times |
| | ○ Exactly | 0,0 | points |
| Line height | ⦿ At least | | |
| | ☐ At most | 0,0 | points |
| Inter-line spacing | | 0,0 | points |
| Paragraph spacing | before | 0,0 | points |
| | after | 0,0 | points |

( Cancel )  ( OK )

It is possible to adjust parameters like:

- The height of the text line based on the size of the font

- The spacing between lines

- The spacing before and after paragraphs

**Lists** ▼

The **Lists** drop-down menu will autonumber the selected text lines within a shape.

There is a set of predefined list styles like numeric lists, alphabetical lists, bulleted lists, and finally the ability to define your own list.

To use this function, just select the text lines within a shape and apply the preferred list type.

▶ ◆ ◀ ◉

You can drag any of the tabstop controls down to the ruler line.

From left to right, you have *Left Tab Stop*, *Center Tab Stop*, *Right Tab Stop* and *Decimal Tab Stop*.

# The Canvas rulers

The Canvas rulers are shown in the selected measurement unit set in the *Canvas Size property inspector*.

When you move a shape around the canvas, you'll see three lines on each of the rulers indicating the left, right, top, bottom, and center placement of the selected shape.

The canvas origin is normally in the upper-left corner. It's possible to change the origin by dragging the upper left corner into the canvas itself — or use the *Canvas Size property inspector* (details of this inspector are found in *Chapter 8, Canvases and Canvas Layers*).

The new origin will be visible as a set of blue lines crossing each other.

To reset the origin back to its default, just double click in the upper-left corner of the rulers. You can of course drag the blue line back to the origin and achieve the same result.

For OmniGraffle Professional users, the canvas rulers have one more function: You can drag a vertical or horizontal guide from the ruler and onto the canvas. To remove a ruler, you can of course drag it off the side of the the canvas.

# Connecting shapes

In Chapter 1, you learned how to connect two compound shapes using the line shape. You even changed the way the shapes connected to each other by changing the **Connection property** palette.

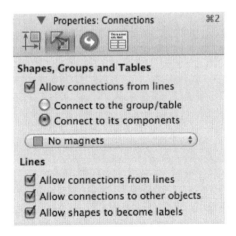

Let us examine the various connection properties for shapes available in OmniGraffle. The **Connection property inspector** handles connection settings for shapes (line shapes, compound shapes and the text shape), groups and tables. For more information on tables, see *Chapter 5, More on Editing Diagrams*.

| | |
|---|---|
| ☑ Allow connections from lines | The **Allow connections from lines** checkbox controls if the connection lines will "stick" to the shape. |
| | If you allow connections from lines, the connector line will always be attached to the shape, even if you move the shape around the canvas. |
| | If you do not enable this checkbox, you can still draw a line to the shape—the line may look like it's connected to the shape, but as soon as you move the shape the connection line will not follow the shape. |
| ○ Connect to the group/table<br>◉ Connect to its components | These settings handle the **Group and Table Connections**. |
| | If you have a grouped shape (or a table), it is not always desirable to let connection lines attach to the single shapes making up the group, or to the single cells of the table. |
| | If you want your connection lines to attach to the group, then select the **Connect to the group/table** option. |
| | If your need is to let connections go to the single objects within a group, select the **Connect to its components** option instead. |
| | These options are only available if you have selected a grouped shape or a table. |

The **Magnet selection** drop-down menu contains several presets for shape magnets. As you learned in Chapter 1, magnets are attachment points on a shape that connection lines will attach to.

You can choose to have

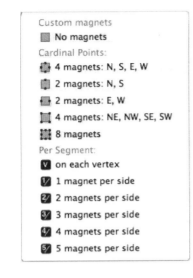

- **No magnets** – lines will still attach to the shape. However, when moving its connected shape around – the connetion point will also move.

- **Cardinal point** based magnets – magnets are placed according to the cardinal compass points (North, South, East, and West) and 2, 4 and 8 magnets per shape are possible.

- A number of magnets on each side, including the corner (vertex) of the shape.

If you find the predefined magnets lacking, you can create your own custom magnets. The simple way is to first select one of the dropdown options, then hold down the *Shift key* (⇧) and then select another option from the drop-down list.

As a last resort you can use the Magnet Tool to really do some hard customization. This tool is covered in *Chapter 4, More Tools for Editing Diagrams*.

The **Line Connection** options are only active if you have selected a line shape.

The **Allow connections from lines** toggles if the line will take on connections from other lines. The line will still connect to other shapes and behave like a connection line.

The **Allow connections to other objects** controls if the line is a connection line or not.

The **Allow shapes to become labels** will control whether or not (text) shapes dragged onto the line will be converted into a line label.

Now on to some experiments.

Before continuing, you will want to switch on the visibility of your magnets. Use the **View** | **Magnets** menu command to toggle the visibility on or off.

Continue using the document with your grouped shapes. Under the grouped shape, add a square, and add two cardinal points magnets (East and West) using the **Magnet selection** drop-down menu. Your square should have two pink circles, indicating the magnets on each side.

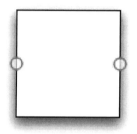

Now, hold down your *Shift* key and select the **on each vertex** (a magnet on each corner). You should now have three magnets on each side of the square for a total of six magnets.

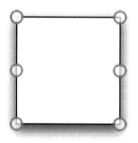

The next thing you should do is create a connection line between the two connection points on the top of the square to the circle and the rectangle in the grouped shape. If you just click on the square shape and then the rectangle, a connection will be made with the shortest distance between shapes. In this scenario, it's the right connection point from the square that will be used. You can set this correctly by dragging the connection line from a connection point to another shape, or connection point. Without too much work, your diagram should now look like the following one:

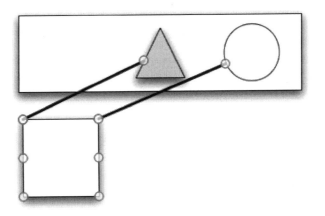

The connection points you see on the rectangle and the circle really belong to the connection lines – not the shapes as both of these shapes have the **No magnets** selected in the Magnet selection drop-down menu.

Now, select the grouped shape and change the **Group and Table Connection** settings to **Connect to the Group/Table**.

You can now try to drag a connection line from the bottom right connection point on the square to the circle. You will not be able to do that; as soon as you try to drag the connection line to the circle it immediately attaches itself to the shape group.

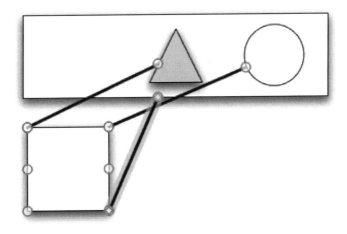

With the two connection lines crossing each other, this diagram is not very good looking. Let's fix this.

Click on the group shape and add **5 magnets per side**.

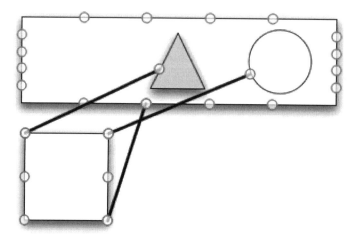

The lines are still crossing each other, but you should now just have to drag the problematic connection line to one of the other magnets on the grouped shape.

Just click on the line and drag the end of the line to the rightmost magnet on the grouped shape.

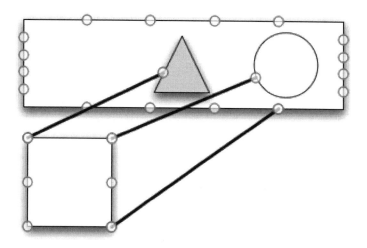

If you resize and drag the square shape around your canvas, you will see that the connections to the rectangle and the circle are very dynamic, while connection lines to fixed connection points are of course not moving about.

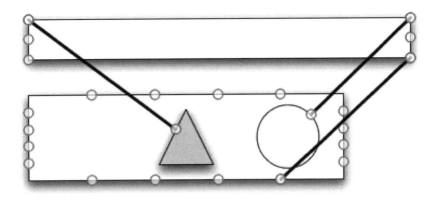

# Summary

In this chapter, you learned about the building blocks that make up a diagram—shapes.

Shapes come in three types: Lines, Compound, and Text shapes. You learned that the text shape is just like any other compound shape. You also learned that if you group several shapes together, this group is considered to be a new (complex) compound shape.

You learned to change the appearance of compound shapes and the properties of lines. You also learned that the text shape is just a special version of the compound shape.

You learned about the time saving feature of using the favourite shape functions.

We also looked into Shape style properties, and learned that most of these can be applied to all kinds of shapes.

Grouping shapes is both time saving and pretty nifty—use this feature often and your diagramming becomes very efficient.

Adjusting shapes using only the mouse is fine and dandy, but often you'll need more control—this is where the *Geometry property inspector* comes into play.

What are diagrams without line connectors? There are several ways to manage line connectors through the number of magnets you use—or the decision to use no magnets at all.

You have not learned the very basis of diagramming with OmniGraffle. The next chapter will give you even more tools to become efficient with the program. This is a chapter you should not skip.

# 4

# More Tools for
# Editing Diagrams

So far you have learned to create a diagram *the hard way* to learn the basics of what goes into making a diagram from nothing to the finished drawing. This chapter is going to teach you to use time saving tools when working with your diagrams.

These tools are found in the Expanded Canvas Toolbar.

For certain kinds of diagrams, you can use OmniGraffle without even touching the mouse.

In this chapter, you will cover the following topics:

- The Expanded Canvas Toolbar and its keyboard shortcuts
- The Canvas Toolbar tools not covered so far like the pen tool, the diagramming tool, style brush tool, and so on
- How to make an interactive diagram using the Action Browse Tool and the Action Property Inspector
- Automatic layout and mouseless editing
- How the outlines and list functions will let you create hierarchical diagrams the easy way
- How to apply diagram styles to quickly change your diagram's appearance.

# The Expanded Canvas Toolbar

OmniGraffle Version 5 deploys something called the **Expando-collapso technology**. This is basically a very nifty way of getting access to more functionality on limited screen real estate.

To the right of the tools palette, you see a bar with a rectangle making up an arrow. This widget is called the expando-collapso technology. Clicking on this arrow expands the toolbar. This is the *expando* part of the technolgy.

You'll notice that the arrow has now changed direction, and clicking on the arrow once more contracts the canvas toolbar into its original form with only the four basic tools available. This is the *collapso* part of the technology.

Big parts of this chapter are devoted to these tools. The tools are, from left to right: the Pen Tool, the Diagramming Tool, the Style Brush Tool, the Rubber Stamp Tool, the Magnet Tool, the Zoom Tool, the Move Tool and the Action Browse Tool.

# The floating Canvas Tool palette

If you are accustomed to have your drawing tools as a floating palette – you can either issue the **Window | Tool Palette** menu command or use the ⌥+⌘+*T* keyboard shortcut command.

A new **Tool Palette** will now appear. You can now resize this palette as you wish. If you drag the Tool Palette to one of the canvas borders, it will attach itself to that border. The tools you have in the Canvas Toolbar are still visible and there for your convenience.

# Customizing the Canvas Toolbar

OmniGraffle allows for customization of your *Canvas Toolbar* to have other tools present than the same tools found in the *Toolbar Palette*. If you right-click on the Canvas Toolbar, you'll see a menu command called **Customize Toolbar...**

This way of customizing the toolbar works the same way as a lot of Macintosh software programs: Drag and drop the tools you want to add or remove from the toolbar. When you are done, press the **Done** button.

The changes you make to your *Canvas Toolbar* will appear next time you start OmniGraffle.

# The Canvas Toolbar preferences

It is possible to change which tool belongs on the expanded toolbar and not. To do this go to the **OmniGraffle | Preferences** menu command and click on the **Drawing Tools** icon. A super-quick way to get to the **Preference** menu is to press the ⌘+, keyboard shortcut command.

On the left-hand side you see a list of all the Canvas Toolbar actions (**Selection**, **Shape**, **Line**, **Text**, and so on) along with a divider line between the **Text** and the **Pen** tool. You can now drag the divider line to whereever you want it. The changes you make to the toolbar are immediate—no need to save your work and re-open OmniGraffle.

If you drag the divider to the very top—the whole slew of toolbar actions can be expanded and collapsed. In the two upper rows from the following screenshot, you'll see the toolbar action both collapsed and expanded.

However, if you drag the divider to the very bottom of the list of toolbar actions, then the expando-collapso tool disappears completely from the canvas toolbar menu. This is seen in the bottom row of Canvas Toolbars in the following screenshot:

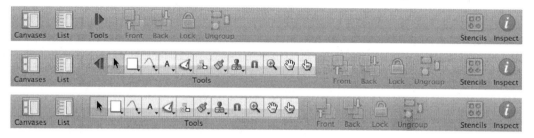

On the right side of the Tools Preferences pane, you can set the preference for how a tool should behave when it is single-clicked or double-clicked. The default settings make perfect sense for most people's diagramming needs, except the **Line Editing** preference; This should really be set to **Double-click to add a label**. The book author does create everything from simple box diagrams to elaborate and complex technical diagrams with a lot of lines, and in almost of all his diagrams he needs line labels—and adding line labels the way you did in chapter one is tiresome.

However, if your main diagramming consists of using the line tool—then you should stick to the **Double-click to add a point** setting.

# Keyboard shortcuts for the Canvas Toolbar

By pressing the number keys *1* to *0* on your keyboard, you will quickly select the corresponding tool on the Canvas Toolbar. By pressing twice on the number key, you can select the tool, for multiple uses, in the same way as if you had double-clicked on the tool with your mouse.

| | Tool | Hot Key |
|---|---|---|
| ▶ | Selection | v |
| ☐ | Shape | s |
| ⌒ | Line | c |
| A | Text | t |

When you investigated the Tool Preferences in the previous section, you may have noticed the **Hot Key** column.

These keyboard shortcut commands *temporarily select a given tool.*

Try this on your own by creating a new blank canvas.

Press the numeric 2 key twice to select the **Shape Tool** for multiple use. Then draw a couple of shapes.

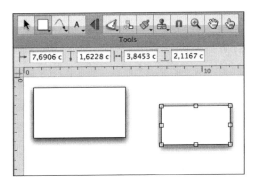

Now, hold down the C key on your keyboard. Notice how the *Line Tool* is now selected. You can now draw a line or two.

If you release the C key, then OmniGraffle reverts back to the *Shape Tool.*

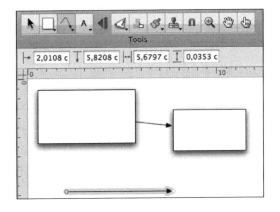

# Using the Pen Tool to create your own shapes

There are a couple of ways to create your own shapes, but only two are preferred. Unfortunately, the easiest way, using binary operations on shapes (which is covered in a later section) is only available in OmniGraffle Pro.

Using this tool requires some planning ahead as the shape you'll create will be a closed shape from the start. This can be very confusing—and of all the tools available in OmniGraffle, this is the most difficult one to use.

This tool will let you draw both straight lines and Bézier curved lines. You learned about the characteristics of Bézier lines in *Chapter 2, Stencils*.

You can start the creation of a new shape by clicking on the canvas where you want the starting point of your shape to be. A good starting point can be an angle, the start or ending of a curve – really any place not in the middle of a curve or a straight line.

There are four basic operations in creating new shapes, straight lines, curved lines and undoing your last point:

- To create a straight line between two points, just move your mouse pointer to the new point's location and click once with your mouse
- To create a curved line between two points, just click-and drag your mouse pointer to the new point's location and release the mouse button
- Pressing the *Delete* key during your line and curve drawing will remove the last point you added
- Double-clicking when adding a point will end the task of creating the shape

When you want to work with a previously created shape, you have the following operations at hand:

- Double-clicking on an existing line segment will add a new point and divide the line segment in two
- Holding down the *Option* key (⌘) and double-clicking on an existing line segment will add a new Bézier point and divide the line segment into two Bézier curved line
- Selecting a line segment point and pressing the *Delete* key will remove the point and join the line segments on each side of the deleted point into a new line segment

Straight lines between points are easy to grasp, but Bézier curved lines may not be equally easy.

In Chapter 2, you have learned that the start and end of a Bézier line will have a handle that will control its part (that is, half) of the line segment. It is the length and direction of these handles that controls the curvature of the line segment.

Let's start experimenting with this tool by creating a triangle.

1. Click on the **Pen Tool** once and place a point on the canvas, and move your mouse pointer to the right of the first point you created. Holding down the *Shift* key works as expected (that is, creating a straight horizontal or vertical line).

2. Now click once and move your mouse pointer below the newly created line segment.

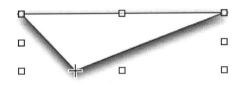

3. Double-click on when you have reached your preferred location—and now you have your own version of a triangle.

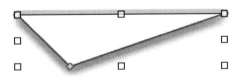

Notice the blue diamond—this is the indication of a shape-point—these are the same midpoints you worked with regarding lines in *Chapter 3, Shapes, Building Blocks for Diagrams*.

The two other points from the first line segment you created are hidden behind the shape selection points. Just click on any visible points and you will have access to all the points on the shape.

 **When the resizing handles get in the way**

If you need to change one of the selection points that is covered by a resizing handle, you may first click on one of the other selections points.

Now let's continue with something more advanced — a shape formed as a drop of water.

1. Again you start with a new blank canvas.

2. Place the first point on your canvas — move the mouse pointer to a new place below your starting point:

3. Next you click once and drag your mouse to the right:

4. Now release the mouse button:

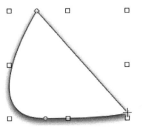

5. Double-click your mouse button to finish working on the shape:

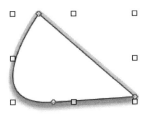

You will now see the three points that your shape consists of.

6. Click on the right-most blue diamond to select this point:

7. Now hit the *Delete* key on your keyboard to delete this very point. The resulting shape does indeed resemble a water drop:

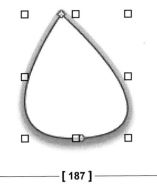

# Fast diagramming using the Diagramming Tool

If you are used to diagramming with other tools, you may miss the functionality where you can put shapes on the canvas and they immediately connect to the previous shape. Creating diagrams with this kind of functionality makes for super-quick diagramming.

In OmniGraffle using the **Diagramming Tool** will give you this functionality.

When using this tool it makes sense to double-click on the icon to set the tool into the *multiple usages*.

Clicking anywhere on the canvas will place the shape currently selected by the *Shape Tool* in the *Canvas Toolbar*.

Notice the mouse pointer symbol to the right of the shape. The mouse pointer will give you a visual clue on how the connecting line will behave in conjunction to the connecting shapes. The pointer seen above indicates that the start of the line will be connected from the previous shape, and that the end of the line will be connected to the new shape.

Clicking next to your shape will create a line between the two shapes. The line type used will be the one currently selected by the *Line Tool* in the *Canvas Toolbar*. For illustrative purposes, we're going to have an arrowhead at the end of the line.

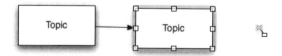

If you double-click instead of just clicking once with your mouse — the next shape you place will not be connected to the previous shape you just placed. This will also happen if you have not selected any shapes and click on a new spot on the canvas.

If you hold down the *Shift* key (⇧) on your keyboard, you will notice that the mouse pointer changes shape. This mouse pointer indicates that the start of the line will be connected from the new shape, and that the end of the line will be connected to the previous shape:

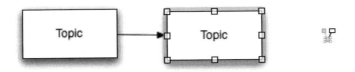

The resulting diagram is as follows:

However, if you hold down the *option* key (⌥) — your new shape will be connected to the parent of your previously selected shape.

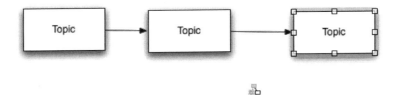

Notice the mouse pointer. Also, notice that we have changed the direction of the line (indicated by the arrowhead) between the middle and the right oblong shape. If the start and end points of the line were the same as the previous example — using the *option* key (⌥) would have simply resulted in a new and disconnected shape.

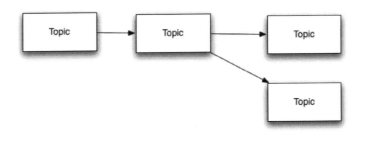

Depending on the kind of diagram you want to create—you should turn on **Automatic Layout** found in the **Diagram Layout** palette (covered in detail in the section called *Automatic Layout* in this chapter), or enable the **Snap To Grid** function found in the *Grid Property inspector* palette (covered in detail in *Chapter 8, Canvases and Canvas Layers*).

# Diagramming Tool Modifier keys

The following table is an overview of how the various modifier keys will change the behavior of the *Diagramming Tool*:

| Modifier key | Pointer | Explanation |
|---|---|---|
| Unmodified | | The connecting line goes from the existing shape to the new shape. |
| ⇧ (shift key)) | | Reverse connection of the line. |
| | | The connecting line goes from the new shape to the existing shape. |
| ⌥ (option key) | | The line will be connected to the parent of the selected shape. |
| ⌘ (command key) | | Create a completely disconnected shape. |

Holding down the command key *should* give you a completely disconnected shape, but as of the time of writing using OmniGraffle Professional version 5.2.3, this behavior is still buggy.

# Style replication using the Style Brush Tool

The **Style Brush Tool** will copy the style from a selected shape and apply the style to other shapes on your canvas.

This tool is very handy if you need to selectively decide on which shapes you want to copy a style to. Compared to using the *Style Tray*— this tool is quicker to use for tasks involving deploying the whole style from one shape. However, if you need more fine-grained control the *Style Tray* is probably the quicker tool to use.

This does not mean that the *Style Brush Tool* does not have the ability to apply only a few styles from one shape to another—it has, and you will learn to do this in a few moments.

Let's learn to use the *Style Brush Tool* by experimenting.

1. Create five different shapes (rectangle, circle, diamond, cloud, and star), and fill the rectangle shape with some light blue background color.

2. Double-click on the **Style Brush Tool** as you will be using it more than once.

   When you first click on the **Style Brush Tool** icon in the Canvas Toolbar—the mouse pointer shows a paintbrush with arrows (✤) indicating that the brush is ready to absorb styles from a shape. Click on the square shape and watch the arrow disappear and the paintbrush change color (✤ )

3. Now you can click on the circle—watch it change into a square.

   This is not what you intended to do. What you want is to copy the color of the shape – not the shape itself.

4. Use the **Edit | Undo Brush** menu command or press the ⌘+Z keyboard shortcut command.

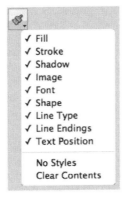

5. At the bottom of the *Style Brush Tool* icon, you'll notice a small triangle. This is an indication that the tool in question has a context menu attached. Click on the tool icon, hold down the mouse key and this menu will appear.

   This menu shows you which styles will be applied when using the *Style Brush Tool*. As you can see, the default is to apply all styles, including the **Shape**.

   You can now choose which of the styles you want to apply to your shapes. You will recognize most of these selections from the **Canvas Style Tray** you learned about in *Chapter 1, Getting Started with OmniGraffle*.

   In your case, use the **No Styles** selection first to clear all the selected styles — then only select the **Fill** style. Notice that the paint brush mouse pointer changes into the one with the arrows indicating that the brush is ready to take on the selected styles from a shape.

6. You can now click on the square as you did earlier and then continue to paint the circle, the diamond, and the star blue.

   Leave the cloud unchanged.

7. You now decide that the circle should have the same color as the cloud.

   Hold down the *option* key (⌥) and watch the mouse cursor change into the brush with the arrows indicating that the brush is ready to absorb styles from a shape.

8. Now click on the cloud – notice that the brush changes into the color of the cloud.

   You can now easily paint the circle.

It is unfortunately not possible to paint more than one shape at the same time — that is, you cannot absorb the color from the square shape and then select the circle, the diamond, the cloud, and the star and then apply the style to these shapes.

# Replicating shapes using the Rubber Stamp Tool

The **Rubber Stamp Tool** is an efficient tool if you need to copy or replicate one shape more than once.

The *Rubber Stamp Tool* has two states—one state where the tool is ready to copy another shape, and the other state where the tool is ready to place copies of the shape on the canvas. You can see which state the *Rubber Stamp Tool* is in by looking at the small rectangle on the stamp. If the rectangle is empty (🔲) the tool is ready to copy a shape. If the rectangle is filled (◼), the tool is ready to place copies on the canvas.

Lets use the *Rubber Stamp Tool* to copy some of the shapes in the previous section.

When you click on the tool, the mouse pointer changes into a rubber stamp icon.

Click on the tool and place it over the circle—notice that the rectangle on the stamp is not yet filled.

Now click with your mouse and watch the rectangle on the stamp icon become black.

As you move the stamp-shaped mouse pointer around, you'll notice that there is a square right beneath, and to the right, of the pointer. This square is a indication of the size of the shape you just copied. The size is based on the outer extremities of the copied shape (for the circle this is the top, bottom, left and right—for the diamond it is its corner, and so on).

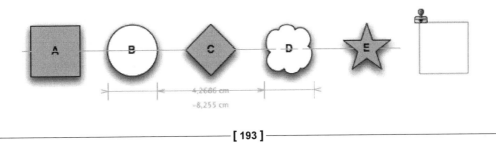

Also see how both the **Smart Alignment Guides** and the **Smart Distance Guides** kick into action when placing the copied shape.

When you need to copy another shape you hold down the *option* key (⌥) while the mouse pointer is over another shape and then click with your mouse.

If you need to clear the copied shape from the tool, you can click-and-hold your mouse over the toolbar icon. A context sensitive menu will appear, and you can choose the **Clear Contents** menu command.

The *Rubber Stamp Tool* is now ready to copy another shape.

# Editing magnets using the Magnet Tool

In Chapter 1 you added magnets to shapes in your first diagram. In Chapter 3, you learned about the Connection Property palette. You learned to add a set of predefined magnets to your shapes using the choices in the Connection property inspector.

Magnets are a great way to control exactly where the connection lines will attach to your shapes. For everyday use, the predefined magnet setups found in the Connection property inspector may be more than adequate for you.

But what if you need to change the location of the magnets? What if you create a completely new shape and you need to add magnets on your preferred points? What if you import some graphics (that is, clip-art) and you want to add magnets to the graphics?

This is where the **Magnet Tool** comes into play. The Magnet Tool lets you control exactly where the magnets are placed on a shape.

If a shape has no magnets—connection lines may be not placed where you want them to be.

The Magnet Tool can do three things:

- It can add a new magnet to a shape: To add magnets to a shape you have to select the Magnet Tool and then just click on the location where you want your magnets to be placed. You cannot place magnets outside the shape's boundaries.

- It can remove an existing magnet from a shape: To remove a magnet from a shape, hold down the *option* key (⌥) while you move your mouse pointer over the magnet to be removed. The mouse pointer will change its look and feel as seen next to indicate that you are about to delete the magnet.

- It can move an existing magnet to a new location: To move a magnet around just click and drag the magnet to its new location.

Let's experiment with the magnets of a shape.

Before you start, turn on the visibility of the shapes magnets by using the **View | Magnets** menu command. You cannot really use the *Magnet Tool* efficiently without seeing the magnets associated with the shape.

Start by creating a new OmniGraffle document and add a star shape. Connect the star shape to a number of surrounding circles. Without magnets – your diagram may look like the one that follows:

When you connect the circles to the star, you'll notice that the lines will connect to the shortest path between the star and the circles. The shortest path is **not** really between the vertex of the star and the border of some of the circles. The shortest paths between *any shapes* are measured from the center of each shape.

What you want to achieve is to connect each circle to the two arms of the star shape.

You can now experiment with the **Magnet Selection** drop-down menu found in the Connection property inspector.

The closest pre-defined setting in the **Magnet Selection** drop-down menu is the **on each vertex** choice.

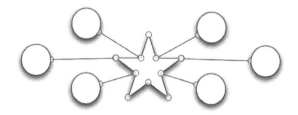

At least these magnets will give you the result you are looking for by re-attaching the connection lines to the points of the star as seen next:

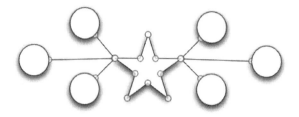

This is fine, you have achieved what you needed to do.

However, the star shape is to be used in your organization and due to internal policy, the only connections allowed to the star shape are to its "hands".

Your next task is to remove the magnets that are not to be used by anyone in your organization.

Double-click on the Magnet Tool to enable multiple use of the tool.

Holding down the *option* key (⌥) while you click on a magnet with your mouse pointer, will remove the magnet from the shape. When you hold down the *option* key, you'll notice that the mouse pointer changes into small cloud.

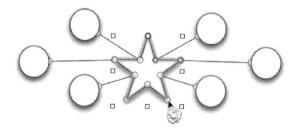

Notice that the connections in the previous diagram are the same as what we used the *Magnet Selection Dropdown*.

Now for something pretty cool: If you remove a magnet which has a connection line attached, the connection line will re-attach itself to the nearest magnet. Let's use this magic to our advantage.

As you remove magnets that have connection lines, you'll see that the lines will attach themselves to the remaining magnets. No need to manually move the connection lines around.

# Zooming the Canvas

There are a couple of ways to zoom in to the very details of your diagram.

The most obvious way is to use the various **View | Zoom** menu commands. There are even a few keyboard shortcuts available to zoom in (⇧+⌥+⌘+=) and zoom out (⇧+⌥+⌘+-) in 100% steps increments. Unless you are using an American keyboard layout, none of these two keyboard shortcuts will be very intuitive to you.

A more intuitive keyboard shortcut is ⌥+⌘+0, which will bring the canvas back to the actual size of your diagram.

The second way is to use the **Zoom** button () at the bottom of your canvas. You can use the **Zoom** button to zoom to a certain percentage—this also includes a customized value.

The last, and maybe most visual and versatile method is to use the **Zoom Tool** found in the *Canvas Toolbar*.

Clicking on the **Zoom Tool** will change the mouse pointer to a magnifying glass with a plus sign inside (⊕), indicating that you are about to zoom into your diagram.

If you hold down the *option* key (⌥), the mouse pointer changes into a magnifying glass with a minus sign inside (⊖), indicating that you are about to zoom out from your diagram.

If the mouse pointer changes into an empty magnifying glass (🔍), this is an indication that you have reached the maximum or minimum zoom level available. The maximum zoom level you can achieve is 800%, and the minimum zoom level is 5%.

There are several zoom operations you can perform using the Zoom Tool:

- Clicking on the canvas will double the zoom level (percentage) you have currently set

- Holding down the *option* key while clicking on the canvas will halve the zoom level

- Holding down the *shift* key (⇧) and clicking on the Zoom Tool in the Canvas toolbar will reset the zoom level to 0, giving you the actual size of your diagram

- To visually decide which part of the canvas you want to zoom into, just click on your starting point and then hold down the mouse button and drag your mouse pointer to where you want your zoom to end

When you click or *Shift* click to double or halve the currently selected zoom level, OmniGraffle will try to center the visible part of the canvas where you clicked with the mouse. However, if you try to do this near the edge of the canvas, the program will adapt the center of the visible canvas accordingly.

When you click and drag to zoom your canvas, you will notice not only the rectangle showing you where you started and ended your zoom operation, but also a shaded area that gives you the area which will be zoomed. This area represents the canvas proportions.

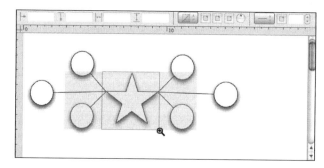

In the previous screenshot we try to zoom in to just the star shape (thin rectangle around the star). However, due to the canvas proportions we will not only get the star—but also the part of the diagram behind the shade.

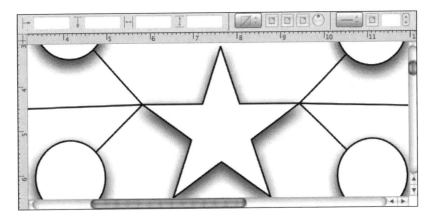

There are a few extra tricks you can apply while zooming your diagram using this particular method:

- Clicking and holding down the *option* key (⌥) before you start your zoom operation, will center the rectangle on where your mouse pointer was when you started
- Pressing the *Shift* key (⇧) while you perform the zoom operation will let you move the zoom area around your diagram

It is well worth investing the time to learn the various shortcuts when performing zooming operations, as it is much quicker than to fiddle around with the **View | Zoom** menu or using the **Zoom** button.

# Moving around the canvas

You use the **Hand Tool** to move around your canvas.

This is very handy if you need to move around a zoomed canvas where only part of your diagram is visible.

To use the tool, you click anywhere on your canvas, hold down your mouse button and drag the visible canvas viewpoint around.

# Using the Action Browse Tool and the Action Property Inspector

The **Action Browse Tool** is used in conjunction with the **Action Property Inspector**.

Using the *Action Property Inspector* you can assign certain actions to happen when the user clicks on a shape using the *Action Browse Tool*.

Shapes associated with an action will show a small icon when the *Action Browse Tool* mouse pointer (🖑) is moved over the shape:

The following actions can be assigned to a shape—along with its corresponding icon.

| | |
|---|---|
| **General action** <br> Jumps elsewhere in the current OmniGraffle document, this includes zooming, going to a specific layer, etc. | |
| **Layer action** <br> Hides, shows and toggles the visibility of a specific layer within the current canvas. | |
| **URL action** <br> Opens a specific URL. | |
| **AppleScript action** <br> Performs an AppleScript. The script will have to be written inside OmniGraffle. | |
| **Open file action** <br> Opens a file or directory. The icon shown will be dependant on the file or directory associated with the action. | |

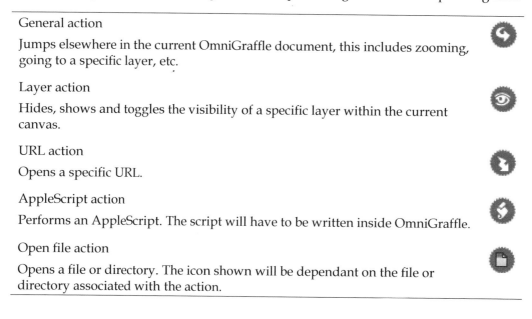

# The Action Property inspector

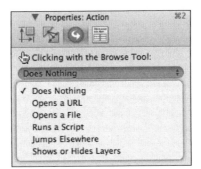

You will now learn how to use the **Action Property inspector** to configure the various actions available in OmniGraffle. Some of these actions may be straightforward; others may require a bit more effort to get working correctly.

The **Does Nothi**ng action is the only way to delete a previously assigned action.

This is thus the default action for a given shape.

The **Opens a URL** or **Opens a File** action will open an URL in your browser or a file from your hard drive.

When the user clicks on a shape with an associated URL, a web browser will open and show the content of the URL.

When the user clicks on a shape with an associated file, the file will be opened by its associated application. What application opens which files is a setting in your operating system.

To associate a file with this action, click on the **Choose File...** button and you'll get access to a file browser where you can select the file you want to associate with the action.

If you click on the **Open** button, you will either open the URL or the file associated with the action.

Instead of choosing a file using the **Choose** file... button or writing in a URL by hand you can simply drag and drop any file or any URL on top of a shape in OmniGraffle. The URL or the file will thus be the associated actions for the shape you dropped the file or URL onto.

When a user clicks on a shape with the associated **Runs a Script** action, OmniGraffle will execute the AppleScript in the text box.

You have two buttons that will help you in writing your AppleScript: **Check Syntax** to see if your syntax is correct, and **Run Script** to test the script without using the *Browse Tool*.

OmniGraffle is very scriptable using AppleScript. By using the *Runs a Script* function, you could for all practical purposes have OmniGraffle drawing a diagram on its own based on various parameters you have entered.

If you are well versed in AppleScript, you'll be happy to know that the self object refers to the current instance of OmniGraffle.

The **Show or Hide Layer**s action will let the user change the visibility of a layer.

You can even hide the layer where the shape associated with this action resides.

The **Jumps Elsewhere** action consist of six actions in a separate drop-down menu:

- **Highlight an Object**
- **Center on a Point**
- **Zoom to Display a Rectangle**
- **Switch to the Previous Canvas**
- **Switch to the Next Canvas**
- **Switch to a Specific Canvas**

The details of these six actions are covered in the next section.

You also have access to a drop-down menu that lets you select which canvas you want the **Jumps Elsewhere** action to apply to.

Except for the actions that switch to another canvas—you'll have access to a **Mini canvas view** along with a zoom slider.

# The Jumps Elsewhere action in detail

The **Highlight an Object** action will, when the user clicks on the action, point to another shape in your document.

You can select a shape on your current canvas, or use the **Canvas** drop-down menu to select another canvas from your OmniGraffle document.

You then use the **Mini canvas view** to select the shape you want to point to.

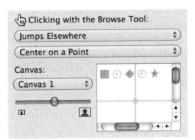

You can use the **Zoom** slider to zoom the **Mini canvas view** to a size where you actually see the various shapes.

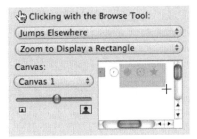

You can use the **Center on a Point** action to change the center of the canvas.

Select which canvas you want to place the new viewpoint on using the **Canvas** drop-down menu, then use the crosshair on the **Mini canvas view** to accurately position your new center.

The **Zoom to Display a Rectangle** will perform a zoom action based on the rectangle you selected in the **Mini canvas view**.

Use the **Canvas** drop-down menu to select which canvas you want to zoom into, then use the crosshair on the **Mini canvas view** to accurately position your starting point. Hold down your mouse button and drag to where the zoom should end.

Due to the canvas height and length properties the action might not work as expected.

The **Switch to the Next Canvas** and the **Switch to the Previous Canvas** actions will simply move the user back and forth between canvases.

If you are on the first canvas—clicking on a shape with the **Switch to the Previous Canvas** will not do anything.

The same is true if you are on the last canvas, and clicking on a shape with the **Switch to the Next Canvas**.

Neither the **Canvas** drop-down menu, nor the **Mini canvas vi**ew are active for these two actions.

The **Switch to a Specific Canva**s behaves exactly as the name implies.

You use the Canvas drop-down menu to choose which canvas to switch to.

After all this – you may ask yourself what's the point in having the *Jumps Elsewhere* action. The answer becomes apparent if you have very big OmniGraffle documents with a lot of canvases and you need to direct your users to the right canvas.

A lot of people are using OmniGraffle as a tool for creating *Wireframe*s. A Wireframe is a mockup of a proposed application user interface. This could be a desktop application, a web page or even a mobile application.

If you need to demonstrate an interactive version of your wireframe—then the *Jump Elsewhere* action will really impress your customers (or co-workers).

You are now going to create an interactive wireframe of a simple iPhone application.

Start by searching, downloading and installing a stencil named **Ultimate iPhone Stencil** from Graffletopia. The easiest way to do this is by using the search function in the Stencils palette. You should also download two other iPhone related stencils—both excellent for making iPhone mockups: They are called **Mobile iPhone** and **iPhone 3G**. Not every GUI element on the iPhone is found in all stencils—thus it will make sense to have all three handy.

All of these stencils are very big—they have a lot of elements, so the only sane way to deal with these stencils is by enabling the grid view by clicking on the **Grid View Mode** button (see the section named *The Stencil Library Controls* in *Chapter 7, Property Inspectors*).

You will first start by making the mockup of the software—then add the interactivity.

1. Start by selecting the iPhone with the startup screen from the *Ultimate iPhone* stencil.

2. Put it on a canvas called **Start**.

3. Create a new canvas named **Application start screen**.

4. On this canvas you add the iPhone frame, the white background, a gray header and the list of photos. Change the title of the header to **My photos**.

5. Duplicate the current canvas, remove the list of photos and add the photo overview page.

6. Change the canvas name to **Photo Library**. This should also be the content of the gray heading.

7. What we lack now is a back button. In the *iPhone 3G* stencil, there are several back buttons. Find the blue one and put in on the header—to the left of the text. On the button—enter the text **Back**.

It's great how simply you have created a mockup for a photo gallery application.

You are now ready to add some interactivity.

1.  Go back to the canvas named **Start**.

2.  Select the background. In the Action property inspector, choose **Jumps Elsewhere** and the second drop-down menu should read **Switch to Next Canvas**.

3.  Select the canvas named **Application start screen**.

4.  Double-click on the element named **Photo Library**. This element is part of a group, and we are now going to add an action to a group element.

5.  Select **Jumps Elsewhere** and **Switch to the Next Canvas** in the *Action Property inspector*.

6. Lastly, in the canvas named **Photoclusters**, select the **Back** button and in the *Action property inspector*, choose **Jumps Elsewhere** and the second drop-down menu should read **Switch to Previous Canvas**.

7. Deselect any selected elements in your three canvases and go to the first canvas (named **Start**). You may also want to adjust the canvas size so the whole iPhone mockup is visible.

8. Double-click on the **Browse Tool** button in the Canvas toolbar. You are now able to move around in the application – but it is only possible to click on certain elements, and not others.

You can now extend your application mockup by adding more screens and jump between screens.

This iPhone application mockup is also available as a file named `Interactive experiments.graffle` found in the `Chapter 9` folder in the download bundle.

Later in this chapter, you will be introduced to the *Presentation Mode*. The *Presentation Mode* makes it possible to show your canvases in full screen—just like a presentation. In this mode, all your actions are available, and this can make for pretty impressive demonstrations. Unfortunately the *Presentation Mode* is only available in the professional version of OmniGraffle—you can skip this section if you are not using the professional version.

# Using Automatic layout

The **Diagram Layout inspector** controls how OmniGraffle automatically will layout hierarchical diagrams.

Within hierarchical diagrams there are certain relationships between the connected shapes. Some of the shapes have offspring; some shapes have the same ancestor and are thus siblings, and so on. At the end of this chapter you will make a genealogy diagram to teach you the coherence about ancestors, descendants, siblings, and so on.

It's when you are using tools like the *Diagramming Tool*, or using *Mouseless Editing* functionality (which you will learn about in the next section), that turning on automatic layout really make sense. Both these tools automatically create connections between shapes, and having OmniGraffle do the hard work with regards to automatically re-arranging shapes based on their relationship is a very nice time saver.

☑ Automatic layout

The **Automatic layout** checkbox toggles if automatic layout should be done or not.

You have access to four different layout methods controlled by four **Layout** buttons.

The first button is the **Hierarchical Layout** button—enabling this button will create a diagram where shapes on the same level in the hierarchy will align to each other.

The second button is the **Force-directed Layout** button. Enabling this button will re-arrange your diagram in random directions from the center of your diagram. Your diagram is no longer a hierarchical diagram, but more a network of connected shapes.

The third button is the **Circular Layout** button. Using this button will re-arrange shapes with the same ancestor (that is, siblings) in a circle with the ancestor sitting in the middle. Given the complexity of your diagram, the results may not even resemble a circle at all.

The fourth button is the **Radial Layout** button, which works much the same way as the Circular Layout button: Except for arranging your shapes in a circle, this button will try to re-arrange your shapes into a semicircle around their ancestors.

The **Direction** buttons, **Rank Separation, Object Separation** and the **Selected Object Rank** controls are only available when the **Hierarchical Layout** button has been activated.

The **Direction** buttons arranges your diagram as the name implies, and the iconography on the buttons: **Top-to-Bottom, Bottom-to-Top, Left-to-Right**, and **Right-to-Left**. Which object is starting top, bottom, left, and right is controlled by which of the **Select Object Rank** are activated.

The **Rank Separation** controls the spacing between the levels in your hierarchy.

The **Object Separation** controls the spacing between shapes on the same level in the hierarchy.

**Selected Object Rank** buttons:

It consists of four additional buttons, which will let you control which node(s) in your hierarchy are going to be the starting shape for the **Direction** buttons. The rank for the consecutive shapes is based on the number of connections each shape has.

 Default object rank button

 Minimum object rank button

Maximum object rank button

Same object rank button

- Selecting one or more shapes, and then enabling the **Default object rank** button will make OmniGraffle arrange your diagram based on the number of connections— this is the natural order of your hierarchy.
- Selecting one or more shapes, and then enabling the **Minimum object rank** button will make OmniGraffle put these shapes at start of your hierarchy.
- Selecting one or more shapes, and then enabling the **Maximum object rank** button will make OmniGraffle put these shapes at the end of your hierarchy. This is the opposite behavior compared to using the **Minimum object rank** button.
- Selecting one or more shapes, and then enabling the Same object rank button will make OmniGraffle put these shapes on the same level in the hierarchy.

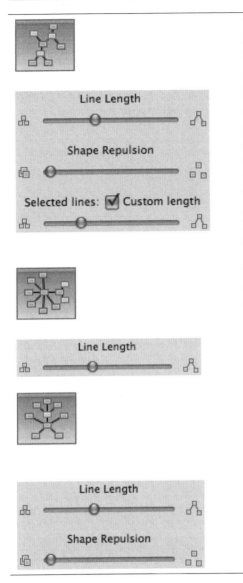

The **Line Length**, **Shape Repulsion** and **Custom Length** sliders are only available when the **Force-directed layout** button has been activated.

The **Line Length** slider controls the length between the shapes in the diagram.

The **Shape Repulsion** slider controls how eager the shapes are to be close to each other. If both the line length and the repulsion values are small enough — the shapes become very cozy with each other.

The **Custom line length** slider controls the length of selected lines. Even if you change the general line length using the **Line Length** slider, the selected ones will keep their specific length.

The **Circular Layout** button has only one control available, and that is the **Line Length** slider.

The slider controls the length between the shapes in the circular diagram.

The **Radial Layout** button has only two controls available: the **Line Length** slider and the **Shape Repulsion** slider.

The **Line Length** slider controls the length between the shapes in the diagram.

The **Shape Repulsion** slider controls how eager the shapes are to be close to each other. If both the line length and the repulsion values are small enough — the shapes become very cozy with each other.

After all this theory on how automatic layout is working — let's experiment. Enable the **Automatic layout** checkbox to experience the magical layout powers of OmniGraffle.

If not enabled, enable the **Hierarchical Layout** button along with the Top-to-Bottom direction button.

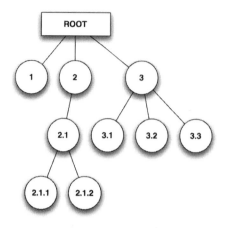

Using the Diagramming Tool on the Canvas Toolbar, create a diagram that looks like this one.

If we where to define a hierarchy there are at least two basic truths that must be upheld:

- No element can be its own master or ancestor — they cannot have any circular relationships, either directly or indirectly. In fancy speak this is known as *transitive* relations.
- One node must be the master or ancestor for all other nodes — this is also known as the *root* of the hierarchy.

The previous diagram upholds these two truths. It is a very typical diagram where the root itself does not have any value except for anchoring the levels of the diagram.

A good analogy is how the book you are reading is organized. You have chapters (1, 2, 3 and so on), sections (2.1, 3.1, 3.2, 3.3 and so on), sub-sections (2.1.1, 2.1.2 and so on). There is however no *überchapter* that rules the other chapters — however, there is the concept the *book* which contains all the chapters. In our analogy the root of all the chapters is the book (that is, a book is a collection of chapters).

So about the name *root* — and why is the root on top of the diagram? It's really a terminology that has existed for many, many years. Think of the concept root as the start of a sequence — such as *the root of this cause consists of the following elements in this very order*.

Let's play around with the various controls.

Pressing the **Bottom-to-Top direction** button places the root at the bottom of the diagram.

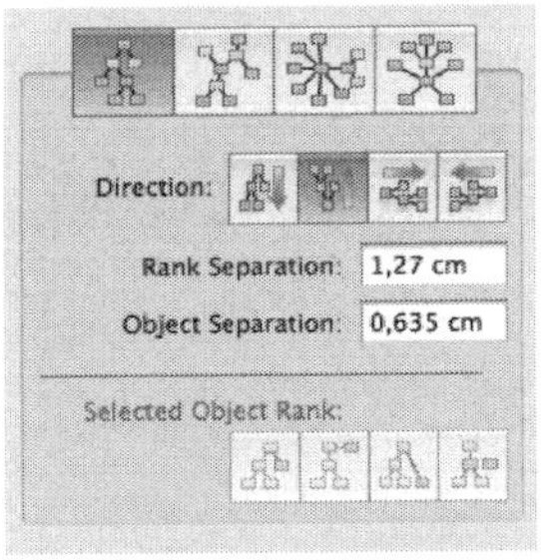

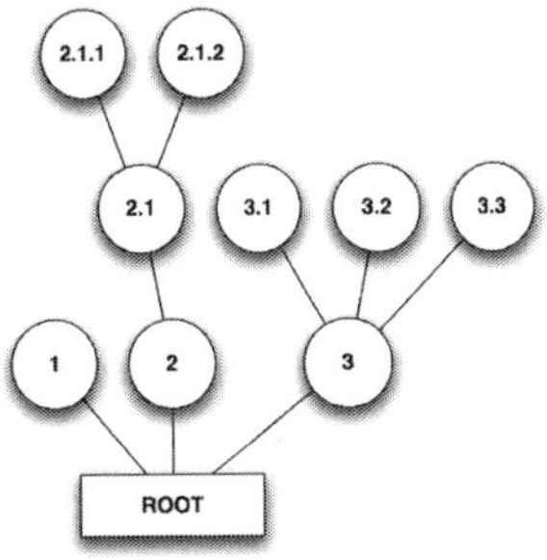

Clicking on the **Left-to-Right direction** button places the root of the diagram on the left.

A diagram with this layout can also be used to map out various events and the possible outcome further down the path.

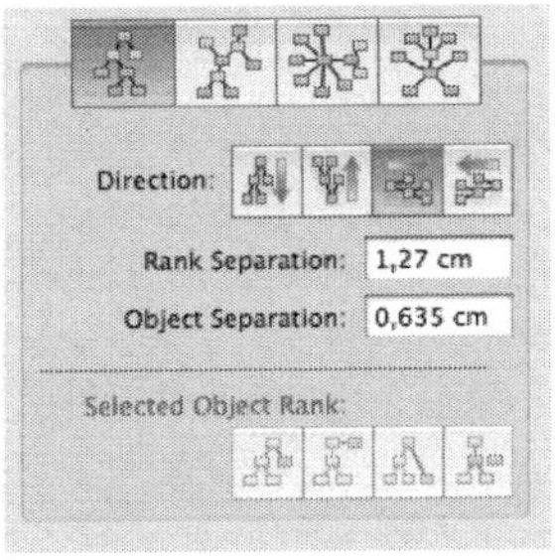

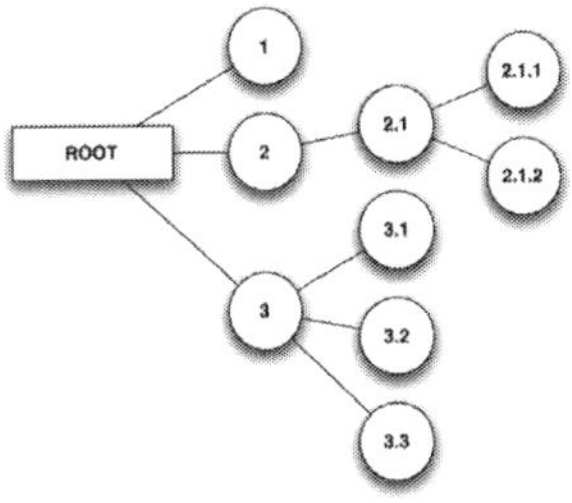

Selecting element **#2** and clicking on the **Minimum object rank** button make this the top element.

In a true hierarchical diagram, you can take any node and make this node the new root node. Again, it's all about the concept of what is *root* and not numbering or naming schemes.

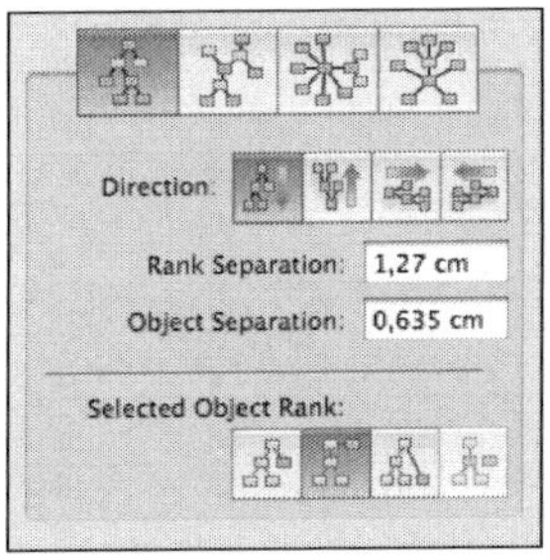

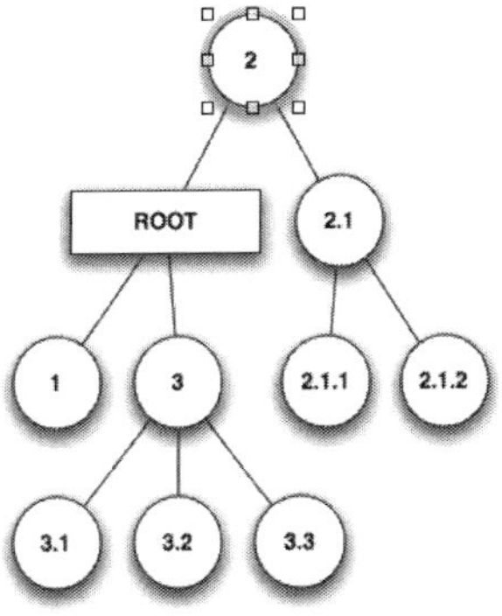

Selecting both the *root* and
element **#2**: Then clicking on
the **Minimum object rank**
button will give you two top
elements.

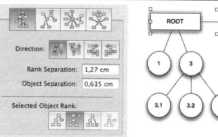

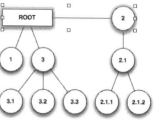

This does not look like a
hierarchical diagram in the
purest sense anymore (that is,
having two *root* elements).

However, for business and
organizational use—these
diagrams can make a lot of
sense.

The **Force-directed layout**
button arranges the diagram in
a seemingly random way.

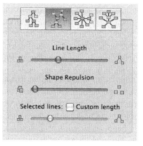

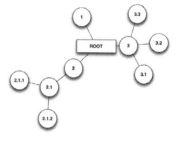

The **Circular layout** button
arranges the diagram in a
circular fashion.

Unfortunately our diagram has
too few nodes to really show
the circular aspects of this
control. Add more nodes and
watch it become a full circle.

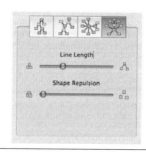

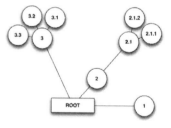

The **Radial layout** button
arranges the diagram in radial
fashion.

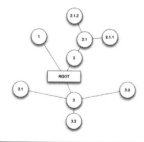

# Mouseless Editing

Learning to use keyboard shortcut commands is, in most programs, including OmniGraffle, a real time saver. It may seem like a bother to learn all these commands—but your brain will thank you in the long run. At the end of this book section, there is a longer explanation of why keyboard shortcuts matter in the long run.

# Keyboard shortcuts and OmniGraffle

The same is true when using OmniGraffle. Remember the first diagram you made in Chapter 1. You used the mouse a lot, mousing back-and-forth-and-back-and-forth to finish your diagram.

This book is trying to teach you all the keyboard shortcuts OmniGraffle has.

If you are a beginner with OmniGraffle, or once-in-a-while user of the program, there is probably no sense in learning all these keyboard shortcuts.

However, if you create a diagram at least once a week (and this is probably not your most enjoyable task at work), then you should go ahead and learn all the keyboard shortcuts—if not for any reason other than to get the job done as fast as possible.

The keyboard shortcuts you have been learning so far have been used to amend existing shapes and diagrams.

Now you are going to learn to create a diagram with minimal mouse involvement.

**A word of caution**

If you feel that you are not very structured, you should consider planning how your diagram will look. In Chapter 2 you learned to plan using pen and paper or a white board before starting to draw your first shape using the computer. This tip is more true when it comes to using only the keyboard.

There are few reasons why this is a good idea. The primary reasons are diagramming speed and not slowing down your thought process. In other words you can use this technique to quickly sketch out a bit part of your diagram, and then use the mouse to finish the diagram.

You are now going to recreate most of the diagram from Chapter 1 using only your keyboard.

Start by placing the first shape in your diagram on a new canvas:

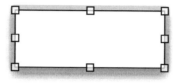

Press the *Enter* key (↵) on your keyboard and notice that you can now enter the text in the first shape (**Start new article**).

Start new article|

Now hold down the Control key (^), the Command key (⌘) and press the right arrow key (→) and you'll get a new connected shape to the right of your current shape (keyboard combinations like these are written as ^+⌘+→).

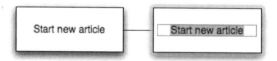

Not only are you getting a new shape—you are also getting right into editing the shape's text. You can now enter **Editing article**, which was the text for the second box.

Before you go on and rush away with keystroke combinations like ^+⌘+→, and ^+⌘+←, and ^+⌘+↑, and ^+⌘+↓ (creating a connected shape to the right, left, above, and below the current shape)—what if you wanted to wanted to have arrows automatically appearing between the shapes? In the original drawing there were arrows between shapes.

You have the choice of making one arrow right now—or to wait it out to most of the diagram is ready and use the *Canvas Style Tray* and the *Canvas Selection property* inspector to amend your diagram afterwards.

Let's turn the connected line into an arrow using the *Line and Shapes inspector palette*. In fact, why don't you go ahead and style the shapes right now (bold text is a good choice).

When done styling, select the **Editing article** shape.

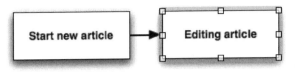

Now hit the ^+⌘+→ keyboard sequence again. Not only are you getting a brand new oblong shape to the right, ready for editing the text—but you'll also get the arrow between the shapes. This is pretty cool.

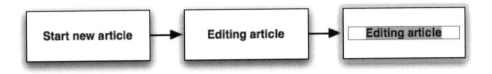

Change the text to **Done editing article** and press the ^+⌘+↓ keyboard combination to create a shape below the **Done editing article**. This shape should have the name of **Publish article**.

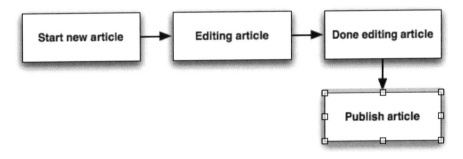

At this moment do not bother to change the look of the shape – you are on a roll to finish the structure of your diagram in double-fast time.

If you change the shape into its intended diamond shape, then the next shapes will become diamond shapes also. This would be fine if most of the shapes present in your diagram were diamond shapes.

Continue your diagram by hitting the ^+⌘+↓ keyboard combination to create yet another shape below the **Publish article** containing the text **Front page worthy**.

Repeat the process to get to the **Published on the company web** shape. Your diagram should now look like the following one:

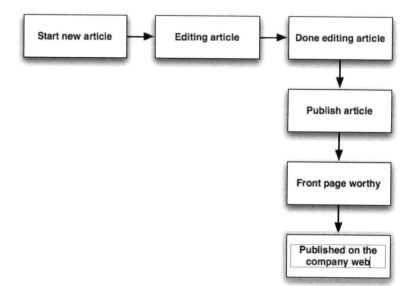

You are now at the bottom of the diagram. Have you literally moved yourself into a corner?

If you now hit the ⌘+↑ keyboard combination, you'll move to the previous shape (and still put the edited text into the shape.

Just continue to hit the ^+⌘+← keyboard combination to create a shape on the left. This shape has the text **Notify DoC**.

To the left of this shape there where the **Publish article** shape. Create this shape by using the ^+⌘+← keyboard combination.

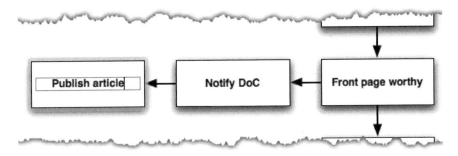

Finish your diagram structure by using the ^+⌘+↓ keyboard combination for the last time and enter the text **Publish article on the front page**.

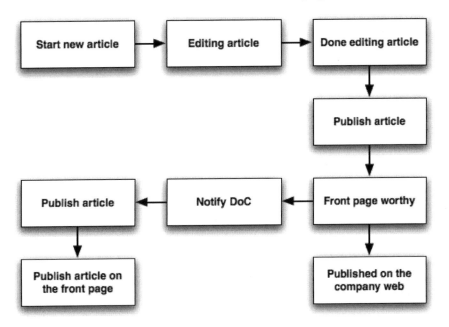

You are now done with the labor-intensive part of your diagram. You did it all with minimal use of the mouse, and in super-fast time compared to copying and pasting shapes around.

Finishing the diagram is mostly eye candy: Just add some colors to the boxes, a few extra connection lines and the line labels. For the diamond shapes – just select all the relevant shapes and click on the diamond shape in the *Lines and Shapes inspector palette* and you are done.

Most of the mouseless editing keyboard shortcuts are found in the **Edit | Mouseless Editing** menu. There are a few not mentioned there—so we have created a table with all the keyboard shortcuts you can use when editing your diagram without the aid of a mouse.

| TASK | Direction | | | |
| --- | --- | --- | --- | --- |
| | Left | Right | Above | Below |
| Move selected shape one pixel at a time. | ← | → | ↑ | ↓ |
| Move selected shape 10 pixels at a time. | ⇧+← | ⇧+→ | ⇧+↑ | ⇧+↓ |
| Select shape. | ⌘+← | ⌘+→ | ⌘+↑ | ⌘+↓ |
| Create a disconnected shape. | ⌥+⌘+← | ⌥+⌘+→ | ⌥+⌘+↑ | ⌥+⌘+↓ |
| Create a connected shape. | ^+⌘+← | ^+⌘+→ | ^+⌘+↑ | ^+⌘+↓ |

# Your brain may thank you for using keyboard shortcuts

The reason why your brain is going to thank you is to do with *usability*. Usability is the wisdom of making things easier to use. Not beginner-friendly but user-friendly. It's only at one point in life we are a beginner when it comes to do certain tasks. These tasks may be anything from using a word processor like OpenOffice Writer or Microsoft Word—to driving a motorcycle and a car.

If you want to learn about usability, there is a small and well-written book by Steve Krug called *Don't make me think*. The book deals primarily with the usability factor when designing web sites—however, the book points out a few universal truths when it comes to any kind of usability: Making the brain spend even the tiniest amount of time on non-relevant tasks make the whole experience of doing a particular job stuffy at worst.

Let's make a thought experiment: You are out driving your car. The cars available cannot turn to the left, or to the right, without first coming to a complete halt. So for every turn you need to make—you have to stop the car, change the direction, then you will have to start it again. You can see how tiresome this is even when driving for a short distance.

This is exactly how your brain feels when you are using your word processor and want to turn some text into bold, italics, or even a heading.

It's a true fact that most long-time (we're talking about years of experience here) word processor users will first write the word they want to make into bold. Next they instruct their brain to stop writing when they have done writing the word, even if it's in mid sentence—then find their mouse—then locate the mouse pointer—then locate the word—then move the mouse pointer to the beginning of the word—then click on the mouse button—then drag the mouse to the end of the word—then locate the bold button on the word processor tool bar—then move the mouse pointer to the located bold button on the word processor tool bar—then click on the bold button.

Phew! And Double Phew!

That's a lot of tasks just to make a single, small, word stand out. You can now finally instruct your brain to go back to typing on your keyboard. The interesting thing is that your brain probably knows where all the keys on your keyboard are no matter if you are a full fledged touch typist or even use the Eagle method of circle three times and strike. The question then becomes: Why not teach your brain to use the one single keyboard shortcut for making text bold?

Most word processor programs use the ⌘ B keyboard command to start and end a sequence of bolded text. Basically – you write along as normal - then hit ⌘ B just before you type the word you want to make bold. When you are done with your word, your fingers automatically hits ⌘ B once again and you can continue writing. Much better for your brain, much better for your workflow, and finally much better for your well-being.

# Using the Outline and List functions to create diagrams

## The Outline function

If you thought using only keyboard shortcuts whetted your appetite for quickly creating diagrams, you'll love this section.

If you need to create a strictly hierarchical diagram, or if part of your diagram is hierarchical, the **Outline function** is very handy.

Let's learn by doing hands on work. A good learning experience using the Outline function is to create a very strict hierarchy – and what's stricter than a family tree?

Your task, if you choose to accept it, is to make a diagram of the Norwegian Royal Family Tree.

The modern royalty in Norway started in 1905 when the union between Sweden and Norway was dissolved and Norway chose its own monarch: King Haakon VII. In fact, the people of Norway by a plebiscite elected the king – thus becoming a true king of the Norwegian people.

Your family tree will start with King Haakon VII and end with Their Royal Highness' Crown Prince Haakon & Crown Princess Mette-Marit, and their common children.

Start a new OmniGraffle document and turn on the Automatic layout found in the Diagram Layout inspector.

To enable outline editing of diagrams, you can click on the Outline icon on the Canvas toolbar ( ), use the **View | Outline** menu command, or simply press the⌥+⌘+2 keyboard shortcuts command.

On the top of the sidebar, you have two buttons: One for the **Outline** function (left button) and one for the **List** function (right button). You can also select which canvas you are working on by using the canvas drop-down menu to the right of the two buttons.

As you are going to only work with one canvas, you can hide the canvas sidebar.

Your canvas workspace should now look like this:

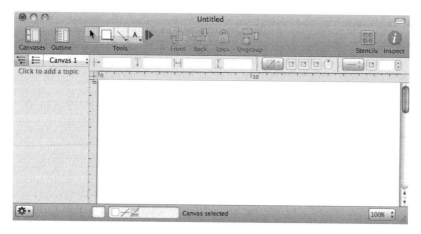

Notice that on your left side you have sidebar with the text **Click to add a topic**.

Go ahead and click on this text and enter **King Haakon VII**. Between the word **King** and the word **Haakon** hold down the *option* key (⌥) and press the *Enter* key (↵). This will result in a line shift in the box.

For clarity we have not added the line shift to our boxes in the screenshots seen in the book.

The red circle around **King Haakon VII** is called the **Outline marker** and shows the currently selected outline item. As you add more and more items to your outline, you can use your arrow keys on your keyboard to move around the outline.

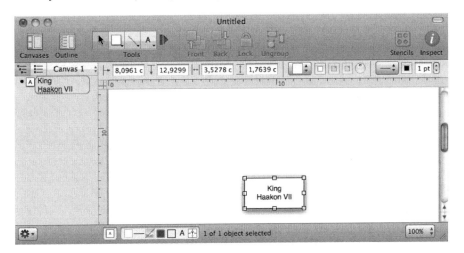

When done, press the *Enter* key. You get a new shape next to **King Haakon VII**.

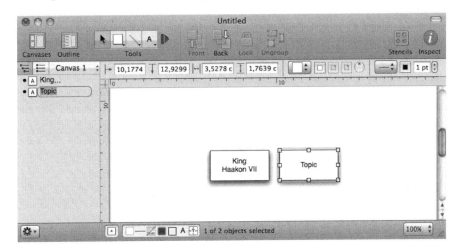

If you hit the *Tab* key (→) your new shape is connected to the **King Haakon VII** shape.

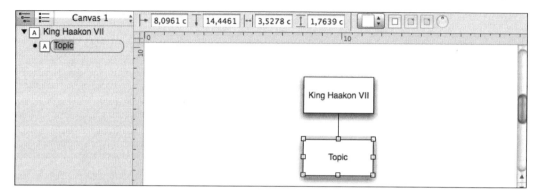

The son of King Haakon VII was King Olav V — so this is what should be entered in the outline.

King Olav V had three children: Ragnhild, Astrid and Norway's current king, King Harald V. Both Ragnhild and Astrid are princesses.

When done entering King Olav V in the outline — hit the Enter key (↵) and then the tab-key (→) and in succession enter **King Harald V**, **Ragnhild**, and **Astrid**. Each name should be on a line on its own in the outline:

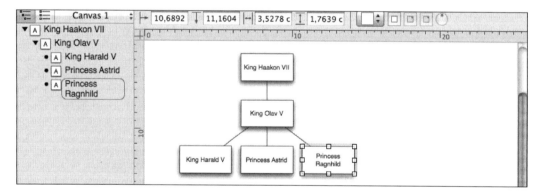

You may need to adjust the zoom level and the page orientation (**File | Page Setup**) to get the diagram to fit in your canvas.

Let's continue adding people to our family tree.

King Harald V has two children: Haakon and Märtha Louise. Move to **King Harald V** by using your up arrow key on your keyboard to place the Outline marker on King Harald V.

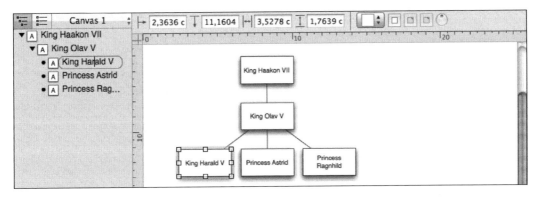

Now hit the *Enter* key (↵) and then the *Tab* key (→) and in succession enter **Crown Prince Haakon** and **Princess Märta Louise**.

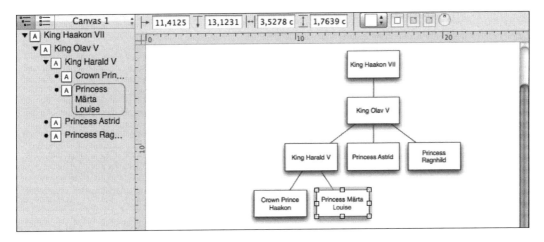

Haakon has two children: Princess Ingrid Alexandria and Prince Sverre Magnus. Add these children like you did with **King Haakon** and **King Harald V** using the *Enter* and the *Tab* keys.

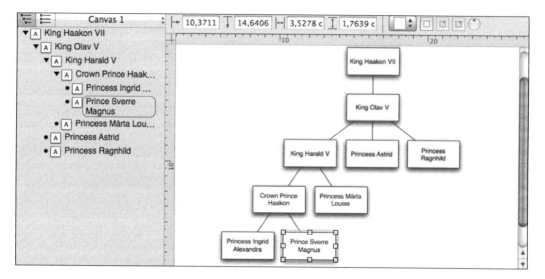

You now have direct descendants from **King Haakon VII**.

What's lacking are spouses. Without spouses in the royal family, there will be no children to inherit the throne—and this is bad for the Kingdom of Norway.

Navigate up to **King Haakon VII**.

The spouses are added using the ⌥+⌘+/ keyboard shortcut command. This keyboard combination is probably fine and dandy if you have a US, or comparable, keyboard layout. If you belong to the 95% of the rest of the world population your only choice is probably to use the **Edit | Outlining | Add Spouse** menu command.

It is however, much quicker to right-click on the small square with the letter **A** to the left of **King Haakon VII**. Notice how there is a red line surrounding all the descendants. If you right-click when the diagram is in this state, you can add any kind of valid relationship to the selected entry (that is, since **Kong Haakon VII** is the root of our hierarchy, you cannot add an aunt to him).

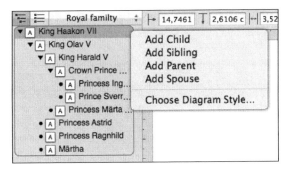

Using this method, you can now add Maud as King Haakon VIIs spouse, Märtha as King Olav Vs spouse. King Harald V is married to Sonja and finally Crown Prince Haakon is married to Crown Princess Mette-Marit.

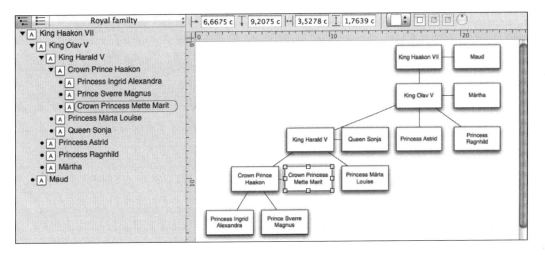

There are a couple of other operations you may find handy when dealing with the Outline function.

If you hold down the *Shift* key (⇧) and then hit the *Tab* key, your selected outline item will decrease its indentation, with the result of also changing the hierarchy. This is the same as using the **Edit | Outlining | Outdent** menu command, and of course this command has its own keyboard shortcut: ⌘+[.

There is also the **Edit | Outlining | Indent** menu command with the keyboard shortcut of ⌘+[. However, using the Tab key is much more intuitive to remember.

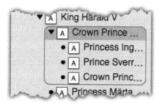

Earlier in this section you clicked on the rectangle with the A next to the king's name, and then left-clicked your mouse to get to the context sensitive menu to add new relationships (child, aunt, parent, and so on).

If you hit the *Delete* key (⌫) you will delete the outline item. Any items (that is, shapes) that have any child-parent relationships with the deleted shape will be rearranged on their own in your diagram.

You may also have noticed that to the left of the rectangle with the **A**, there is a small triangle that will collapse and expand a given part of the outline hierarchy.

If you collapse part of the outline hierarchy you will see that all the corresponding shapes in your canvas are selected.

Pressing the *Delete* key will of course delete all the selected shapes.

You can also use the operations such as copying (⌘+C), cutting (⌘+X), pasting (⌘+V), and duplicate (⌘+D) shapes directly from the outline without first reverting to the canvas.

If you want to learn more about the story of the modern Norwegian royalty and their continuing ties to the common people of Norway, you should go to the English pages of the Norwegian Royal Family `http://www.kongehuset.no/english/vis.html`. At this website you'll also find a more elaborate family tree, which includes relationships such as Princess Märtha Louise is married to Ari Behn and that they have three children.

The family tree you have worked on so far is found in the folder named Chapter 9 in the download bundle. The diagram is named Norwegian royal family.graffle.

# The List function

The List function is available in the same sidebar as the diagram outline.

Click on the **List** button on the Outline sidebar header to switch to the list mode. You can also use the **View | List** menu command, or simply press the ⌥+⌘+3 keyboard shortcuts command.

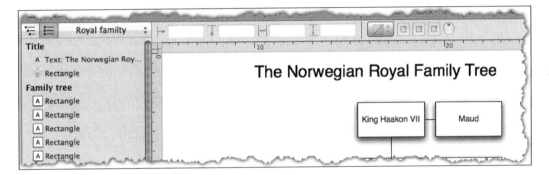

The shapes are ordered in front to back — with shapes on upper layers ordered first.

You use the list function to get an ordered view of shapes belonging to a given canvas. It is possible to reorder the shapes as you please.

At the bottom of the sidebar, you have four arrows at your disposal for moving the shapes up and down. You can also drag and drop shapes using your mouse and you can even drag a shape from one layer to another layer.

If you are using OmniGraffle Professional, you can turn on the visibility of a unique identifier for the shapes in your diagram. This may be useful if you plan to interface your diagram with AppleScripts.

# Diagram Styles

So far you have been working with plain OmniGraffle documents. All the shapes have a distinct style—all the lines start with the same thickness and the font is set to Helvetica Regular.

These defaults are tied to which **Diagram Style** you are currently using. A Diagram Style has a definition for shapes, fonts, colors, and so on. The cool thing about a Diagram Style is that you can apply a style to an existing diagram.

If you take a look at the family tree diagram you created on the Norwegian Royal Family it's not very good looking. Everything is white and the lines are thin. Your work is not very appealing to look at.

However, fixing this is very easy.

Use the **Format | Choose Diagram Styles** menu command and you'll have access to a whole slew of ready-made styles from the **Diagram Style Chooser**.

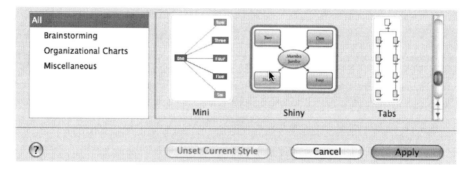

Locate and select the style named **Shiny**, then click on the **Apply** button.

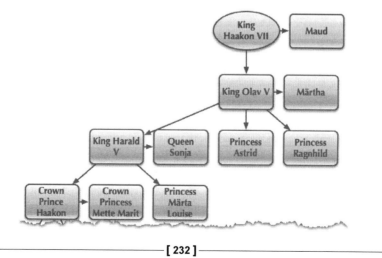

This may not be perfect — but it's a good start and you can work your way from here.

On the other hand this may not be the perfect look and feel for something as serious as a royal family tree.

Creating your own diagram style is really not very difficult. It's as easy as creating your own OmniGraffle document and styling it as you please — then save it as a new Diagram style.

First things first, revert back to your bland family tree using the **Edit | Undo Apply Style** command. You can also use the ⌘+Z keyboard combination.

Now issue the **File | New Resource | New Diagram Style...** You'll be prompted with the Diagram Style Chooser. Locate the **Basic** style and click on the **New Diagram Style** button. The title bar of the canvas should now read: **Diagram Style: Untitled.**

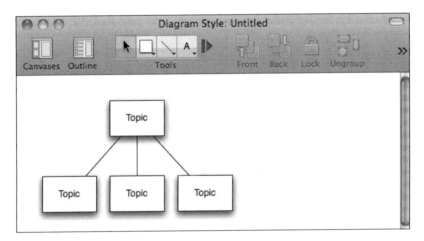

Notice the hierarchical nature of the *Diagram Style* document. When applying a Diagram style to an existing document OmniGraffle will try to match the hierarchical styles in the Diagram style with the one found on the current canvas. The hierarchy in the Diagram style document must be 100% strict — that is, no circular connections are allowed.

Delete all shapes from the document in the canvas.

Now, copy the whole royal family tree over to this new document.

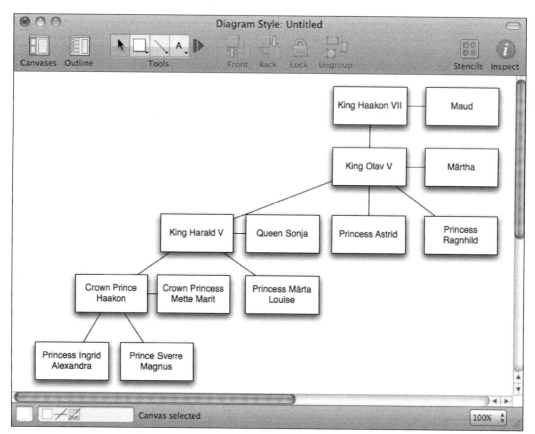

Style this document as you please—and change the various names to a generic text like *Topic*.

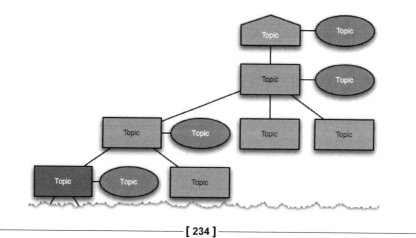

Now save this document as **Family tree**.

This document style is now available from the Document Style Chooser.

Let's try to apply this style diagram to a new family tree.

Create a family tree resembling the following diagram.

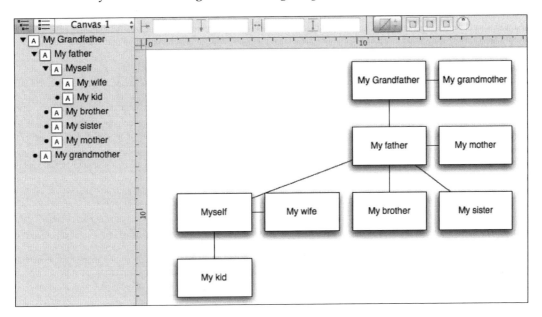

Now apply the Diagram style you made earlier by calling up the Diagram Style Chooser using the **Format | Choose Diagram Styles...** You'll find your **Family tree** style, select this one.

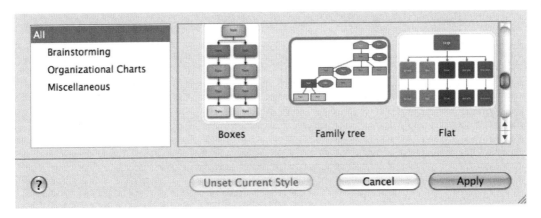

Your resulting diagram should now resemble the one next. This may not be perfect, but is quicker than applying the style by hand.

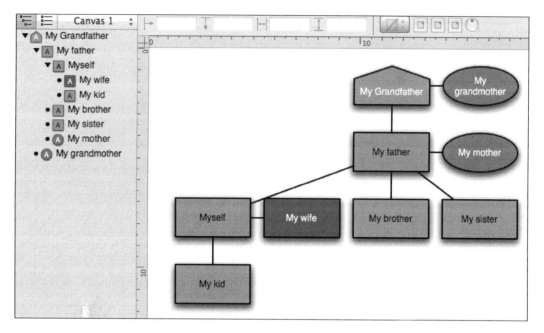

# Diagram Templates

**Diagram Templates** are used every time you start a new OmniGraffle document. If you start a new document by using the **File | New** menu command, or the ⌘+N keyboard shortcut command — a default Diagram Template is used.

OmniGraffle comes with a few templates built in. You can take a look at these templates by using the **File | Template Chooser** — or use the ⇧+⌘+N keyboard shortcut.

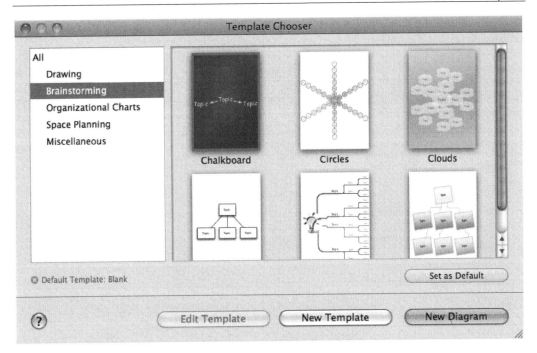

If you choose a to create a new diagram based on one of the templates in the template overview — you'll get a new diagram containing the shapes you saw in the overview. Using templates can be a big time saver.

Templates contain not only the size of your canvas, but also the grid layout, layers, and so on.

You can also make your own template based on an existing template by selecting a template from the template overview, and the clicking on the **New Template** button. Edit your template as you see fit and when you save, the template will appear in the **Miscellaneous** section next time you choose to use the **File | Template Chooser** menu command.

You can also create a new template by using the **File | New Resource | New Template** menu command. You will be presented with the Template Chooser to select an existing template to build upon.

If you select a template from the overview, and use the **Set as Default** button, this is the template you'll be using every time you use the **File | New** menu command. If not, you'll always get the **Template Chooser** when using this command.

# Summary

You have now learned everything there is to about creating diagrams in OmniGraffle. The rest of the book will cover various properties and styling options not covered so far.

This chapter explained the rest of the tools on the canvas toolbar, including how to customize the toolbar keeping only the tools you normally use.

By deploying Diagramming Tools, Mouseless Editing, and using the Outline function you can create your diagrams amazingly fast. The Diagramming Tool lets you create new connected shapes using your mouse—and the Mouseless Editing and the Outline function gave you the opportunity to edit your diagrams without using a mouse at all.

You learned how to quickly absorb a style from one shape and paint the style onto other shapes—this may be quicker than using the Canvas Style Tray and the Canvas Selection inspector palette.

You learned everything you ever need to know about magnetic connection points—including how to customize these to fit your particular shapes.

You also took a look at how to efficiently zoom and move around your canvas.

The next chapter will cover functionality only found in OmniGraffle Professional. If you are not using the professional version you might want to skip this chapter. On the other hand it is a very in-depth examination on what you are missing if not using the professional version.

# 5

# More on Editing Diagrams

So far in the book, you have encountered a few options that are available in both the Standard and Professional versions. There are however, a few diagramming functions that are exclusive to OmniGraffle Professional. If you do not use the Professional version, you may skip this chapter. If you are curious about what functions you would be missing—please keep on reading.

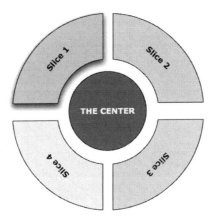

This chapter will teach you how to use the professional version of the program to:

1. Make new shapes using **binary operations on shapes**.
2. Divide your diagram into subgraphs.
3. Structure out tabular information with the table function.
4. Create and manage full screen presentations.
5. Apply ColorSync profiles to your document.

# Creating your own shapes the easy way

A fancy way of saying what you are now going to learn is called *binary or Boolean, operation* on shapes. When something is binary it can be either on or off. What this section will teach you is that you can create new shapes by either adding new parts to a shape, or removing existing parts from a shape.

This method works by using a set of basic shapes (circles, oblongs, triangles, and so on) and the combining of these into new shapes. We are not talking about simply grouping shapes here—but creating new shapes from the bottom up.

In the **Edit | Shapes** menu there are four commands which will aid you in creating a new shape.

# The Subtract Shapes menu command

As the name implies, the **Subtract Shapes** menu command will create a new shape that is based on two or more shapes subtracted from each other.

Start by creating two shapes: One square and one circle. The circle should be put on top of the rectangle.

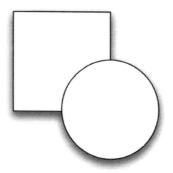

Select both shapes and issue the **Edit | Shapes | Subtract Shapes** menu command. The result below, left, is what you get when the circle is on top of the square. The result on the right is when the square is on top of the circle—and by rotating the shape you could in fact create a Pac-Man lookalike shape.

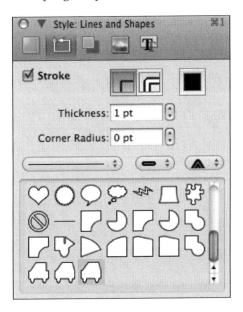

So the rule when subtracting shapes is that the top-most shape will delete the overlapping part of an underlying shape.

A very cool side effect of creating a new shape is that it will appear in the Style inspector Shape Collection. This means that next time you need this very shape—you only have to draw an oblong and the click on that shape.

Any custom shape you have made that is found in the Shape Collection will not be saved from one document to the next. You will thus not be able to re-use these shapes. To re-use these shapes, you will have to create a stencil instead.

# The Union Shapes menu command

An union of two or more shapes is the area of the shapes combined into one big shape. It does not matter which shape is on top of another shape—they will all be combined into one shape.

If you revert back to your square and circle from the previous section, select both and issue the **Edit | Shapes Union Shapes** menu command—the result should be like the following one:

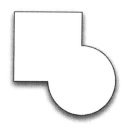

By using just three different basic shapes—two circles, two triangles, and two oblongs—you can in fact quickly create a car-shape (finished product on the right):

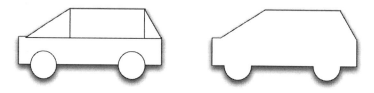

# The Intersect Shapes menu command

As the name implies, the **Intersect Shapes** menu command will create a new shape that is the intersection of two or more shapes. This means that the area covered by all the selected shapes will become the new shape.

If you go back to your square and the circle lying on top of the square—select both shapes and then issue this menu command, the result will be a new shape that is covered by the circle and the square, as seen next:

In fact it does not matter which shape is on top—only the *common area* shared by both shapes matters.

# The Make Points Editable menu command

The **Edit | Shapes | Make Points Editable** menu command will reveal the various points a shape is made up of. By issuing this command, you can edit the details of any shape.

Example: If you do not feel that the cloud shape is "cloudy" enough—mark the shape and issue the **Make Points Editable** menu command.

Notice the small blue diamonds indicating where the shape has its shape points. You can now click and drag these blue diamonds around to make the shape more "cloudy".

Clicking on any of the points may show two control handles (such as the cloud shape above). These handles let you control the behavior of the very point. These handles are only available when the point is a *Bézier Point*.

In *Chapter 2, Stencils* you learned a great deal about Bézier lines and the same principles you learned there, apply here.

# The Big Wedge Experiment

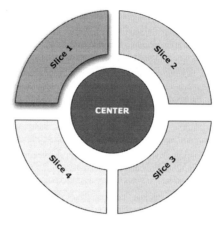

You have now learned everything there is to Boolean operations on shapes. Let's put this knowledge into use for creating a special kind of diagram using a special version of the wedge.

Every time you dive into these kinds of diagramming tasks, you should sit down and analyze how to proceed. As you will see later in this chapter, the most obvious way to create this diagram is not the correct one.

Start by eliminating obviousness—like the circle in the center. It's a plain circle—nothing exciting about this.

How about the wedges then? The four different fill colors and the fact that only one wedge has a shadow show us that these are in fact four different shapes. We also notice that basically, it's the same wedge shape that has simply been copied and rotated into three other positions.

Actually, why rotate something that you can easily *mirror*? The top-right shape is a mirrored version of the top-left shape, and the two bottom shapes are mirrored versions of the two wedges on the top.

This brings us to creating the first wedge.

Start by creating two guides, and then two circles. Make the inner circle smaller than the outer circle.

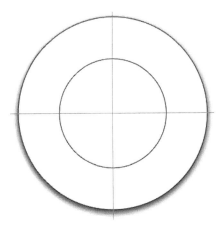

Mark both shapes and issue the **Edit | Shapes | Subtract Shapes** menu command.

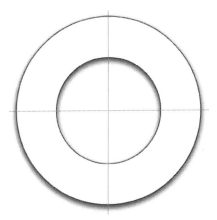

For illustrative purposes we have left the shadow turned on so that you can clearly see that this is one shape. Notice the shadow on the inside. This is a nice donut shape.

The next thing you need to do, is to remove the bottom half plus some extra space.

Add an oblong to the bottom half plus the extra space. You do not want to just cut the circle in half as this will not give you the proper wedged shape.

Subtract those shapes by using the **Edit | Shapes | Subtract Shapes** menu command. The resulting shape after subtraction is shown below on the right.

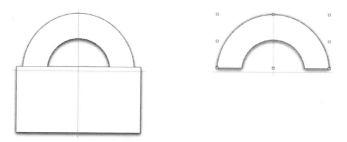

Given the half-circle you now have—repeat the process of covering the right half of the half-circle. The amount you cover over the center-line should be at least as much as you covered over the center - line in the previous operation.

Again you can see the result of the shape subtraction, below, on the right.

Congratulations – you now have the first wedge in your diagram.

As you learned earlier on – the three other wedges are actually mirrored versions of this wedge. All you have to do is to duplicate the shape and then play around with the Flip Buttons ( ⬦ ⬦ ) found in the Geometry Inspector (this was covered in detail in *Chapter 3, Shapes, Building Blocks for Diagrams*).

Now duplicate the shape and press the *Horizontal Flip Button*. Realign the shape to the left of your first wedge.

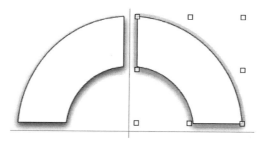

You are fast approaching your goal. Mark both shapes, duplicate them and click on the *Vertical Flip Button*. You can now realign the shapes below the center-line.

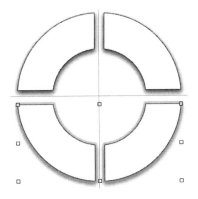

Add a circle, some text and color gently. Finish off by removing the shadow from three of the wedges and the circle. You will then make one wedge stand out—an easy trick to make a certain wedge become the focal point of your diagram.

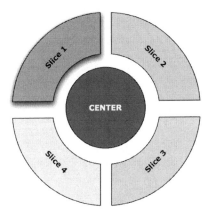

If you are inclined, you may even rotate the text.

If you want to see the diagram in its full glory, you can open the file named `Wedge experiment.graffle` from the Chapter 5 folder in the download bundle.

You may ask—why do I really need to create four different wedges, then move and flip those faster than the world champion of burger flipping? Why do I need four single wedges? After all, if you take the two joined circles and divide them into four different parts you should get the same result as above.

Let's try to do that.

Start by creating two guides, and then two circles as you did earlier. Make the inner circle smaller than the outer circle.

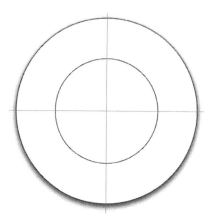

Mark both shapes and issue the **Edit | Shapes | Subtract Shapes** menu command.

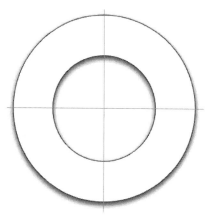

You now have the same shape as you made earlier.

For illustrative purposes we have left the shadow turned on so that you can clearly see that this is one shape. Notice the shadow on the inside. This is a nice donut shape.

Now add the two oblongs to your shape, one covering the horizontal center-line and one covering the vertical center-line.

If you now select all these shapes and issue the menu command **Edit | Shapes | Subtract Shapes** you get all four wedges in a single step.

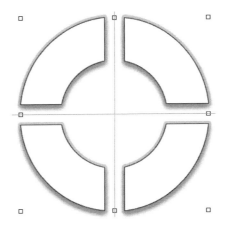

Actually, you do not get four different wedge shapes you get one shape, which consists of four wedges. If you try to fill just one of the four wedges, all four will be filled at the same time with the same fill color.

This is a very good example that demonstrates an important issue relevant to creating diagrams using your own shapes — you must try to find the smallest part of your diagram, and build it from there.

# Subgraphs

The features described in this section are only available in the OmniGraffle Professional version. If you do not have the professional version, you can skip this section.

If you've ever created a really big OmniGraffle diagram with hundreds of shapes, you'll soon find that zooming in and out, and moving around your diagram all the time, is on the brink of annoying.

If your diagram is built in a way that makes it possible to group certain parts of your diagram together—you can create a **subgraph**.

A subgraph is a special kind of group for shapes that can be collapsed and expanded on command. Shapes within the subgraph are hidden and shown accordingly. Any lines to shapes within the subgraph will become lines to the subgraph when collapsed.

To make a subgraph is as simple as selecting a few shapes, then using the **Arrange | Group as Subgraph** menu command. Your shapes will now be enclosed in a rectangle which can be styled as you want.

To ungroup a subgraph, use the **Arrange | Ungroup** menu command.

To collapse and hide the shapes in the subgraph, use the **Arrange | Collapse Subgraph** menu command.

To edit shapes within a subgraph—use the same technique as you used when grouping shapes earlier. Click once to manage the whole group, then click on the shape within the subgraph that you want to edit.

You are now going to experiment with the subgraph features. You are going to create a two-dimensional flow chart explaining the steps needed when replacing a damaged car tire.

The main steps are, in sequence: Change damaged tire, get new tire, and replace tire.

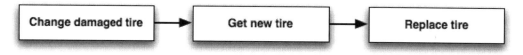

The steps that go under the *Change damaged tire* are:

1. Find jack and spare tire
2. Jack up car

3. Un-mount damaged tire
4. Mount spare tire
5. Jack down car

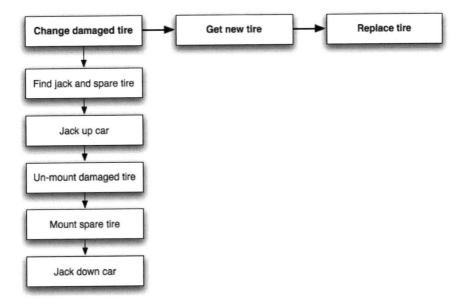

Under **Get new tire** the steps are:

1. Drive to the mechanic
2. Buy new tire

Under **Replace spare tire** the steps are:

1. Find jack and new tire
2. Jack up car
3. Unmount spare tire
4. Mount new tire
5. Jack down car

These steps should result in a graph much like the following one (you are free to style it with colors as you please).

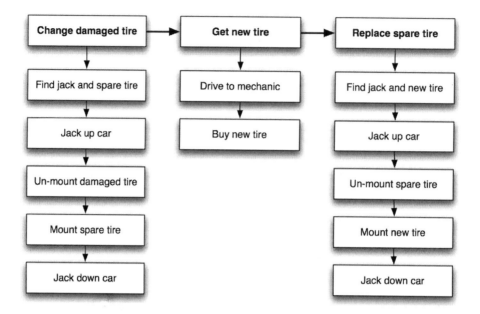

The next thing is to select the row of shapes under the **Change damaged tire** and use the **Arrange | Group as Subgraph** menu command.

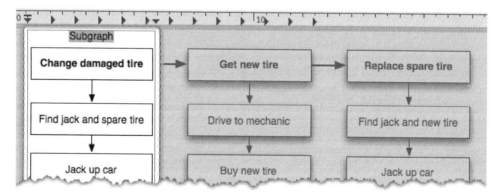

Notice how the rest of the canvas is dimmed down.

You can now change the title of the subgraph to **Change damaged tire**. You can also style it with colors as you please. Fill the subgraph using the **Fill Style inspector** as you would have filled any other shape.

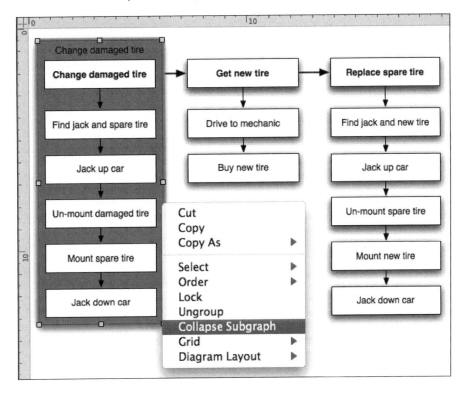

We have used a red to represent damage.

You can now right-click on the subgraph and use the **Collapse Subgraph** menu command.

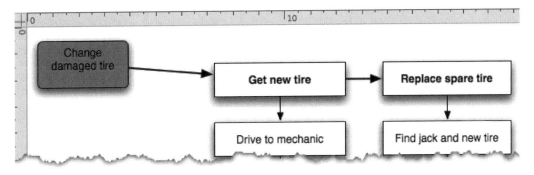

Repeat the process with the two other columns (**Get new tire** and **Replace spare tire**).

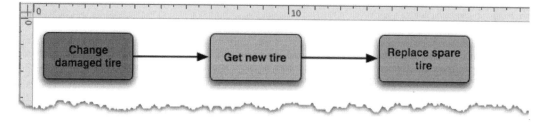

You can find this diagram in the Chapter 5 folder as a file named `Experiments with subgraphs.graffle` from the download bundle.

# Tables

The features described in this section are only available in the OmniGraffle Professional version. If you do not have the professional version, you can skip this section.

This is another special case of grouping shapes together. The difference between this method of grouping shapes and the Subgraph and the ordinary shape grouping is that the table grouping organizes your shapes in columns and rows.

You can take any shapes on your canvas and make these into a table. It is as simple as selecting the shapes you want to use as a table and issuing the **Arrange | Make Table** menu command.

Since the table is just another special case of a group—you can use the **Arrange | Ungroup** menu command to dismantle an existing table.

Let's make a table.

Start with a new blank canvas.

Add an oblong shape just a tad larger than the text field inside the shape:

The next step is to issue the **Arrange | Make Table**, or you can use the ⇧+⌘+*T* keyboard shortcut command. Your shape gets four new resizing table handles—left, right, top, and bottom.

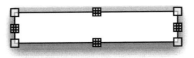

If you drag the right handle further to the right, you extend your table with more columns:

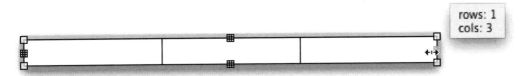

You can now of course enter some text into these table cells.

| One | Two | Three |
| --- | --- | --- |

When you expand the table by dragging the table handles, you copy the column or row you are dragging from.

If you drag the bottom handle further down—you'll end up with more rows like the one you already have.

| One | Two | Three |
| --- | --- | --- |
| One | Two | Three |
| One | Two | Three |

Drag the right handle once more to the right to add another column.

| One | Two | Three | Three |
| --- | --- | --- | --- |
| One | Two | Three | Three |
| One | Two | Three | Three |

Amend your table to have a table looking like the one below:

There are certain operations you can do on your table.

You can select a row or a column by using the **Edit | Tables | Select Row** or **Edit | Tables | Select Column**. You can then hit the *Delete* key (⌦) to delete the selected row or column. Note that you cannot use the **Edit | Tables | Select** menu commands while you have selected more than one cell in the table.

You can even delete a single cell in your table—remember that a "table cell" is really a shape within a group.

Click once on the table, and then click once on cell number **5**.

This behavior works and looks exactly like when you select a shape from within a group of shapes.

You can now hit the *Delete* key and watch cell/shape number **5** disappear.

The commands for inserting a row or a column can also be found in the **Edit | Tables** menu. Select a single cell and issue one of the following commands.

If you insert a row (⌘+↵ keyboard shortcut command), it will be copied from the row where you had selected the cell.

If you insert a column ($\mathcal{A}$+$\mathcal{H}$+$e$ keyboard shortcut command), it will be copied from the column where you had selected the cell.

Resizing the whole table is done in the same way as resizing a group of shapes—just grab hold of one of the corner handles and drag the table to its new size.

If you need to resize one single column, select one of the shapes in the column and drag the side handles to the new horizontal size.

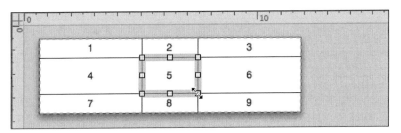

The same applies to resizing a single row. Select one of the shapes in the row and drag either the top or bottom handles to the new vertical size.

You can also drag one of the corners of a selected shape and adjust both the column width and the row height in one operation.

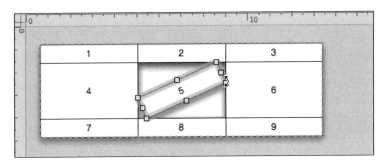

And finally, you can hold down the command key ($\mathcal{H}$) and drag the shape in the direction of your preferred rotation.

Even if you can rotate a shape (cell) within a table-group—you cannot add a rotated shape when you create a new table.

Crate a new OmniGraffle document—and add two oblongs on either side of a circle. Rotate the oblongs so that they slope towards the circle.

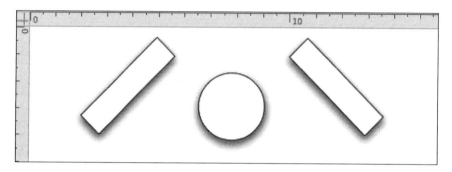

Select all three shapes and use the **Arrange** | **Make Table** menu command.

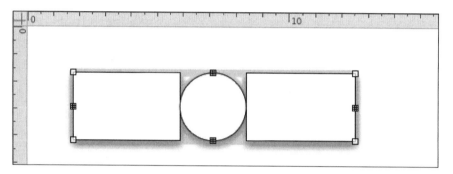

Not only will the rotation be reset to 0° but the oblong shapes will also adjust their height to the circle.

Consider the following before and after pictures of shapes made into a table:

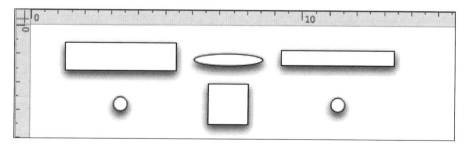

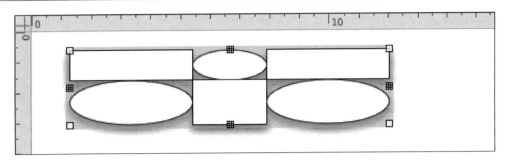

It is thus clear that OmniGraffle adjusts shapes to both the height and width of the biggest shapes per row, starting with the top-most row.

# Using OmniGraffle as a presentation tool

If you feel that Microsoft PowerPoint or Apple Keynote is not the tool you are most comfortable with, why not use OmniGraffle as a presentation tool?

## Creating a presentation

Creating presentations is as simple as using a canvas for each of the slides you want to have in your presentation.

As most of the computer screens and projectors operate in the landscape mode, you can save yourself a lot of headache by setting up your OmniGraffle document in the landscape mode. This is achieved by using the **File | Page Setup...** menu command (the corresponding keyboard shortcut is ⇧+⌘+P).

## Starting, navigating, and stopping your presentation

You can start your OmniGraffle presentation by using the **View | Start Presentation** or by using the ⌥+⌘+P keyboard shortcut command.

OmniGraffle will now go into **full screen mode**.

You stop the **presentation mode** by pressing the *Esc* key.

You can navigate between the canvases by using the arrow keys. Another way of doing the same is to click anywhere on the canvas to advance to the next slide (that is canvas).

When in presentation mode, the default behavior of OmniGraffle is to highlight any objects on your canvas when you move your mouse over the shape. You can use this feature to highlight just the objects you want your audience to focus on.

A nice feature to call up is the navigation bar while in presentation mode. The navigation bar will pop up if you move your mouse to the bottom of the canvas.

The navigation bar will give you a preview of all the canvases you have in your document/presentation. The preview is a thumbnail representation of the content of your canvas. You can click on any of these previews to go directly to that very canvas.

You can also click on the small arrow key on top of the navigation bar to move backwards or forwards between canvases.

The **X** in the upper left-hand corner will close your presentation if clicked.

# Advanced presentation mode

When giving a presentation using a projector and your laptop, you have in effect two different screens (unless you have set your *Macintosh Display Preferences* to *Mirror* the two displays).

You can show your OmniGraffle document in presentation mode on one screen, and edit the same document on the other screen.

If your computer is connected to two screens (it does not have to be a projector—an extra monitor will do just fine), you can open the file named `Presentation.graffle` found in `Chapter 5` in the download bundle.

| | |
|---|---|
| Minimize | ⌘M |
| Zoom | |
| **New Window on "Presentation.graffle"** | |
| Stencils | ⌘0 |
| Tool Palette | ⌥⌘T |
| Workspaces | ▶ |
| Bring All to Front | |
| ✓ Presentation.graffle: Canvas 1 | |

Use the **Window | New Window on "Presentation.graffle"** menu command.

You now have the same OmniGraffle document open in two different windows.

Put the window titled **Presentation.graffle (2)** on your 2nd monitor.

Navigate both documents to show **Canvas 1**.

Click the window on your 2nd monitor to activate this, and then use the **View | Start Presentation** menu command. OmniGraffle is now showing your document in presentation mode on this monitor. You can now move back and forth between slides (that is canvases); you can also use the presentation toolbar at the bottom of your screen as you learned in the previous section.

On your primary monitor (the window with the title **Presentation.graffle (1)**)—take the Pac-Man shape and move it around your canvas. Notice how this very shape will also move around the canvas on your 2nd monitor.

Given this unique capability, you can actually edit your presentation "live".

# Actions and presentation mode

In *Chapter 4, More Tools for Editing Diagrams* you learned how to use the **Action Browse Tool** to set up various actions when a shape is clicked.

These actions are immediately available when using the presentation mode, and the actions performed are the same as you set up with the **Action Property Inspector . . .** and as if you had used the **Action Browse Tool**.

Using actions within the presentation mode can make for pretty interesting and impressive presentations. These combined features may, for example, allow you to conduct a real-time collaborative session with your audience where you make changes "on the fly."

# Changing the color and behavior of the presentation highlight

The default behavior in OmniGraffle is to highlight any shape you move your mouse pointer over.

The color used by default is the color that is defined by your system preferences as your **Highlight color**. You'll find this in the *Appearance* section in the operating systems' *System Preferences*.

For reasons dependant on where you are holding your presentation, you may not want this particular color.

Likewise, you may not want shapes to be highlighted as your mouse moves over the shape. If you open up the iPhone software mockup you made in Chapter 3, you'll quickly realize that given the number of shapes each canvas consists of the presentation will very quickly, look messy.

You can easily change this behavior by using the **Presentation Preferences** section in the **OmniGraffle** preference pane.

Use the **OmniGraffle | Preferences...** menu command or press the ⌘ , keyboard shortcut combination.

You can change the highlight behavior and the highlight appearance. The appearance is controlling the color of the highlight.

The behavior controls how highlighting will occur:

- You can highlight by moving your mouse pointer on a shape. This is the default behavior.
- You can highlight only shapes that you are actively clicking on.
- You can also turn off any highlighting.

Even if you turn off highlighting—associated actions will still perform as expected.

The **Show link badge when highlighted** checkbox controls where an appropriate icon will be shown over the highlighted shape.

# The ColorSync support

Your Apple Macintosh comes with a very cool feature called ColorSync. If you are using your Mac for graphics work, you are probably already familiar with the ColorSync concept.

ColorSync will ensure that what you see on a ColorSync enabled monitor and what's being printed on a ColorSync enabled printer will look exactly the same.

ColorSync support is controlled from the ColorSync preference pane. Use the **OmniGraffle | Preferences...** menu command to open up the preference panel.

If you enable ColorSync by checking the **Use Color Profiles** checkbox, the program will save color profile information along with the OmniGraffle document – or any of your exported graphics files.

If you try to import graphics files that have embedded color profile information, OmniGraffle will use this information accordingly. The same applies if you open an OmniGraffle document that is color profile enabled. You can control what OmniGraffle will do in these circumstances by using the drop-down menu found in the preference pane.

# Summary

You have now dived into the various tools that are exclusive to the Professional version of OmniGraffle.

You learned how easy it is to create your own shapes using binary operations—rather than using the Pen Tool.

You saw how you could use Subgraphs to hide larger parts of your diagram.

One of the most versatile functions of the Professional version is the ability to create tables—not only of text shapes but really of any shapes.

Lastly, you saw how you could use OmniGraffle as a presentation tool, somewhat akin to what PowerPoint and Keynote do.

In the next chapter, we're back to functions and options found both in the standard and the professional versions alike. You are going to learn how to make your diagram look good easily using color, size, and alignment functions.

# 6
# Making your Diagram Look Good

OmniGraffle has several methods of quickly styling your diagram. This chapter will introduce you to methods and techniques you can use for this purpose.

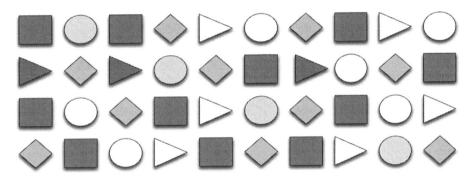

In *Chapter 1, Getting Started with OmniGraffle* you were introduced to a few tips on making your diagrams visually appealing. Some of these were:

- **Colorize gently**: Do not flush your diagram full of colors. It is best if you can keep to just a few colors. Use colors that match each other — if you feel that you are not good at choosing colors, you can use the ColorJack and Kuler websites mentioned in Chapter 1.

- **Use few fonts**: Try to use only two different fonts. These fonts should be without serifs, also known as sans serif. The text you are reading right now is a serif font — the titles in this book are written without serifs.

- **Consider your output media**: The thickness of lines, the color (or lack there of) fill of shapes, and so on, means different things when used in a screen presentation, on a web page or in a printed report.

- **Symmetry is better than asymmetry**: A balanced diagram is a good-looking diagram. However, any educated graphics designer will tell you there is a difference between visual and mathematical symmetry. If you are unsure about this – just do what looks correct.

- **Have one and only one focus point**: The focus point is the most important part of the diagram.

- **Use titles, figure captions and legends**: A diagram without a title is not telling the reader exactly what they are looking at. The exception to this rule is if the diagram is part of a report or a book.

- **Be liberal with white space**: Avoid cramping shapes together, as this will make your diagram look busy and messy. If space permits – use a whole page exclusively for your diagram if needed.

In this chapter we will cover the following topics:

- Resizing shapes based on existing shapes on your canvas
- How gridlines might improve your diagramming
- How to efficiently align shapes to each other
- Selecting and re-styling shapes based on similarity
- Selecting and re-styling connected shapes
- Various color picker tricks

# Manually adjusting diagram elements

So far you have manually moved shapes around your diagram. You have also learned that you can use visual guides in your diagram to align elements. However, for the majority of tasks, you used the **Smart Alignment Guides** and the **Smart Distance Guides** found in the **Arrange | Guides** application menu.

Next you see a shape that is aligned with both the Smart Alignment and Smart Distance guides enabled.

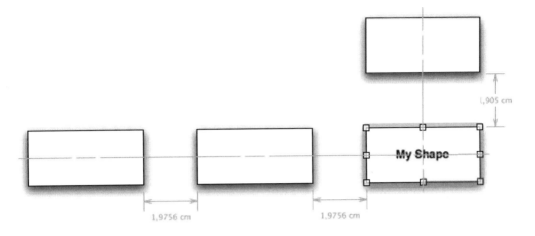

The thin blue lines going through **My Shape** in the previous diagram are a visual indication that the shape is aligned both to the shapes to the left and above. If you have a diagram with a lot of shapes close to each other, the Smart Alignment Guides may not seem so smart anymore. In fact, the guides will not align to whatever shapes you wish they should align to. In these circumstances, using manual guides is the only good solution for very precise shape alignments.

The Smart Alignment Guides will appear when you align two or more shapes to each other.

Between the shapes you see the visual measurements that appear when the Smart Distance Guides kicks into action. The guide shows that the distances between **My Shape** and the two other horizontal shapes are equal to each other—creating horizontal symmetry. The same is also true for the vertical distance guide.

The Smart Distance Guides appears when you try to distance three or more shapes from each other.

# Resizing shapes

Until now you have resized shapes manually by dragging on the shape's resize handles (the small squares found on each corner and on each edge).

If you wanted to make two or more shapes the same size, you've had to do a lot of work manually. Instead of manually working on each shape, you can use the **Arrange | Size** menu commands. You can also find the same commands using the context sensitive menu that appears if you right click on any shape, or selection of shapes.

There are all together five sizing commands available (Make Same Width, Make Same Height, Make Same Size, Make Natural Size, and Size to Fit Image). You can size shapes to the same height, the same width, the same width and height, to their natural size and finally you can resize a shape to fit an imported image.

# Size to Fit Image

Executing this menu command will resize the shape to cover the length and height of an associated image. How to add an image to a shape (that is, filling a shape with an image) is covered in *Chapter 3, Shapes, Building Blocks for Diagrams* in the *Style shape properties* section.

# Make Natural Size

A natural sized shape is a shape where the height and the width of the shape are the same.

The resizing is done based on the longest length, either vertically or horizontally. If you resize a shape which is wider than it's tall—then the *Natural Size* is calculated based on the width of the shape. The same applies if the shape is taller than it's wide—the *Natural Size* in this case is based on the height of the shape.

The shape is always resized from the center line (either vertically or horizontally).

Let's learn by doing.

Start with a new canvas – add a rectangle to the canvas, and place a manual guideline through the shape's horizontal center line.

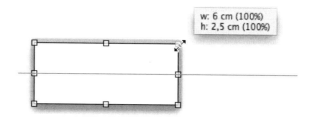

After either using the **Arrange | Size | Make Natural Size** menu command, or right clicking and using the **Size | Make Natural Size** menu command, the shape is resized into a perfect square where each side has the same length and width.

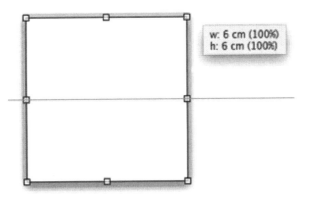

As you can see, the horizontal center is still intact.

# Making shapes the same size

You have at your disposal three resizing commands that can only be used if you have selected more than one shape. The commands are to make the shapes the same width, height, and both width *and* height at the same time.

We cannot stress this enough, but the order in which you select the shapes affects the end result.

Start by creating an OmniGraffle document with an ellipse, a rectangle, and a triangle.

1.  First select the ellipse *and then* select the rectangle.
2.  Issue the **Make Same Width** menu command.

3.   The result is an oblong the same length as the ellipse.

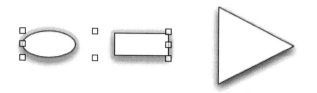

4.   Now – first select the triangle, and then select the rectangle.

5.   Issue the **Make Same Height** menu command.

The result is that the rectangle is now the same height as the triangle, as seen in the screenshot below:

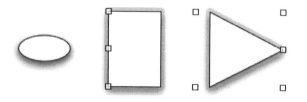

Let's try to select all the shapes and then use the **Make Same Size** menu command.

You can select all the shapes by using the ⌘+*A* keyboard shortcut command.

If you got the following result, this is because the rectangle and triangle where already selected (remember that the order in which the shapes are selected matters).

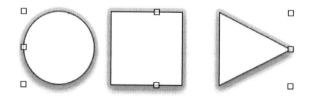

If you instead had deselected any shapes prior to using the keyboard shortcut, the result would have been as expected because the ellipse was the first shape you drew on the canvas.

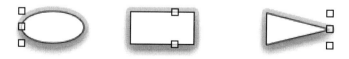

To complicate matters even further, as you drew the ellipse first, this shape was the top-most shape in your diagram.

If you add a new cloud-shape to the right of the triangle, and order this shape to be the uppermost shape using the **Front** function ( ) on the **Canvas** toolbar, your diagram should now look as shown next:

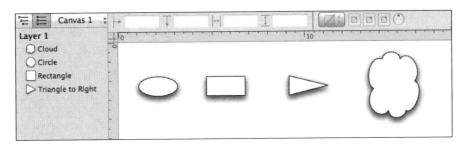

Now, hit ⌘+A to select all shapes on the canvas, and then issue the **Make Same Size** menu command.

The following screenshot is the resulting diagram:

# Gridlines

So far in this book you have worked without using a visible grid on your canvas. With the aid of the Smart Alignment Guides and the Smart Distance Guides, you have made perfectly aligned and good-looking diagrams. If your diagrams are much like the ones you have created so far, you may never have to use a grid when placing shapes.

However, if you are making diagrams, which represent "real life objects" – using a grid is a must. These kinds of diagrams can be anything from a diagram showing the new office layout – to a diagram for showing office visitors where various parts of the building are.

# Enabling gridlines

You turn the visibility of grid lines on or off by using the **View | Gridlines** menu command. You could also use the ⌘+\ keyboard shortcut command.

In the previous screenshot, you see the canvas with grid lines. The thick grid lines are called the **Major Gridlines**, while the thinner lines are called the **Minor Steps**.

# Adjusting gridlines

You can control the measurement unit in the **Major Grid Spacing** input field using the **Canvas Size Property inspector**. We'll cover this inspector fully in *Chapter 6, Making your Diagram Look Good*.

The default spacing for the Major Gridlines is 2,54 cm / 1 inch. Between Major Gridlines, there are eight Minor Steps as default.

You can adjust the Major Gridlines and the Minor Steps by using the **Grid Property** inspector found in the Canvas selector.

The details of this property inspector are covered in *Chapter 8, Canvases and Canvas Layers*.

# Aligning shapes to the document grid

By using the Smart Guides, you really do not have to care about where your shapes are placed relative to the canvas grid. However, if you create diagrams that involve shapes that have to be correctly sized to match the "real world", you can get a lot of help from OmniGraffle by enabling the **Snap to grid** checkbox and the **Edges on grid** button on the Grid Property inspector.

The following discussion will demonstrate how OmnniGraffle will help you create a floor plan (as seen in the previous picture) for an exhibition your company is holding.

- Your company, which sells maritime gear, is arranging an exhibition for your customers. You have invited all your suppliers, and they will exhibit products and goods.

- The exhibition is held in a room measuring 20 X 30 meters (65.62 X 98.42 feet).

The first thing you have to set up is a grid that will help you in drawing your diagram. A normal measurement in this regard is letting 1 cm on paper equal 1 m in real life (or the equivalent of imperial units, that is, 1 inch on paper equals 1 foot in real life). A meter is divided into 100 cm, but as your diagram is not really a builder's diagram, you do not need the high resolution of 1 cm in real life. A resolution of 10 cm will suffice.

So basically, your Major Grid Lines is set to 1 cm, and Minor Grid Steps is set to 10. Each minor grid step equals 10 cm.

To see the complete grid in all its glory, you may have to zoom in to the canvas. You can zoom by using either the **Zoom** button at the bottom right on the canvas (100%), or using the **View | Zoom | Zoom In** menu command.

The following screenshot facilitates the canvas with a 200% zoom. Notice that the rules on the top and to the left are nicely numbered from 1 onwards. This is a pretty cool indication that you can easily create a room of 20 X 50 meters.

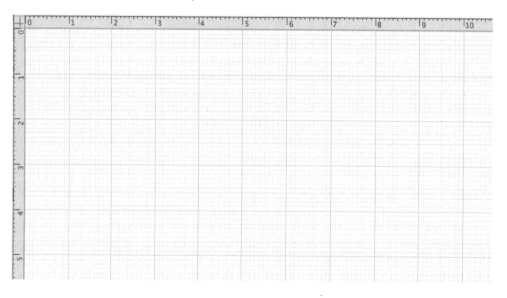

The one thing that might hinder us is the diagram's origin (that is, the upper-left corner). It will be easier to work with the diagram if you move the origin a bit into the canvas. Dragging the blue cross on the upper left into the canvas achieves this:

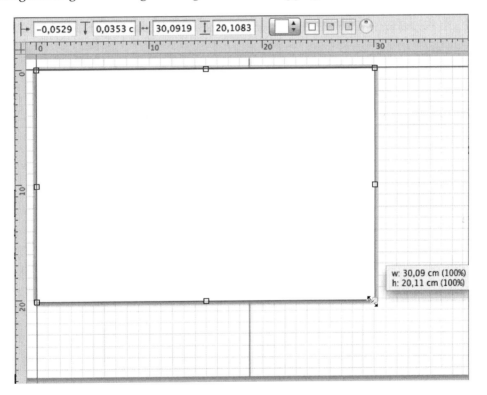

Use the **Zoom** button to zoom out to 50% to get the full overview.

Next, create an oblong measuring 20 X 30 meters. This is simply done by placing an oblong starting on the diagram origin and the dragging it to the canvas.

Notice how difficult it can be to have the oblong starting in the origin when you have zoomed out to 50% also notice how time consuming it can be to get an exact measurement of 30 X 20 cm (representing 30 X 20 meters).

There are two things you can do to aid you in getting the correct measurements. One is to use the **Snap to Grid** checkbox we discussed earlier. The second thing you can do is to use the **Inspector Bar**.

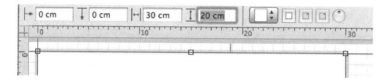

The left side of the Inspector Bar displays both the origin of a shape and the width and height of the shape. You can enter the correct measurement and placement information in these boxes. If you now enter **0** and **0** in the two first boxes; **30** and **20** in the next boxes, your shape should now be correctly set.

To make our floor complete, we need to add a door and thicker walls. The walls should be 7 points thick. We need to add a door to the room—the door is 4 meters wide and is placed on the left wall, 3 meters from the top. Basically, the door is just an opening in the wall.

Zoom back to 200% using the **Zoom** button, and add an oblong shape with the correct size and without any strokes. This rectangle will represent the door in our building.

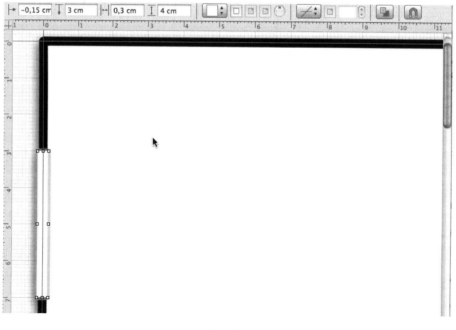

Notice the various numbers in the Inspector Bar to place this shape correctly.

Now our floor is complete, and to prevent yourself from accidently messing up your diagram as you work on it, rename this layer to **Floor** and lock it to prevent changes. You use the **Arrange | Lock** menu command to prevent shapes from been accidentally moved around. You can also use the lock icon on the canvas toolbar, or the ⌘+L keyboard shortcut command.

Now add a new layer—this layer is where we are going to place the exhibition booths and other infrastructure.

First off, we need a couple of registration desks.

Given that this is a high level diagram, we're not going to add the detailed level of the desks themselves—but an indication of where the registration area is.

The registration area is just another rectangle near the door, as seen next:

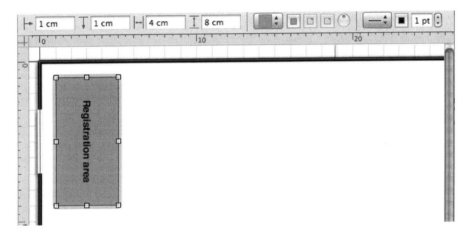

Remember that one of the "rules" we stated earlier is that symmetry is a good thing. Notice that our registration area shape is 8 cm high—and exceeds the door by 2 cm on each side.

If you have the standard version of OmniGraffle, you will need to rotate the whole shape 90°. However, if you have OmniGraffle Pro, you only need to press the overflow **text fitting** button, and then rotate the text 90°.

Even if the physical room is not really set this way, we must take some liberties with our diagram. The main reason for creating these kinds of diagrams is usability: The diagram should be easy to understand and easy for visitors to use for navigating the exhibition ground.

Next out is creating a few exhibition stand aisles.

There will be two rows of stands on each side of the room. The widths of these rows are 4 meters, and the length is 20 meters. One row should be named **Sailboat vendors**, the other **Motorboat vendors**.

The row of stands in the middle is 18 meters long and 6 meters wide (that is, 17 cm and 6 cm). The name of these stands is **Equipment vendors**.

Fill each stand row with a different color for easy indication and identification, as shown next :

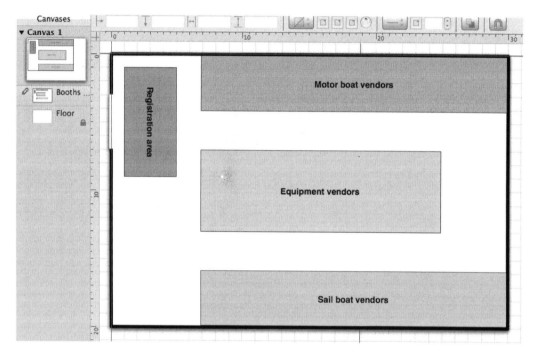

The only things lacking now are the concession kiosk, the toilets, coat check, fire extinguishers, and so on. The standard way to indicate these things is by using a special set of symbols from the

Download and install a stencil named **AIGA Symbols** from GraffleTopia. If you are unsure about how to do this, take a look at Chapter 2.

Place the kiosk, the coat check and the toilet on the left wall—use the appropriate AIGA symbols to indicate which is which.

For more information on these symbols, check out the AIGA website at
http://www.aiga.org/content.cfm/symbol-signs

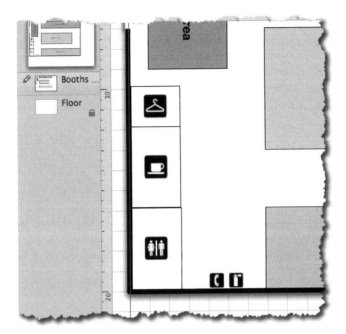

Every diagram of this kind **must** have a legend explaining the various part of the diagram. Add the legend below, and you should be done.

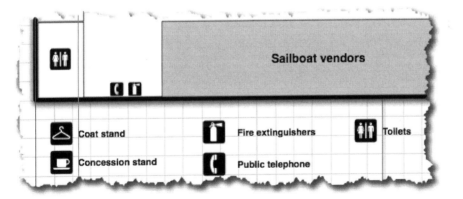

Notice the use of the vertical guide to align the legend text. The reason for this is that the **Smart Alignment Guides** did not work as expected due to the number of shapes on the canvas.

This may look like a very simple diagram—and it is. However, it's also very clear and easy to understand.

There is only one very glaring error with this diagram: The texts of the three stand rows are not aligned. True, they are aligned to the center of each oblong but not to each other. We'll need to fix this.

Unless you have OmniGraffle Professional, you will have to remove the text inside each shape, and then create stand-alone text shapes. You can then align these stand-alone text shapes to each other.

If you have OmniGraffle Professional, you just have to use the **Text Offset** controls in the Text style inspector.

However, for this very diagram, doing it the non-professional way gives you much more control than the percentage adjustments you can do with the Text Offset controls. It is often more desirable to use other means than percentage adjustments for finer controls over objects and their positioning.

And here is the complete exhibition map—observe that we have added a title to the diagram

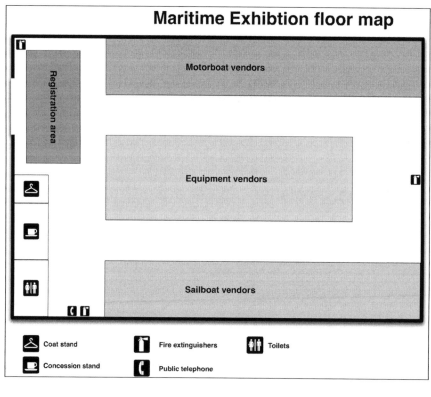

To spice things up, we should add a list of suppliers and add this to the map also.

In the final version, we have a list of suppliers beneath the map, and the legend to the right of the map. The main reason for this is that if the vendors were to be placed to the right of the map, this could easily become the main focus point—which is a no-no.

## Maritime Exhibtion floor map

| | |
|---|---|
| Registration area | **Motorboat vendors** |
| | Motorboat vendors |
| | Absolute |
| | Bayliner |
| | Dominator |
| | Falcon |
| | Poly Marine |
| | Regal |
| | Rinker |
| | Sunseeker |
| | **Equipment vendors** |
| Equipment vendors | 3M Products |
| | Harken |
| | Helly Hansen |
| | Lewmar |
| | Mustand |
| | Raymarine |
| | Spinlock |
| | UK Sails |
| | **Sailboat vendors** |
| Sailboat vendors | Bavaria |
| | Bénétau |
| | Catalina |
| | Comfortina |
| | Laser |
| | Privateer |
| | Quest Yachts |
| | X-Yachts |

Coat stand   Fire extinguishers   Toilets
Concession stand   Public telephone

If you want to see the finished diagram in full color, please open the file named Exhibition.graffle. The file is found in the Chapter 7 folder in the download bundle.

# Aligning shapes to each other

You will sooner or later need to quickly align a series of shapes. OmniGraffle has several ways of doing this.

Start by placing a few shapes randomly on the canvas.

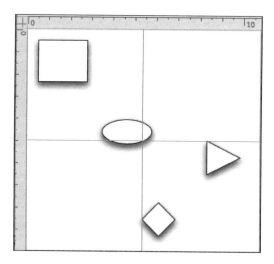

From the **Arrange** | **Align** menu, you have several choices on how you want to align your shapes. It is also possible to right-click and get a context sensitive menu appearing with the various alignment choices.

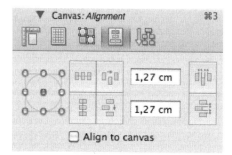

Most of the same choices are also available from the Canvas: **Alignment inspector**.

However, there are a few extra choices available like offsetting shapes either vertically or horizontally.

The behavior of the Alignment buttons is controlled by the **Point of Alignment** matrix.

The Alignment buttons may thus be used to align shapes to the lower-right corner, or to the center-bottom of the shapes – it is all controlled by the active point (blue) in the Point of Alignment matrix.

You will find a sub-set of the alignment options in the **Arrange | Align** menu, this also holds true for the context sensitive menu that appears on right-clicking the selected shapes.

The **Alignment** buttons are what actually control the alignment of two or more selected shapes.

The **Horizontal Shape Alignment** button (that is, the upper button) controls the horizontal alignment of shapes. The leftmost and rightmost shape will limit the horizontal alignment.

The **Vertical Shape Alignment** button (that is, the lower button) controls the vertical alignment of selected shapes. The top shape and bottom shape will limit the vertical alignment.

The red line associated with the buttons shows to what respect the shapes will be aligned to each other, and the selected button in the Point of Alignment matrix controls where the line appears.

The **Spread** buttons distributes selected shapes evenly between the leftmost and the rightmost shapes. The buttons will only work if you have selected more than two shapes.

The upper button is the **Horizontal Spread** button, and as its name implies; clicking on this button with three or more selected shapes will distribute those shapes horizontally without altering their vertical placement.

The lower button is the **Vertical Spread** button. Clicking on this button will evenly spread out three or more selected shapes in the vertical direction without altering the shapes' horizontal placement.

The **Spacing** button is used when you need to manually set the vertical or horizontal space between shapes.

The upper button is called the **Horizontal Space** button, and will set the horizontal space based on the value entered in the input field to the left of the button. Clicking on this button when two or more shapes are selected will not alter the shapes' vertical placement.

The lower button is called the **Vertical Space** button. Clicking on this button will set the vertical space entered in the input field to the left of the button without altering the horizontal placement of the selected shapes.

The **Align to canvas** checkbox overrides the outermost shapes and will use the canvas edge as the left, right, top, and bottom edges for the alignment.

The following table shows the resulting alignment when some of the alignment controls are used. All actions performed in this table, are on the basis of the shapes displayed at the beginning of this section.

Clicking on the **Vertical Shape Alignment** button:

Clicking on the **Horizontal Shape Alignment** button:

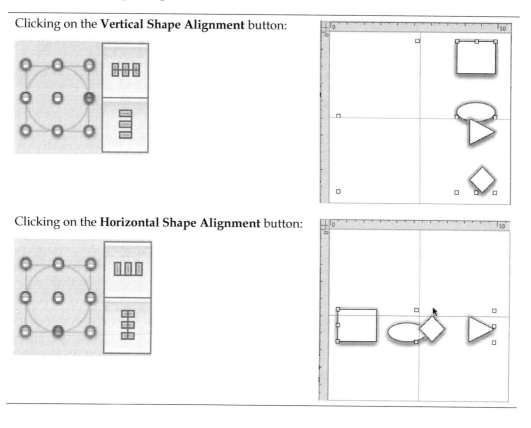

Entering **0,01 cm** in the **Horizontal Space** button offset field and clicking the button:

Notice that the vertical alignment has not changed.

# Easy shape selection

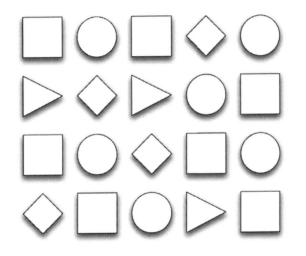

When diagrams become complex and you want to change the appearance of many of the same objects, you can either hold down the shift key on your keyboard and select the shapes you need to change, or you can use the built-in selection functions in OmniGraffle.

There are three built in methods of selecting shapes:

1.  The **Edit | Select | Similar Objects** menu command.
2.  The context sensitive menu when right-clicking on selected shapes (**Select | Similar Objects**).
3.  Using the Canvas: **Selection inspector**.

If shapes are connected to each other, it's also possible to select connected shapes from the application menu or the context sensitive menu. You will deal with connected shapes later.

# What OmniGraffle defines as similar shapes

**Similar shapes** are shapes that have **exactly** the same styling, not the form, type or size of the shapes. The styling can be; the filling color or blend of the shape, the stroke thickness, the corner radius, the stroke color, the shadow, if the shape is filled with a picture and if the shape has an associated text.

Neither the size of two or more shapes, nor the content of the text will make OmniGraffle define the shapes as dissimilar.

If you change the font type, weight or color – then OmniGraffle will define the shapes as dissimilar.

As the few examples in the table below show more often than not, shapes that are of the same type (rectangle, circle, and so on) are dissimilar.

| Shapes | Explanation | Result |
|---|---|---|
| Rectangle / Oblong | Same font, color and weight, but different text. | Similar shapes. |
| Rectangle / Oblong | Difference in the fuzziness of the shadow. | Dissimilar shapes. |
| Rectangle / **Oblong** | Different font size. | Dissimilar shapes. |
| Rectangle / Oblong | Different color. Different text, but same font, color and weight. | Dissimilar shapes. |

Let's explore how easy it is to select similar shapes.

Create an OmniGraffle document with only 4 shapes: Rectangle, Circle, Diamond, and Triangle. Mix them all together so it's not easy to manually select various shapes.

In the download bundle, Chapter 7, there is a file named Experiments in shape selections.graffle—you can open this if you do not want to create your own version.

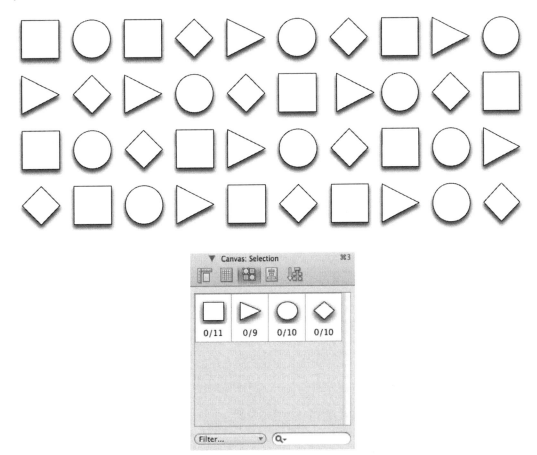

In the Canvas: **Selection inspector** (seen in the previous screenshot), you will see the four different shapes. Under each shape, there are two numbers separated by a forward slash (/). The number on the left indicates how many of the given shape are selected, and the number to the right of the slash is the total count of shapes on the current canvas.

As you can see in the Selection inspector, we have 11 rectangles, 9 triangles, 10 circles, and 10 diamonds.

To select all the diamonds on the canvas, click on the diamond shape in the Selection inspector. Notice that the numbers below the shape are now reading **10/10**. If you click on the Fill style inspector and use the color named **Honeydew** from the **Crayon color palette**—all the diamonds change into this color.

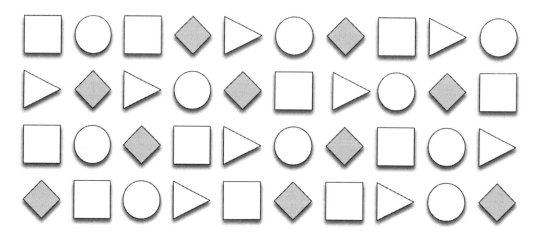

Now, click on the rectangle in the upper-left corner and right-click to get the context sensitive menu. Then select then use the **Select | Similar Objects** menu command, as seen next:

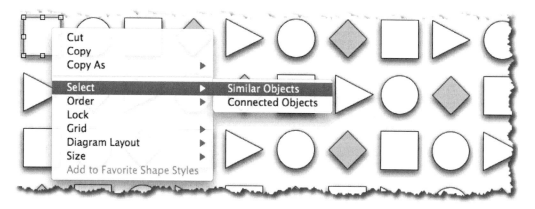

Now all the rectangles are selected.

Fill the rectangles with the color named **Tin** from the **Crayons color palette**.

The next thing you are going to do is to select four of the circles and fill these with a yellow color.

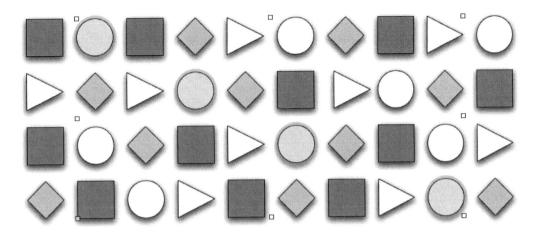

Notice that the Selection inspector now has five different shapes:

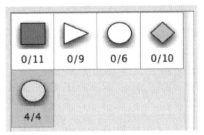

You can now continue on your own to experiment changing various style properties to the shape groups.

# Selecting connected shapes

You are now going to perform some experiments with connected shapes. Start with a diagram like the one next. You can either create this by hand, or you can open the file named Experiments in shape selections.graffle found in the Chapter 7 directory in the download bundle.

The diagram is found on the second canvas. Notice that all shapes are connected to each other.

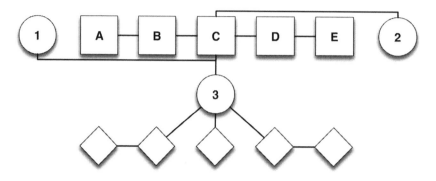

If you look at the Selection inspector, you'll see four shapes, where the lines are one of those shapes.

> OmniGraffle defines descendants to a selected shape as all shapes that are either connected to the right of or below the selected shape.
>
> OmniGraffle defines ancestors to a selected shape as all shapes that are either connected to the left of or above the selected shape.

The following table lists a few actions and their corresponding results while working with connected shapes.

| Action | Result |
|---|---|
| Choose (select) circle number **1** and execute **Descendants** from the **Edit \| Selection** menu.<br><br>This action results in the selection of the shapes connected below and to the right of the chosen shape. | 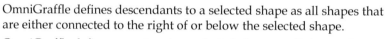 |
| Select circle number **2** and choose **Ancestors** from the **Edit \| Selection** menu.<br><br>This action results in the selection of shapes connected to the left of the chosen shape. | 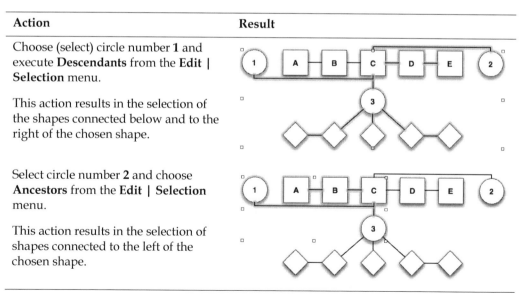 |

| Action | Result |
|---|---|
| Select circle number **3** and choose **Ancestors** from the **Edit \| Selection** menu.<br><br>This action results in the selection of shapes connected above and to the left of the chosen shape.<br><br>Notice that circle number **2** is not selected. The reason is that this shape is on the right of the chosen shape. | 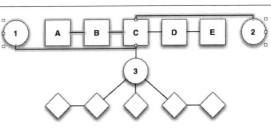 |
| Select square **B** and choose **Descendants** from the **Edit \| Selection** menu.<br><br>This action result in every shape except circle number **1** and square **A** being selected. | 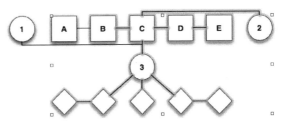 |
| Select square **C** and choose **Ancestors** from the **Edit \| Selection** menu.<br><br>The shapes connected to the left of the chosen shape are selected. | 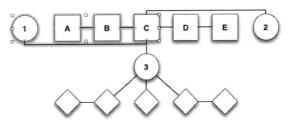 |
| Select square **C** and choose **Descendants** from the **Edit \| Selection** menu.<br><br>The shapes connected below and to the right of the chosen shape are selected. | 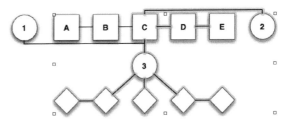 |
| Select any shape and choose **Connected Objects** from the **Edit \| Selection** menu.<br><br>This action results in the whole diagram being selected since every shape is connect to every other shape, either directly or indirectly. | 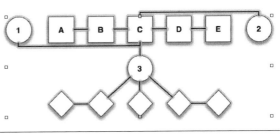 |

Selecting all these shapes—either by form or by connections seems like a very powerful tool, and indeed it is.

With this way of selecting shapes, you can easily change the look and feel in a consistent manner throughout your whole diagram.

# Easy re-styling of shapes

Instead of selecting similar shapes, and then changing their appearance by using the style inspectors, you can also drag and drop styles from the Style Tray directly onto the Selection inspector.

Start your experiments in the easy re-styling of shapes by creating various shapes, and fill some of these with various colors.

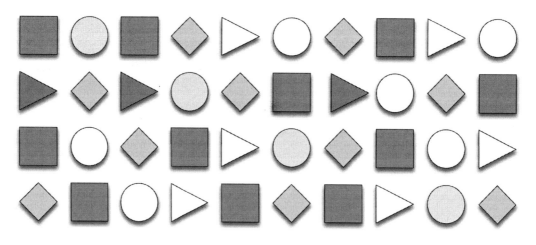

To save you some time and get right into the experimentation, you can also open the file named Experiments in re-styling shapes.graffle, which is found in the Chapter 6 folder of the download bundle.

We're not quite happy with only having four yellow circles.

Your first task is to make the rest of the circles yellow. Unfortunately, you do not know which yellow color these circles are – you could work with the color picker to get the right yellow. This is too much work. Let's do this the simple way.

In the Selection inspector, you will see all the different shapes, including the four yellow circles. If you use the file from the download bundle, you should have the yellow circles as the first shape in the inspector.

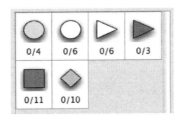

To select all the yellow circles, you could click on one of the circles and then use the **Edit | Select | Similar Objects** menu command. This is too much work really.

Just click on the shape inside the inspector.

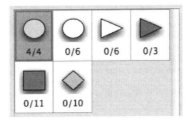

What happens now is that all the yellow circles have been selected.

In the Style Tray, the styling for these shapes is now shown:

You can now drag the color chit (▢) on to the white circle in the Selection inspector.

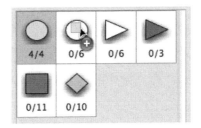

Suddenly all your circles have this shade of yellow.

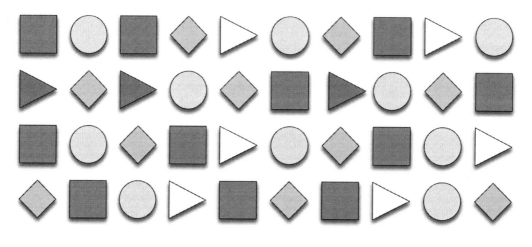

And it's not only the color we can change in a second like this. In fact, your next job is to eradicate all of those gray and boring squares and instead replace these with the green and happy diamonds.

This is also just a two-step process.

Start by clicking on one of the diamonds in your canvas.

Now, drag the **Complete Style Chit** (the leftmost of all the chits) onto the gray squares inside the selection inspector.

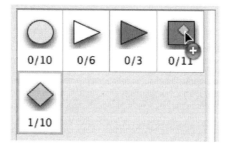

Not only does this change the color of the square shapes— but it also changes the shapes into diamonds.

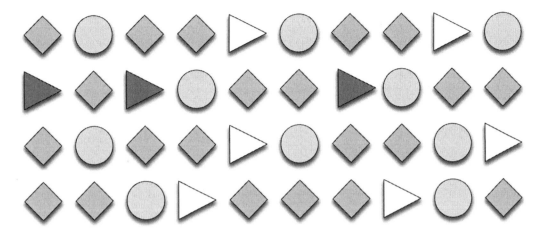

You can thus drag any chit from the Style Tray onto any shapes both on the canvas (as you did in Chapter 1), and also onto the Selection inspector.

This is a very powerful tool to aid you in getting a consistent look for your shapes.

You can also use this method to search and replace a lot of shapes in one go. No need to manually hunt around on a shape-by-shape basis.

# Color picker tricks

So far in the book you have changed the color of a shape, lines and text by first clicking on a color well, and then selecting the preferred color. This process can be quite tedious, and OmniGraffle will, for most tasks involving color-change, let you drag a color from the color picker directly onto a shape, the text or a line.

Start by drawing a rectangular shape on your canvas – and place the text **This text belongs to this shape** inside. The stroke thickness is set to 5 points, and the font is 18 points Helvetica.

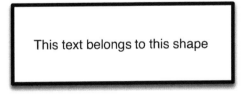

This text belongs to this shape

You are now ready for some color picker magic.

Hide all the inspectors by using the **Inspectors | Hide Inspectors** menu command. If you prefer to use the keyboard shortcut, this is ⇧+⌘+*I*.

If the color picker is not visible— use the **Inspector | Color** to make it visible (the keyboard shortcut command is ⇧+⌘+*C*).

You should now have just the color picker and the shape on the canvas visible.

Select the **Color palette** (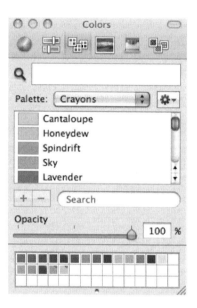) on the color picker. Then select **Crayons** in the **Palette** drop-down list.

Click on the **Cantaloupe** color and drag this over the oblong. Notice how the inner side of the oblong will pulse in a red hue. This is an indication that you are about to fill the shape.

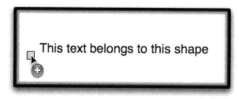

When releasing the mouse button, the shape is now filled with the Cantaloupe color.

Dragging a color onto the border of a shape, will in fact color the border with the chosen color. If you drag the **Lavender** color onto the border, the whole border will glow with a red hue.

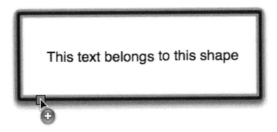

Finally, you can drag and release the **Honeydew** color onto the text inside the shape. Notice how not only the text will glow with a red hue, but the whole shape.

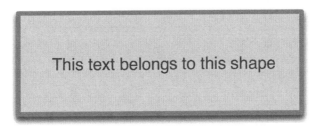

If you have dragged and dropped the three colors as suggested in the text above, you'll see that the text (Honeydew color) on the background (Cantaloupe color) is not very readable.

This is a very clear example of two colors that do not have enough contrast when put together. A better color for the text may be a dark color like Eggplant, Midnight, Licorice, or Lead:

This text belongs to this shape

# The color picker in detail

The color picker consists of five sections.

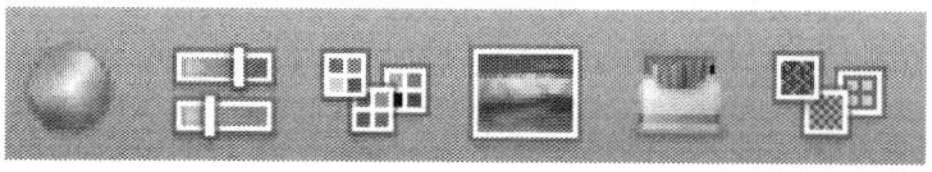

The **Color Picker Selector** lets you choose the various ways to pick colors.

From left to right you can choose between:

- **Color Wheel**
- **Color Sliders**
- **Color Palette**
- **Image Palettes**
- **Crayon Palette**

If you are using OmniGraffle Professional, the last selection lets you choose between various patterns.

This section is divided into two tools.

The **magnifying glass** can be clicked and then used anywhere on your screen to pick a color.

The area to the right of the magnifying glass is the **Current Selected Color**.

You can drag a color from this tool and onto parts of your shape as you did in the previous section.

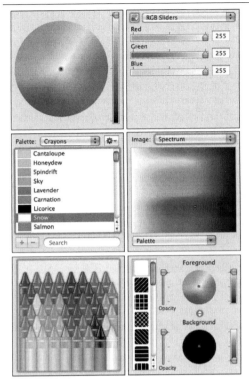

The next section on the color picker is dependent on which tool in the *Color Picker Selector* you have chosen.

From top left the selection tools are as follows:

- The **Color Wheel**
- The **Color Sliders**
- The **Color Palette**
- The **Image Palettes**
- The **Crayon Palette**
- The **Pattern Palette**

The Pattern Palette is only available in OmniGraffle Professional.

Excepted for the Color Palette, where you can drag color chits directly onto your shape, you must use the Current Selected Color for all the other palettes. So basically, you choose your color, and then drag the color from the Current Selected Color onto your shape.

The **Opacity Slider** controls the transparency of the **Current Selected Color**.

The **Color Picker Chits** are where you keep your favorite colors. The color palette will be kept for each time you start OmniGraffle or start a new diagram. This is where you should keep your own preferred color palette.

You can at any time drag any of these colors directly onto your shape to fill the background, change the stroke color or the color of the associated text.

To save a color for later use, just drag the **Current Selected Color** into any of the small squares in this section of the **Color Picker**.

Clicking on any of these colors will place that very color into the **Current Select Color** for further manipulation.

# The Color Wheel

The Color Wheel lets you choose colors and adjust their brightness. Unfortunately, there is not much tactical feedback, so for all practical purposes you lose the fine tuned control on the variables that make up a color.

If you are a graphic designer, and you have to work with a set of predefined colors, this is definitely not the tool to use.

However, if you want to play around with any colors, any shades and any opacity – this is the tool to use.

# The Color Sliders

The Color Sliders let you choose color based on a bit more control.

You have access to the following kinds of sliders chosen from the drop-down list – all giving a different tactical screen based on which color space you have chosen.

Unless you are a graphics professional, you will be more than content using RGB Sliders.

If you are a graphics professional, you have the following color spaces available: Gray Scale, RGB, CMYK, and HSB.

If you are using OmniGraffle Professional, you will have support for Apple's ColorSync technology. You can use the ColorSync Widget () to easily switch between the various ColorSync profiles that are available on your system. If you are unsure what to use here, select **Generic RGB**. If you print your OmniGraffle documents or export these to other programs, the color may be incorrect. The probable mistake is using the wrong ColorSync profile.

# The Color Palettes

For most people, this is probably the best tool to use when creating diagrams. You have access to a fair number of different colors with several predefined palettes available.

The predefined palettes are **Classic Crayons, Web Safe Colors, Crayons, Developer,** and **Apple**.

You can also easily create your own palette by choosing **New** using the **Action** button (    ).

The same Action button will also let you rename and remove a user-defined palette.

To add colors to a user-defined palette, just drag the **Current Selected Color** into the palette. Double-clicking on such a color will let you rename it as whatever you like.

# The Image Palettes

This palette will let you choose colors from images you load into the palette by using the **Palette | New From File** drop-down list.

You can then select colors from these picture-palettes to use in your diagram. When selecting a color, this will appear in the **Current Selected Color** tool.

If you have not loaded a picture, the **Spectrum** "picture" will be shown.

Using the **Palette** drop-down list you can also load a image that you have previously copied to the clipboard.

# The Crayons Palette

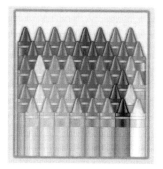

This is the basic Crayon palette, which you will find in a lot of other Macintosh software titles.

A nice thing about this palette is that you have a clear overview of all the colors available.

# The Patterns Palette

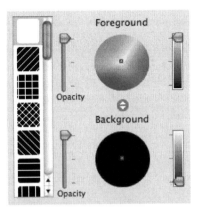

The Patterns Palette is only available if you are using OmniGraffle Professional. If you are using the standard version of the software, you can skip this section.

The patterns palette lets you choose between a set of predefined patterns. You can change the foreground and the background colors along with the respective opacity settings.

The patterns work the same way as colors do: You can fill a shape with a specific pattern, and you can apply a pattern to a line or a text.

# Summary

In this chapter, you have learned to quickly select similar shapes by using the **Edit | Select** menu commands.

You have also learned that the **Selection inspector** can take on shapes, colors, and other style formatting.

Finally, you learned a few tricks on using the color picker so that you do not have to use the various color wells to select and apply colors.

The next chapter is all about property inspectors not covered so far in the book. The inspectors that the chapter will deal with are not really tools on their own, and don't necessarily control any drawing tools—but they will alter several interesting aspects of your diagram. This chapter is a must-read if you are serious about diagramming with OmniGraffle.

# 7
# Property Inspectors

So far in the book you have dealt with only a few of these properties, however, this chapter will teach you about all the available properties in OmniGraffle.

The property inspectors are not proper tools in their own right, but you can consider them as very valuable settings for your diagrams. This is also why we have put them together in a chapter of their own.

We will take a look at the following inspectors in this chapter:

- Whatever we did not cover earlier regarding the Grid Property inspector
- How to use the Canvas Size Property inspector to control the page setup and the unit scale
- How the Document Property inspector controls how files are saved and page margins
- Adding meta data to your OmniGraffle documents using the Data Property inspector
- Leaving comments in your diagram using the Note Property inspector (only available in OmniGraffle Professional)

# The Grid Property inspector revisited

In *Chapter 6, Making your Diagram Look Good* you took a quick look at the **Grid Property inspector**, we are now going to take a look at the inspector as a whole.

In the previous screenshot, you can see that the **Major Grid Spacing** is **2,54** centimeters wide. This means that for each 2,54 cm there is a grid stroke (2,54 cm equals to 1 inch). Depending on how you set up your canvas, your document will normally be set to either Imperial or Metric measurement units. You will learn all about this in the section about the *Canvas Size Property inspector*.

OmniGraffle does not care if you enter your decimals using a comma or a period, as it will convert this to the proper format depending on your system setup.

No matter what you enter in the Major Grid Spacing input field, you will not see these changes unless you make the grid visible. Using the **View | Gridlines** menu command can do this or you can use the ⌘+\ keyboard shortcut command. You can also use the **Show grid lines** checkbox to control the visibility of the grid lines.

The various grid controls are set per canvas inside your OmniGraffle document. You can then have various grid setups for each of your canvases.

**Major Grid Spacing:** 2,54 cm

The **Major Grid Spacing** controls the width of the grid. Another way of looking at this number is the length of a grid square.

The default is 2,54 centimeters, or the equivalent 1 inch.

Instead of using cm or inches as the measuring unit—it's possible to enter pixels as the measuring unit. In these cases, OmniGraffle will translate the number of *pixels* into the appropriate length in centimeters or inches.

**Minor Grid Steps:** 8

The **Minor Grid Steps** divide the Major Grid Spacing into the number of steps found in this input field.

Default number of steps is **8**.

If you enter 1 step into this field, only the Major Grid Lines will be available. As of version 5.2.3, you cannot enter 0 in this field.

There is one **Color Well** for the Major Grid Spacing and one for the Minor Grid Steps.

The default color for the Major Grid Spacing is more fortified than the color of the Minor Grid Steps. Both colors are shades of grey, which for common diagramming tasks are adequate and do not interfere with your diagramming work.

Only in certain situations where you work with diagramming objects that are mostly grey, does it make sense to change the color of the grid.

☐ **Snap to grid**

The enabled **Snap to Grid** checkbox means new shapes you put onto the canvas will snap themselves to the grid. The size of the shape will also align itself to the grid lines.

☐ **Grid in front**

The **Grid in front** checkbox controls if the grid will be shown in front of, or behind the shapes on the canvas.

☑ Show grid lines
☑ Show major
☐ Print grid

This group of checkboxes controls the visibility of the grid, if major grid lines should be visible, and finally if the grid lines should appear when you print your diagram.

The **Show grid lines** checkbox will for all practical purposes achieve the same result as the **View | Grid Lines** menu command.

**Show major** checkbox toggles the visibility of your Major Grid Lines.

The **Print grid** checkbox toggles whether the grid will be visible on any printouts.

○ Center on grid
◉ Edges on grid

The **Center on grid / Edges on grid** toggles the control of how selected shapes on the canvas will be aligned in relation to the grid lines when you either move the shapes around or click on the **Align To Grid** button.

Align To Grid

Clicking on this button after having selected shapes will align those shapes based on the Center on grid / Edges on grid toggle control. Selected shapes will be aligned; either snapped to the edges of the grid lines – or placing the center of the shape on grid line intersections.

Using the **Edges on grid**, may resize a shape to fit within the closest grid lines. This is an excellent option to use if you want your shapes to be "correctly sized" as you draw them.

It is the grid lines controlled by the Minor Grid Steps that actually constitute the grid you see on the canvas. The lines controlled by the Major Grid Spacing are only displayed for your convenience.

However there is in practise no limitation on how you use the major or minor grid lines.

Now it's time to do some experimenting!

Start a new OmniGraffle document and enter **2 inch** for the Major Grid Spacing. This will automatically translate into **5,08 cm** if you are using Metric measurement units.

Now enter **2** in the **Minor Grid Steps** input box.

Your grid should look like this:

We see both the major and the minor grid lines. If you toggle the **Show major** checkbox, the grid will still be there, but no extra visible lines indicating where each whole inch on the diagram is.

For the next step, the **Snap to Grid** checkbox should not yet be enabled.

Draw a circle overlapping a fraction of the major grid lines, but not aligned to the minor ones also.

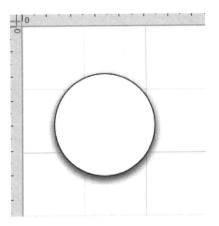

Click on the circle to select it, then select the **Edges on grid** and click on the **Align To Grid** button. Your circle does just that — its edges are aligned to the grid's edges. Notice how the shape also changes its size to accommodate the grid settings — the shape can both shrink and grow according to the size of the minor grid lines.

If you had selected the **Center on grid** and clicked the **Align To Grid** button — the result have would been as seen next:

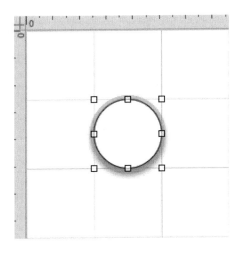

The shape does not change its size, it only repositions itself so that the center of the shape corresponds with a grid point. A grid point is where two grid lines cross each other.

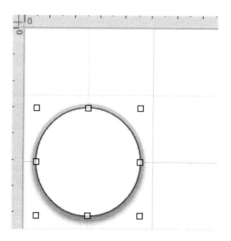

# The Canvas Size Property inspector

The **Canvas Size Property inspector** controls not only the size of the canvas, but also how the canvas will match any printed output.

This is also where you set your measurement units. These units can be Imperial units (inches, feet, yards, and miles), Metric units (millimeters, centimeters, meters, and kilometers), typographic units (points and picas), and finally screen units as in pixels.

| | |
|---|---|
| **Canvas Size** ⟷ 1 page ↕ 1 page | The **Canvas Size** input fields control the height and width of the canvas in whatever measurement unit you prefer.<br><br>The default measurement unit is in *pages*, but you can easily use inches, cm, pixels, points, and so on. |
| ☑ Size is multiple of printer sheets | This checkbox controls whether or not the edges of the canvas will automatically snap to the edges of the page.<br><br>The reason for enabling this checkbox is if your canvas is bigger than your printed matter (page, DVD-sleeve, business cards, and so on). By having a bigger canvas than the printed matter—diagrams can be split over two pages which is something you may want to avoid. |
| ☐ Auto-adjust the canvas size | When **Auto-adjust the canvas** size is enabled, the canvas will automatically adjust to the size of your diagram.<br><br>If you extend your diagram outside the visible canvas—the canvas will automatically resize itself to include all parts of your diagram. |
| ☐ Print canvas on one printer sheet | If your diagram exceeds more than one page, you can enable this checkbox to scale down the diagram to fit the output sheet you are printing on. |
| Orientation: ( Use Page Setup ↕ ) | This controls the orientation of the current canvas regardless of the page orientation set in the **File | Print Setup** dialog.<br><br>This is something you would use if your document is normally set up with the Portrait orientation, but you need use Landscape for your current canvas. |

Ruler Units: ( centimeters (cm)* ‡ )

The **Ruler Units** drop-down menu lets you control the measurement units of the horizontal and vertical ruler of the canvas your diagram is set up to use.

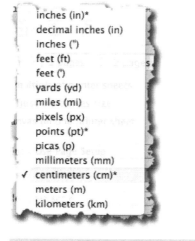

These units can be Imperial units (inches, feet, yards, and miles), Metric units (millimeters, centimeters, meters, and kilometers), typographic units (points and picas), and finally screen units as in pixels.

Even if you change the units you want your rulers to have; the actual size of the diagram does not change.

Some of the measurement units in the drop-down list are marked with an asterisk (*). By choosing any of these units, you can also scale your canvas accordingly by using the Unit Scale drop-down menu.

Unit scale: ( No scale ▾ )

The **Unit scale** drop-down menu is used when you need to control the scale of your canvas ruler.

This property is only available in OmniGraffle Professional.

By changing the unit scaling, the canvas rulers will change accordingly.

Examples of such scales are that 1 cm on the paper equals 1 m in real life or that 1 inch on paper equals 1 foot in real life. If the Unit scale is set to 1 cm = 1 m, then the canvas rulers will scale to indicate meters. A side effect is that the size of the shapes also changes. If a 1 cm long shape is scaled to 1 cm = 1 m, then the shape is physically 1 m long.

As a last resort you can enter a given scaling ratio. Example of such a ratio is 1:4. This means that any shapes on the canvas are now 4 times bigger than prior to the scale change.

Within the drop-down list you can choose **Reset Scale** to remove the unit scale, or to start over.

| Origin: | 0 cm | 0 cm | These two fields let you set the origin of the canvas. Normally, this is in the upper left but—as you experienced in Chapter 7—the origin can be easily moved by hand. |
|---|---|---|---|
| | | | These two **Origin** fields let you set the origin value explicitly. |

# More on scaling your diagram

In *Chapter 5, More on Editing Diagrams* you briefly scaled your diagram when you worked on the maritime exhibition ground map.

When you set a given Unit scale, you learned that the size of the shape would change even if the representation of said shape does not change.

If you set the scale to be 1 cm = 1 m, then your 1 cm long shape is really 1 meter long. If you change the scale to say 2 cm = 1 m, then your 1 cm long shape is now half a meter long. If the scale is set to 1 cm = 2 m, your shape is 2 meter long.

To see how this is behaving in real life, create a new OmniGraffle document with 1 cm as the Major Grid Spacing and 10 Minor Grid Steps. You may have to adjust the zoom-level to see the minor grid lines.

Make a rectangle that should be 1 cm high and 3 cm long.

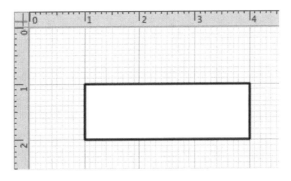

If you change the **Ruler Units** to **Meters**, you'll notice that you cannot see the ruler at all unless you zoom out. However, even if you zoom out to 25%, you will still not see the 1 m mark unless you have a really big computer screen. What you now have is in reality a one-to-one ratio on the sizes you see on your screen and their corresponding real-life sizes.

If you now set a custom size for the Unit Scale as **10 cm = 1 m**, then our 3 cm originally is now in reality 30 cm.

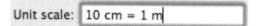

Notice the 1 meter mark on the horizontal ruler:

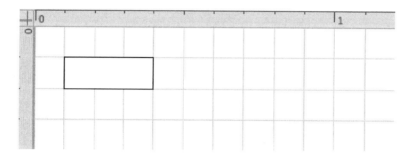

It is not possible to have a different unit scaling on the vertical and the horizontal ruler.

# The Document Property inspector

The **Document Property inspector** controls how your document should be saved and which margins your page should have.

**File format options**

Automatic (package or flat file) ⟷

The **File Format options** drop-down menu controls how OmniGraffle is saving your document. The default setting is **Automatic** — which will select between the **file package format** and the **flat file format**.

☐ Compress on disk

The **Compress on disk** checkbox makes OmniGraffle compress your OmniGraffle document. This can be quite a space saver if your diagram has a lot of shapes.

For normal operations you should never enable this option.

☑ Include Quick Look preview

Your Macintosh operating system has a feature called Quick Look built right into its core functionality. With Quick Look you do not need to open a particular document just to take a look at the content.

This functionality is very apparent in Apple Mail where you can preview attachments without opening the attachments software tool.

For OmniGraffle to support this handy feature, the program must save some extra information with the OmniGraffle document, and the **Include Quick Look preview** checkbox toggles this feature.

**Page Margins**

☐ Use printer margins

| 0,635 cn |
| Top |
| 0,635 cn | | 0,635 cn |
| Left | | Right |
| 1,446 cn |
| Bottom |

This property setting enables you to either use the document margins set in the **File | Print** dialog, or you can override these values with your own.

The default value is to override the values.

# More on file format options

OmniGraffle lets you choose between storing your document as one, single, **flat file** — or storing your document as a **file package**. There are pros and cons for each of these methods.

For normal day-to-day operations, you can let OmniGraffle automatically decide which file format to use.

The main difference between the flat file format and the file package format is that the flat file is one single file, while the file package really is a directory. For plain diagrams without any extra graphics (like the ones you will find in a lot of stencils) the main practical difference is that you cannot email a directory without first making an archive of said directory.

A flat file is easy to attach in your mail client — you can actually do this without resorting to the extra step involving archiving the file first.

Next time you try to attach an OmniGraffle document and your mail program refuses to do this, the most likely reason is that the document was stored as a file package.

Another reason why flat files may be superior to file packages is apparent when you are using a networked file system. A pure local area networked file system (i.e. a pure Macintosh setup) may work without issues, but as soon as you involve other services you may be in trouble. According to the Support Ninjas at OmniGraffle, even the *MobileMe* offering from Apple may create havoc with file packages.

It's when you add stencil elements, include graphics, and so on in your diagram that the difference between the flat file and the file package becomes more obvious.

In the flat file every graphics and elements is *encoded* and added to the file. If you add a picture of your dog, the picture will be encoded and saved in the same file as the rest of the diagram. Because of this encoding such files are a bit bigger than the corresponding file package documents.

In the file package, graphic and element are saved into the file package directory in the same format as they were imported. So if you import a picture of your cat, you can find this picture in the file package directory.

In *Chapter 6, Making your Diagram Look Good* you created a diagram for a maritime exhibition — in the following screenshot this very file is saved as a file package (143 KB) and as a flat file (160 KB) — notice the difference in size: 17 KB.

| Name | Date Modified | Size | Kind |
|---|---|---|---|
| Exhibition flat file.graffle | Today, 23.28 | 160 KB | OmniGraffle document |
| Exhibition flat file – compressed.graffle | Today, 23.34 | 74 KB | OmniGraffle document |
| Exhibition file package.graffle | Today, 23.28 | 143 KB | OmniGraffle document |
| Exhibition file package – compressed.graffle | Today, 23.34 | 111 KB | OmniGraffle document |

We have also saved compressed versions of these file formats and notice that for this very diagram, the compression is much more efficient in the flat file version. The compression equals to more than 53% compared to the 22% for the file package compressed version. Your mileage will vary, as there are several technical factors in play – the one with the highest impact is not only the number of attached graphics, but also the kind of graphics you add to your drawing.

**File format compression—a look behind the scenes (technical stuff)**

Even if you have selected to save your file as **file package**, the **compress on disk** option will still work. However, it's only the `plist` file within the file package that will be compressed.

This behavior makes sense, as compressing file formats that already are compressed is a waste of computing power. The PNG and JPG file formats are already compressed, and PDFs are very often compressed also. PNG, JPG and PDFs are probably the most common file attachments that you will encounter using OmniGraffle.

# The Data Property inspector

You can store a lot of information with your diagram using the **Data Property inspector**. The cool thing about storing at least some of this information is that it is available in the Spotlight indexing feature that comes with the Macintosh operating system.

If you do not care for **Copyright, Version, Subject,** or long and windy **Comments,** at least fill out the **Description** field. As your collection of OmniGraffle diagrams grows on your computer, finding the right diagram after a few months will become both tedious and very time consuming.

You can also, by the aid of the drop-down menu, add **Authors, Organizations, Languages, Keywords,** and **Projects.**

# The Note Property inspector

The **Note Property inspector** is only available in the OmniGraffle Professional version. If you do not have this version installed, you can skip this section.

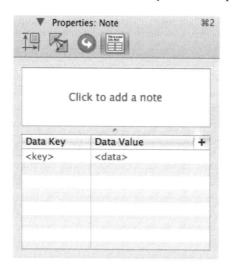

Using this inspector you can add any kind of information to a shape. You can both enter free form information in a note field, or you can add structured information in a data table.

The note field can contain rich text. This means that you are not limited to using one predefined font. You can use various fonts, sizes, colors, and so on. Anything you can do with text inside OmniGraffle—you can also do with this field.

The data table is organized around the concept of *Key/Value pairs*. The **Data Key** is akin to a label in a data entry form, and the **Data Value** is the information you enter into the corresponding field in the data entry form.

There are many uses for associating data with shapes. The most obvious usage is to keep information on components in an infrastructure diagram. If you want to create a diagram about all the computers at your work place, you can use the Data table to keep information like computer name, type of computer, network address, name of primary user, and so on.

When you hover over various parts in your diagram, you will be able to see the data without explicitly consulting the property inspector.

The super nice thing about storing information in the Data table is that the data will be indexed by the Spotlight search system that comes with your operating system.

You are now going to experiment with this feature.

Start by opening a new OmniGraffle document and add a shape. Any shape will do.

In the note field of the property inspector, enter the following text:

**This is my shape—it is a very nice shape.**

**Even line feeds and bold text are possible.**

Enter a **Data Key** with the following text: **ShapeName**. In the corresponding **Data Value**, enter **Oblong**.

If you hover over your shape with the mouse, you'll notice that the data you entered is shown in a popup, as shown next:

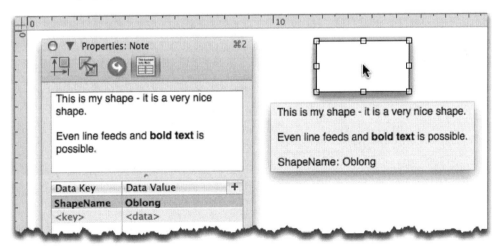

Is it possible to have other uses for these bits of information? One thing you can do is to display the **Data Value** information from the Data table by using **userdata** variables. This is very easy to achieve. In our shape, we want the name of the shape to automatically appear when we change the information.

In the text entry for the shape, you enter **I am the <%userdata ShapeName%> shape**.

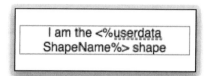

Entering this information will result in the following shape:

I am the Oblong shape

The real clue here is the **<%userdata ShapeName%>**. This syntax tells OmniGraffle to retrieve the userdata variable ShapeName. Any variables, including the system variables found under the **Edit | Insert Variable** menu can be retrieved in this way. By using the system variables you can get shapes to report on their own width, length, and so on.

Entering **I am the <%userdata ShapeName%> shape and my width is <%Width%>** in the oblong will give the following result:

I am the Oblong shape and
my width is 5,8208 cm

# Summary

This chapter expanded your knowledge and experience about all the properties in OmniGraffle that are covered elsewhere in the book. Depending on your use of OmniGraffle, it might be that you never even have to touch most of the properties covered in this chapter.

On the other hand, you did learn all there is regarding the Grid Property inspector. This is the inspector you'll need to make your diagrams very tidy.

The next logical step up from the grid's properties are the Canvas properties, and here we took a close look at the Canvas Size Property inspector. This inspector will aid you in creating very precise diagrams, including advanced scaling options.

By using the Document Property inspector you can control how OmniGraffle is saving its data. You have the choice to save data in one simple file, or as a package file.

There is also another property inspector dealing with the document—the Data Property inspector. Use this inspector to keep information about your diagram and of course this data can be found with the built-in Spotlight search system.

You also covered one property inspector only available in the professional version of OmniGraffle—the Note Property inspector. With this inspector you can keep relevant information about what a given shape actually means.

So far in the book, we have not bothered too much with the intrinsic properties of the canvas. The next chapter will take care of this and will teach you about a very useful feature called Canvas layers.

# 8

# Canvases and Canvas Layers

If you need to work on more than one diagram for your task, you have a few choices: You can either have one diagram per OmniGraffle file, you can place one diagram on each page on your OmniGraffle canvas, or you could use more than one canvas.

A lot of people never get past the idea of working with more than one canvas. They are more than happy using one page for each diagram that they create and exporting or printing just the very page that they need.

You should aim higher and become confident with the notion of one diagram per canvas. This chapter will teach you exactly how to work with multiple canvases.

Another wonderful, time saving, and efficiency booster is the use of **canvas layers**, or just **layers** for short. Using layers enables you to quickly hide and show various parts of your diagram. This is very handy if your diagrams will contain a lot of elements.

In this chapter, you will learn about:

- Naming your canvases
- Managing your canvases
- Managing your canvas layers
- Working with different shapes on different layers
- The joy of shared layers

# Canvases

In *Chapter 1, Getting Started with OmniGraffle* you learned that the canvas is the place where all your diagramming work is done. You make shapes, you edit shapes, and you delete shapes. You even connect shapes to each other using connectors.

Generally you will use only one canvas: You make a single diagram for your report, export it to a JPEG or a PNG file, and then you are done.

However, what if you need to include more than one diagram in your report, presentation, or e-mail? You may end up in creating one diagram per file. There is nothing wrong in having one diagram per file—it may even make a lot of sense. However a more sensible approach may be to have all the diagrams in one OmniGraffle file.

If you have ever created a big diagram, your diagram may inadvertently have spread over two physical pages. A logical step would thus be to use one physical page for each diagram that you need. There's nothing wrong with this but it may become a hassle and you may lose control if you have a lot of diagrams. Having just a few diagrams spread over just a few pages is cool. However, if you have extended this to more than a few diagrams, you may have received a shock when everything goes askew just because you need to have one of your ten diagrams in landscape mode.

This is where using multiple canvases is the right solution.

The cool thing about using one canvas per diagram is that you can easily and quickly navigate between the various diagrams.

Your canvases will appear in the **canvases sidebar** in the main working area of what you probably call the canvas.

There are a few ways to toggle the visibility of the canvases sidebar. You can use the ⌥+⌘+*1* keyboard shortcut command, you can also use the **View | Canvases** menu command, and finally you can click on the Canvases symbol (▯▢) in the **Canvas Toolbar**.

In the following screenshot, you can see the **canvases sidebar** with several canvases of different sizes and configurations:

Each canvas has a preview of the content, a name, and a small triangle in front of its name. Clicking the triangle will toggle viewing of the associated canvas layers — we will cover layers later in this chapter.

To view or edit a canvas, just click on its preview or the canvas name in the sidebar, and the canvas will appear ready for amendments.

# Naming your canvases

If you double-click on a canvas name, the name will be highlighted and you will be able to rename it. Try to keep the name of the canvas short but still descriptive. You can also resize the sidebar to accommodate longer names.

As well as for your own sanity, there is at least one very good reason why you should have good names for your canvases. In the **File | Export** dialog box you have the choice of selecting **Entire Document** from the **Export area** drop-down list.

Let's say you have an OmniGraffle document that contains two canvases named **My canvas** and **My 2nd canvas**. When you export the entire OmniGraffle document, you'll end up with a folder containing both your canvases with file names corresponding to the name of the canvas.

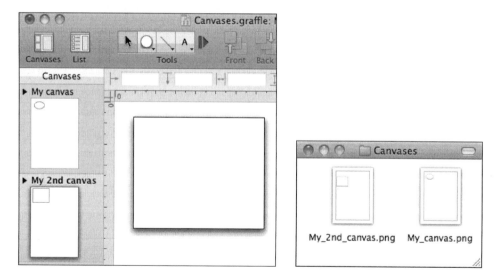

# Adding, deleting, and rearranging canvases

Adding a new, blank, canvas can be done with the aid of the ⌥+⌘+N keyboard combination. There is also the **Edit | Canvases | New Canvas** menu command. Finally, you can also use the **New Canvas** button ( [ + ] ) found to the bottom-left in the canvases sidebar. You will also notice the **Action** button ( [⚙▾] ), which also has a **New Canvas** choice in its context menu.

If you want to copy or duplicate an existing canvas, you can use the ⌘+D keyboard shortcut combination, the **Edit | Canvases | Duplicate Canvas** menu command, and finally the **Duplicate Canvas** found in the **Action** button at the bottom of the canvases sidebar.

You can also copy a canvas from one document to another OmniGraffle document. In the document, you want to copy the canvas from, you click on the canvas you want to copy. Then you issue the **Edit | Copy** menu command – or use the faster ⌘+C keyboard shortcut command. Second, you move over to the document you want to copy the canvas to and execute the **Edit | Paste** menu command or the keyboard ⌘+V shortcut combination. Even cut-and-paste will work as expected.

If you feel that the old copy-switch-document-paste routine is too elaborate – you can simply drag the canvas you want to copy from your current document, onto the OmniGraffle document you want to copy it into. The only caveat is that both documents need to be open at the same time. Just put both documents side-by-side and drag the canvases you need to copy back and forth from the sidebar in your source document to the sidebar in your destination OmniGraffle document.

The easiest way to delete a canvas, is simply clicking on its preview icon to select the canvas, and then press the *Delete* key on your keyboard. The **Edit | Canvases | Delete Canvas** menu command, and the **Delete Canvas** found in the **Action** button at the bottom of the canvases sidebar are of course also available.

To change the order of your canvases, just drag the canvas in the order that you need to the new position in the canvases sidebar.

If you rather want to use a keyboard shortcut to navigate between canvases, ⌘+> takes you to the next canvas, while ⌘+< takes you to the previous canvas in the canvases sidebar. Both these commands are also available in the **View | Display Canvases** menu command.

# Canvas layers

A layer can be defined as a transparent surface upon which you can draw one or more shapes. These shapes are thus associated with their corresponding layer. All canvases in OmniGraffle have at least one layer.

Think of a layer as a transparent plastic sheet where you draw with a pen. If you now visualize that you can put another transparent plastic sheet over the first one — and draw on this second sheet — then you'll have the concept of how canvas layers behave.

Let's say you have a diagram of your new company office. The bottom layer will then have the outer walls. You could the have a layer on the top of this outlining each office cubicle, a layer with the electrical wiring, a layer with air conditioning ducts, and so on. Then you could have yet another layer with the office furniture in place.

So if you wanted to show only the electrical wiring — you hide the layers with the office cubicles, the office furniture, the air conditioning ducts, and so on. Then, if you need to show your co-workers how the new office will look, you just show the relevant layers.

An example of the different layers you want to use when planning your new company office might be:

- Office furniture
- Air conditioning ducts
- Electrical wiring and network sockets
- Office cubicles (that is, movable walls)
- Inner walls and fixed (infrastructure like stairwells and toilets)
- Outer walls including windows and doors

Another way to think about layers is that a layer should contain certain shapes that are related to each other.

Does it always make sense to use layers in your diagrams? If your diagram is a one-off diagram, without a lot of details, then you may not need to use more than one layer. However, if your diagram contains a lot of details, and the various categories of information in your diagram are not for everyone to digest, then more than one layer is suitable.

The need to present different variations over a basic foundation is another reason why layering your diagrams is a good thing. If we use the example of making a diagram of your new company offices, the foundation will be the outer walls. These will be fixed for every variation of the cubical arrangement you draw.

Compare using layers to having various versions in separate OmniGraffle document, and you suddenly had to change the size of the office space (that is, the floor plan). You would then have to change every file—that is, doing the same operation a lot of times. Even if you did copy and paste the floor plan from one document to the next, it would still be quite some work.

Had you instead put the floor plan (defined by the outer walls) as the first layer in your diagram, you would have only needed to do one change—no matter how many variations you were working on.

# A visual explanation of canvas layers

Let's say you needed to create a document with three shapes—a circle, triangle, and diamond. You could place the circle on the bottom layer, the triangle on the second layer, and the diamond on the third layer.

On the screen this would look like the following:

To illustrate the three shapes on three separate layers, imagine placing the shapes on transparent plastic and then placing the plastic sheets on top of each other.

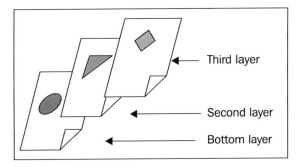

In OmniGraffle your layers will not be displayed like the illustration. Your layers will be displayed in the **Canvases Sidebar**.

To toggle between showing or hiding layers, you need to click on the small triangle next to the name of the canvas (▶). Doing this will show you the various layers associated with a canvas along with a few controls for each layer.

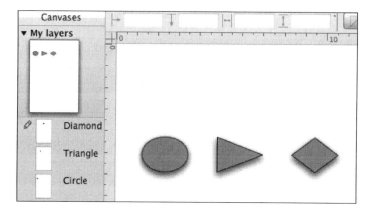

Our layers are named **Diamond**, **Triangle**, and **Circle**. The layers could really be named anything you want.

Also notice the small pencil ( 🖉 ) next to the Diamond layer. This is an indication that this is the **active layer**. For all practical purposes, this is now the layer we are working on.

Even if you are working on one layer (that is, the Diamond layer), clicking on any shape in your diagram will indicate a small rectangle ( ▢ ) next to the layer where the shape is found. In the following screenshot, we are working on the **Diamond** layer, but have clicked on the circle shape.

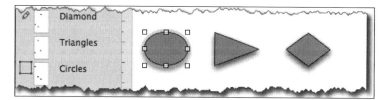

# Working with layers

Before you learn how to work with objects on layers, you will need to get a basic understanding of the various operations you can perform on your layers.

There aren't any keyboard shortcuts dealing with layers. Everything you need to do with your layers is found in the **Edit | Layers** menu. You will also find the most used commands using the **Action** button ( ⚙▾ ) found in the bottom of the Canvases Sidebar.

If you right-click on a layer in the sidebar, you will get access to the same layer menu commands as are found using the **Action** button.

# Adding a new layer

You can add a new layer by either using the **Edit | Layers | New Layer** menu command or using the **New Layer** button ( ▱+ ), found in the bottom of the sidebar. A new layer will appear on top of your current layer, and then become the active layer for editing.

For OmniGraffle Professional users, there is something called **New Share Layer** in the **Edit | Layers** menu — this concept will be covered later in this chapter.

# Duplicating and copying a layer

Duplicating a layer is either done with the ⌘+*D* keyboard shortcut command, using the **Action** button, or using the **Edit | Layers | Duplicate layer** menu command.

Before you can duplicate a layer, you will have to click on the layer you wish to duplicate in the Canvases Sidebar, and then issue the duplicate command. Duplicating a layer will position the duplicated layer above the activated layer. This means that you can in fact duplicate a layer which you are not currently working on.

It is also possible to copy a layer from one canvas to another canvas. Just select, or click on, the layer you want to copy. You can either use the **Edit | Copy** menu command, or use the common ⌘+*C* keyboard shortcut command to initiate the copying of the layer.

The next thing you do is click on the canvas you want to copy your layer into, and then use the **Edit | Paste** menu command, or use the ⌘+*V* keyboard shortcut command. If you're wondering if cut-and-paste works the same way, the answer is yes.

An even faster way is to hold down the ⌥ key while dragging your layer on to another canvas.

An example of copying the **Triangle** layer from the **My layers** canvas to the **My other layers** canvas is seen in the following screenshot:

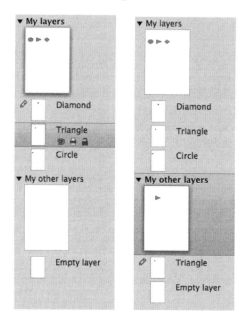

In fact, it is completely possible to copy a layer from one document to another OmniGraffle document. Just copy (or cut) your layer as you learned in the previous paragraph.

> An even faster way to copy a layer from one document to another document is to have both documents open, side-by-side, and then drag the layer you want to copy from one document to the other.

When copying a layer to another canvas (or even another document), all the objects and formatting are copied. No object is left behind.

If you want to play around with a ready-made version of the above diagrams—please open the file named `Layers - 3 shapes.graffle`. The file is found in the `Chapter 9` folder in the download bundle.

# Rearranging and moving a layer

If you want to move or rearrange the order of your layers—just drag and drop your layer within the same document—move it from one canvas to another canvas. If you try to drop a layer onto a canvas which already has a layer with the same name, your moved layer will have a sequence number appended to the end of its name. This means that if you wonder which layer you just moved into your canvas, just look for a 1, or a 2, or a 3, and so on. The highest number is the last layer moved into your canvas with just that name.

If you try to move a layer to another document it will instead be copied.

# How to merge two layers

In the **Edit | Layers** menu you will notice the **Merge Layer Down** command. This is used to merge two layers together. Because OmniGraffle is an object-oriented vector drawing program—you will need to decide which shapes from a layer should go on top of the shapes on the layer you want to merge. This is the reason why the command states that you merge a layer down.

This means that you cannot merge the bottom layer, you can only merge a layer that is on top of another layer, down to the lowest layer. This is also why you may not even see the **Merge Layer Down** while clicking on the **Action** button.

Let's say you have a document containing the layers Diamond, Triangle, and at the bottom, Circle. If you wanted to merge the Triangle and Circle layers, you would have to click on the Triangle layer and then issue the **Merge Layer Down** command.

When you merge two layers, it's the layer you are merging down to that becomes the name for the new layer.

As you can see in the following screenshot, the layer you want to merge does not even have to be the active layer you are currently working on. By using the right-click on your mouse you'll get the context sensitive menu showing you all the operations you can perform on a layer.

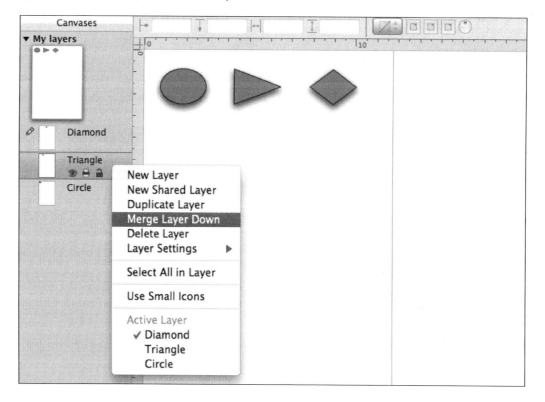

After merging the Triangle and Circle layers, the new layer will be named Circle as this is the layer below the one you want to merge.

If you need to merge two layers that are not on top of each other, you will have to rearrange the layers before merging them.

# Deleting a layer

You can always delete a layer using the *Delete* key, instead of using the various menu commands.

You cannot delete the last layer associated with the canvas. A canvas must always have one layer present.

# Layer settings

There are three settings or states a layer can have. These settings are for visibility, if the layer is to be printed, and if the layer is locked.

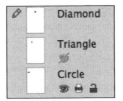

Each of these three settings has its own symbol in the **Canvases Sidebar**. As you can see in the previous screenshot, you have an eye, a printer and a padlock icons, which corresponds to the respective settings.

You can easily toggle these settings on or off by moving your mouse over a layer and clicking on any of the icons. States that are enabled will be easily seen even if the mouse arrow is not currently present in the Canvases Sidebar. As you can see, the **Triangle** layer has its visibility turned off, as there is a slash through the eye-icon.

You can of course use the right-click context menu, the **Action** button menu and the **Edit | Layers | Layers Settings** menu commands to change the layer settings.

## Visibility

You can use the visibility setting to hide or show a layer. This is handy if you have layers that portray different messages, and it will not make sense to mix these messages. This could be something as simple as variations to a diagram—or something as complex as our example with the new office layout earlier in the chapter.

A great way of using the visibility settings is to have a layer where all your internal diagram annotations are placed. Before exporting your diagram, you can just hide this annotation layer, and your final document will appear without your internal annotations and comments.

## Printing

This setting is used when you do not want a particular layer to be printed. This is very useful if you have a layer with internal comments or annotations that should not make it into a printed version.

Instead of having to toggle the visibility setting on your "internal layer" prior to exporting your diagram, you could also make the internal layer non-printable.

Do not forget that even if you can export your diagrams to a graphic file, a PDF file is still an excellent choice, as it will be displayed and printed consistently across computer platforms and printers. Printing a document as a PDF is built into all Macintosh programs.

## Locking a layer 🔒

Locking a layer prevents any changes being made to the objects on the layer.

Locking a layer is very handy when you have diagrams with a lot of shapes—it is simply too easy to grab hold of the wrong object and do something that will require a lot of work to undo. Even if you can press the ⌘+Z (undo) keyboard combination to undo your action—there could be cases where this will fail miserably. It could be something as simple as involuntarily saving the document and quitting OmniGraffle.

# Working with shapes on layers

As long as you take a note of which layer is the active layer by looking at the pencil (🖉) denoting the *active layer,* and which layer has the small rectangle (🔲) denoting the layers your current selected object is associated with, you will save yourself a lot of headache.

There are only two related operations on shapes you will need to perform with regard to layer. The first operation is copying or moving shapes from one layer to the active layer. The other operation is moving all shapes from one layer to any other layer.

Copying or moving one or more shapes from a layer into the active layer is as simple as marking the shapes you want to copy (or move) and either using the **Edit | Copy** or **Edit | Cut**, and **Edit | Paste** menu commands. You can of course use the corresponding keyboard shortcut commands.

If you want to move every shape on one layer to another layer, then you have the **Edit | Layers | Select All in Layer** menu, or the **Action** button, command. This will select all objects on the layer that you perform this command on. Now, select any other layer and issue the **Edit | Layers | Move Selection Into Layer** menu, or the **Action** button, command.

Let's say you have the following documents that contain three layers named **Diamond**, **Triangles**, and **Circles**—each with corresponding shapes.

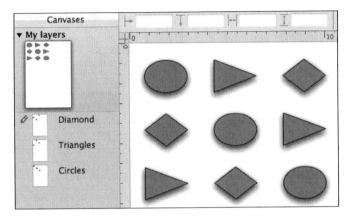

Notice that the **Diamond** layer is our active layer.

By clicking on the **Circles** layer and issuing the **Select All in Layers** command, all the circles will be selected.

In the following screenshot, we right-clicked to get the context sensitive pop-up menu, and then chose the **Select All in Layer** command:

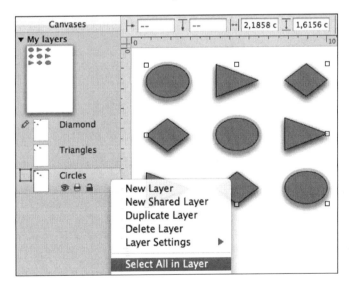

If you click on the **Triangles** layer and then right-click, you'll now notice the menu command. Executing this menu command will move all the circles onto the **Triangles** layer.

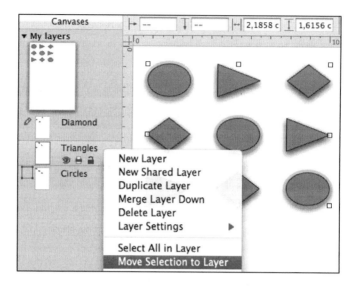

When the operation is done, the **Circles** layer will be empty, and can be deleted.

If you want to play around with a ready-made version of the above — please open the file named `Layers – 9 shapes.graffle` found in the `Chapter 9` folder in the download bundle.

# Shared layers

Shared layers are only found in the professional version of OmniGraffle. If you do not have the professional version, you can skip this part.

A layer can be shared between canvases thus the name **shared layers**. A shared layer behaves a tiny bit different from ordinary layers: When you change the content of the shared layer this change is reflected on all canvases sharing the layer. However, there is no difference when it comes to editing shapes on a shared layer, this works as normal. If you copy, or move, shapes to and from a shared layer, this will of course be reflected on all canvases sharing the layer.

You are now going to learn how to work with shared layers, by doing an example. You can use any of your existing OmniGraffle documents — or you can work with the document from earlier in this chapter. The name of the document is `Layers – 3 shapes` and is found in the folder named `Chapter 8` in the download bundle.

We're going to extend this document with another canvas, but most importantly you are going to add a heading on both canvases.

To create a new, shared layer, you can issue the **New Shared Layer** menu, or Action button, command.

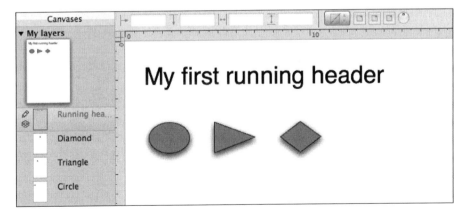

You'll notice that a new layer will appear. The layer will have a different color than your other layers and it will also have a special icon (⬧) on its left to indicate that it's a shared layer.

Rename this layer to **Running header**.

By using the text tool—make a text shape saying **My first running header**.

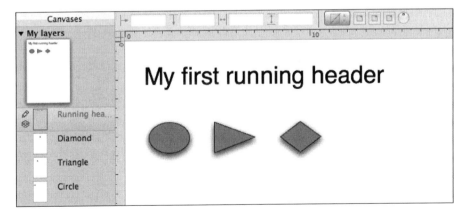

Next, you create a new canvas, call it **My other canvas**. Notice how the shared layer with the header is automatically copied over. This is pretty cool.

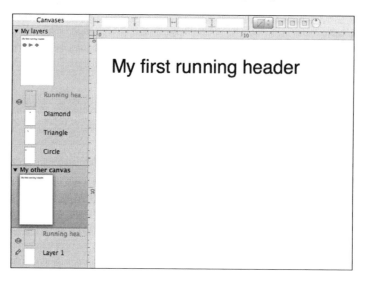

Creating a new canvas will only copy the shared layers from your active canvas. It will not copy shared layers from other canvases.

This behavior can be a bit confusing to begin with.

Let's continue exploring shared layers by adding another canvas. Call this canvas **New Canvas**. Add a shared layer to this new canvas, name this layer **Oblong**, and place an oblong on the shared layer.

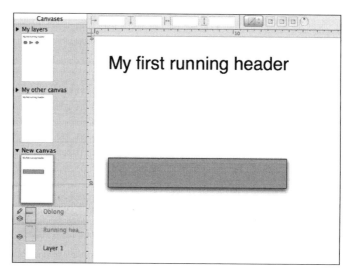

You decide that you like your oblong to be present on the **My layers** canvas. To achieve this, you just drag the shared layer named **Oblong** to the **My layers** canvas. You'll now see the oblong appear in the **My layers** canvas.

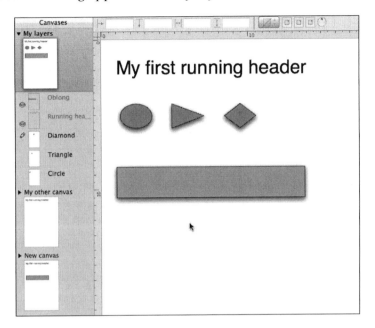

Now, change the shared oblong in the **My layers** canvas to an ellipse. If you are unsure on how to proceed with this operation, please consult *Chapter 3, Shapes, Building Blocks for Diagrams*.

Now watch the ellipse appear on the canvas named **New canvas**.

Any changes you made to shapes on a shared layer will appear on any canvases sharing this particular layer.

# When to use layers

There are of course no hard and fast rules on when to use layers, and when not to use layers. Best practises regarding diagramming may suggest that you should use layers to group all logical parts of a diagram together.

If you are new to diagramming, it may be tempting to place each shape on a layer on its own. OmniGraffle will not stop you from doing this—however, this will take the efficiency and pleasure out of your diagramming work as you will have an overwhelming numbers of layers to deal with.

# Summary

This chapter taught you the ins and outs of canvases and layers.

After reading this chapter you are capable of:

- Adding, copying, and deleting a canvas within the same OmniGraffle document
- Copying a canvas from one document to another OmniGraffle document
- Adding, copying, merging, and deleting layers within the same canvas
- Copying a layer from one canvas to another canvas—either within the same document or to another OmniGraffle document
- Setting layer options (visibility, printing, and locking)
- Copying and moving shapes from one layer to the active layer
- For OmniGraffle pro users: Working with shared layers

The next chapter is also the last chapter in the book and will cover how to get the most out of the OmniGraffle workspace options.

# 9
# OmniGraffle workspaces

This chapter will teach you how to set up your workspace. Having different workspace configurations tailored to various diagramming tasks can be a real time saver.

You can then have a workspace configuration for the times when you are using just your laptop monitor, when you are using more than one monitor, when you are working on huge diagrams, with a lot of shapes, requiring the use of all your screen space, and so on.

## Your workspace

An organized work place is a good thing for both your creativity and your efficiency. The same goes for OmniGraffle. If you set up OmniGraffle the way you feel most comfortable, OmniGraffle won't be in your way.

The most common way of dealing with the program is to have the Canvas on the left side of your screen and then the palettes on your right, with the stencils on top, and the style palette below.

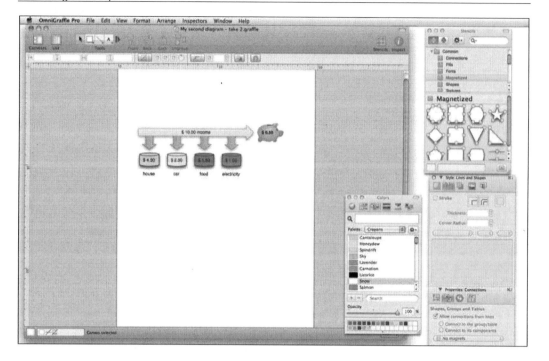

The problem with this way of setting up your workspace is that not only do you constantly need to expand and contract your style palette, but also that the two palettes fight each other for the same screen real estate. Even if you know the various shortcuts for accessing the various styles and stencils it is messy.

Perhaps a better way is to put the style palette to the left of the canvas, and leave the stencils on the right. This way you can expose all the styles, all the time, and have room for a lot of stencils on the screen at the same time.

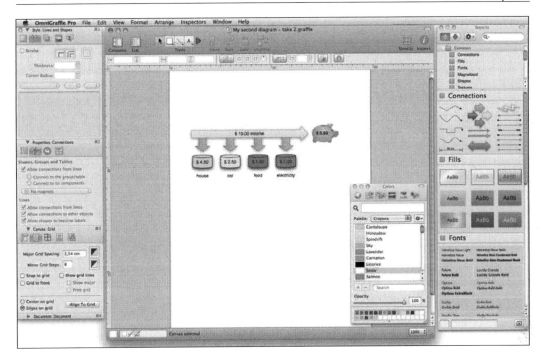

However, you will loose space for the canvas by organizing your workspace like this. So, what do you choose then?

You can have it both ways!

OmniGraffle lets you save your workspace setup. If you go to the **Window | Workspaces** menu, you can define several workspace setups. OmniGraffle will even assign a shortcut key to your workspaces, so that you can easily switch between these.

In the following screenshot, we see three defined workspaces called **Ruben WP**, **All hidden** and **Everything**. All three workspaces have been assigned a function key.

By using one of the defined function keys, you can easily switch between various workspace setups.

You can have a workspace setup, that just displays the canvas and the styles. Maybe you'll prefer to hide every palette in the program—a good choice if you really must concentrate on the layout of your diagram and need the whole screen. Maybe you just want to switch on every palette there is.

If you are using a laptop that is from time to time connected to an external monitor, use this monitor as an extension of your desktop (that is for non-mirrored displays). A good use of your screen real estate is to have the style palette on the left of your main monitor screen along with a big canvas and use the auxiliary monitor screen to host a expanded stencil library along with the color and font picker.

The choice is yours—OmniGraffle will do as you please.

If you want to add your own preferred workspace setup, just place your canvas, stencils and palettes the way you prefer, and then go to the **Window | Workspaces | Edit Workspaces**. You are now presented with a small floating palette where the various defined workspaces are present.

In the bottom of this palette you'll notice a set of buttons, or chits. You can thus use the **+** and the **-** button to add and remove a workspace.

The camera button is to save your current workspace, and the button with something resembling a carpet roll is for restoring (that is rollback) a workspace. These two buttons will only work if you have highlighted an existing workspace setup.

There is one caveat regarding workspaces: The saving of workspaces applies primarily to the various palettes—their state and their position on the screen. It does not save the position, or the size, of the canvas.

# Summary

This short chapter showed you how you can set up OmniGraffle to accommodate various application setups depending on your workspace needs.

This is also the last chapter in this book and we hope that you have enjoyed the journey and that you are now a more proficient OmniGraffle user than you ever expected.

Take care and diagram safely!

# Index

## Symbols

⌥+⌘+2 keyboard shortcuts command  224
⌥+⌘+T keyboard shortcut command  180
⌥ (option key)  190
⌘+A keyboard shortcut command  272
⌘ B keyboard command  223
⌘ C keyboard shortcut command  329, 333
⌘ (command key)  190
⌘+↑keyboard combination  220
⌘+\ keyboard shortcut command  274
⌘+\ keyboard shortcut command, Grid
    Property inspector  308
⌘+L keyboard shortcut commands  279
⌘+N keyboard shortcuts command  236
⌘+R keyboard shortcut command  167
⌘ V keyboard shortcut command  334
⌘ V shortcut combination  329
⌘+Z keyboard shortcut command  191
^+⌘+← keyboard combination  220
^+⌘+↓ keyboard combination  219
⇧ (shift key)  190
.gstencil file suffix  99
.vss file  101

## A

action browse tool
    about  200
    AppleScript action  200
    general action  200
    open file action  200
    URL action  200
Action button  303, 329, 333
action property inspector
    about  200-202
    does nothing action  201
    Jumps Elsewhere action  202-204
    opens a file action  201
    opens a URL action  201
    Runs a Script action  202
    Show or Hide Layers action  202
actions and presentation mode  261
AIGA website
    URL  281
Align Middle button  130
Align to canvas check box  286
Align To Grid button, Grid Property
    inspector  311
Allow connections from lines checkbox
    control  172
annotation
    using  73
AppleScript action, action browse tool  200
Arrange | Align menu  284, 285
Arrange | Bring to Front menu
    command  155
Arrange | Group menu command  157
Arrange | Guides application menu  268
Arrange | Lock menu command  279
Arrange | Send to Back menu
    command  155
Arrange | Size | Make Natural Size menu
    command  271
Arrange | Size menu commands  269
Arrange | Ungroup menu command  158
Aspect Ratio buttons  150
Auto-adjust the canvas size, Canvas Size
    Property inspector  313

# B

Back-button 209
Behind all Shapes button 141, 142
Bevel option 134
Bézier lines 121
big wedge experiment
    about 244
    Edit | Shapes | Subtract Shapes menu
        command 245-249
Blend Direction wheel 138
Blend Position 138
Bottom-to-Top direction button 215
Browse Tool button 209
built in types, stencil
    common stencils 62
    maps stencils 62
    organizations charts 62
    science stencils 63
    software stencils 63
    space planning stencils 63
bundle 49
Butt option 134

# C

Cantaloupe color 298
canvas
    ⌘ C keyboard shortcut command 329
    ⌘ V shortcut combination 329
    about 326
    Action button 329
    adding 329
    copying 329
    copying, from one document to
        another 329
    deleting 329
    duplicating 329
    Edit | Canvases | Delete Canvas menu
        command 329
    Edit | Canvases | Duplicate Canvas menu
        command 329
    Edit | Canvases | New Canvas menu
        command 329
    naming 328
    moving around 199
    New Canvas button 329
    New Canvas choice 329

    order, changing 329
    option-key 198
    View | Display Canvases menu
        command 329
    viewing 327
    zooming 197
    zooming, tricks 198
    zooming, Zoom-button used 198
    zoom operations 198
    Zoom Tool 198
canvas layers
    about 330, 331
    visual explanation 331, 332
canvas, OmniGraffle workspace
    about 8
    components 9
    drawing area 10
    inspector bar 9
    style tray 10
    toolbar 9
canvas rulers 170, 171
canvases sidebar 326
Canvas Size input field, Canvas Size
        Property inspector 313
Canvas Size Property inspector
    about 312
    Auto-adjust the canvas size 313
    Canvas Size input field 313
    diagram, scaling 315, 316
    Origin fields 315
    page orientation 313
    Ruler Units drop-down 314
    Unit scale drop-down 314
Canvas Style Tray
    about 45-47
    Complete Style Chit 45
    style chit 45
Canvas toolbar
    about 129, 180, 273
    customizing 181
    keyboard shortcuts 182, 183
    preferences 181, 182
Center on grid, Grid Property
        inspector 310, 311
Choose file... button, action property
        inspector 201
Circular layout button 211, 213, 216

clear contents menu command 194
Color button 133
color palettes, color picker 298, 303
color picker
   color palettes 303
   color sliders 302
   color wheel 302
   crayon palette 304
   image palettes 304
   patterns palette 305
   sections 300, 301
   tricks 297, 298
Color Picker Chits 301
color sliders, color picker 302
ColorSync support 263, 264
Color Well, Grid Property inspector 309
color wheel, color picker 302
Complete Style Chit 296
compound shapes
   about 111
   copy of existing shape, drawing 113, 114
   favorite shapes and styles 114, 115
   shape types 111, 112
   style properties 111
   text caption, adding to shape 113
Compress on disk checkbox, Document
      Property inspector 317
connected shapes
   selecting 291-293
Connections property inspector 30
connector 110
Connect to the group/table option 172
Corner Control drop-down menu 134-136
Corner Radius field 133
crayons palette, color picker 304
Create a connected shape, task 222
Create a disconnected shape, task 222
Current Selected Color tool 303, 304
Customize Toolbar... 181
Custom line length slider controls 213

# D

Data Property inspector 319, 320
Data Value, Note Property inspector 320
Default line label 128

Default object rank button 212
Delete Style 126, 132
diagram elements
   adjusting 268, 269
diagram layout inspector
   about 210
   automatic layout checkbox 211
   Circular Layout button 211, 213
   Custom line length slider controls 213
   Force-directed Layout button 211
   Hierarchical Layout button 211
   Radial Layout button 211
   Shape Repulsion slider controls 213
Diagramming Tool
   modifier keys 190
   Shape Tool 188
   shift-key (⇧) 189
   used, for fast diagramming 188-190
diagrams
   exporting 51, 52
   saving 49, 50
diagram style
   ⌘+Z keyboard combination 233
   about 232-235
   File | New Resource | New Diagram
      Style... 233
   Format | Choose Diagram Styles menu
      command 232, 235
diagram templates
   about 236, 237
   File | New menu command 238
   File | New Resource | New Template
      menu command 237
   File | Template Chooser 236
   Set as Default button 238
Direction buttons, automatic layout 212
document grid
   shapes, aligning to 275-278
Document Property inspector
   about 50, 316
   Compress on disk checkbox 317
   file format, options 317, 319
   File Format options drop-down menu 317
   file package 318
   File | Print dialog 317
   Include Quick Look preview checkbox 317

Does Nothing action, action property
    inspector  201
Done button  181
Do nothing, lines  124
Double Color Wells  138
Double Linear Blend  137
Double Radial Blend  137
Double stroke button  133
Drawing Tools icon  181

# E

Edges on grid button  275
Edges on grid, Grid Property inspector  310
Edit | Canvases | Delete Canvas menu
    command  329
Edit | Canvases | Duplicate Canvas menu
    command  329
Edit | Canvases | New Canvas menu
    command  329
Edit | Copy menu command  338
Edit | Cut menu command  338
Edit | Delete menu command  122
Edit Delete menu command  119
Edit | Layers | Duplicate layer menu
    command  333
Edit | Layers | Layers Settings menu
    command  337
Edit | Layers menu  333, 335
Edit | Layers | Move Selection Into Layer
    menu  338
Edit | Layers | New Layer menu command
    333
Edit | Layers | Select All in Layer menu
    338
Edit | Mouseless Editing menu  222
Edit | Outlining | Add Spouse menu
    command  228
Edit | Outlining | Indent menu
    command  230
Edit | Outlining | Outdent menu
    command  229
Edit | Paste menu command  334, 338
Edit | Select | Similar Objects menu
    command  295
Edit | Shapes | Make Points Editable menu
    command  243.

Edit | Shapes | Subtract Shapes menu
    command  241, 245
Edit | Shapes Union Shapes menu
    command  242
Edit | Undo Brush menu command  191
expando-collapso technology  180
Export area drop-down list  328
external stencils
    commercial sources  70
    Graffletopia  69
    MS Visio stencils, importing  70
    Omni Group, downloads  69

# F

fast diagramming
    Diagramming Tool used  188-190
Favorite shape style
    about  114
    removing  115
file bundle  49
File | Export dialog box  328
File Format options drop-down menu,
    Document Property inspector  317
File | New menu command  238
File | New Resource | New Diagram
    Style...  233
File | New Resource | New Template menu
    command  237
File | Print dialog, Document Property
    inspector  317
File | Template Chooser menu
    command  236, 237
Fill checkbox  130, 137
Fill property inspector  43
    Blend Direction wheel  138
    Blend Position  138
    Double Color Wells  138
    Double Linear Blend  137
    Double Radial Blend  137
    Fill checkbox  137
    Fill Style drop-down menu  137
    Linear Blend  137
    Radial Blend  137
    Solid  137
    Triple Color Wells  138
Fill Style drop-down menu  137

**first diagram, drawing**
about 13, 14
article editing step, adding 20-22
article, writing 17, 18
blank canvas, starting with 15, 16
Canvas Style Tray 45
editor check, adding 24-32
enhancing, color used 41-44
first task, adding 16, 17
Line Label 32
publishing 39-41
publishing, on front page 33-39
shape, moving 22, 23
shapes, connecting 18-20
**Font button 144**
**Force-directed layout button 211, 213, 216**
**Format | Choose Diagram Styles menu
command 232, 235**
**Front function 273**

## G

general action, action browse tool 200
**Geometry property inspector**
about 66, 128, 160
Flip buttons 162
Line Label controls 162
Maintain aspect ratio checkbox 162
Shapes Coordinate fields 161
Shapes Rotation wheel 162
Shapes Size fields 162
**Graffletopia**
about 69
Library folder, finding 71
stencil import, automatic method 72, 73
stencil import, manual method 70, 71
stencils, importing 70
**Grid in front checkbox, Grid Property
inspector 309**
**gridlines**
about 273
adjusting 274
enabling 274
**Grid Property inspector**
about 275, 308
Align To Grid button 311
Center on grid 311

Center on grid / Edges on grid 310
Color Well 309
Edges on grid 310
Grid in front checkbox 309
Major Grid Spacing controls 309
Minor Grid Steps 309
Minor Grid Steps input box 310
Print grid checkbox 309
Show grid lines checkbox 309
Show major checkbox 309
Snap to Grid checkbox 309, 311
**Grid View Mode button 205, 76**

## H

**Hierarchical Layout button, automatic
layout 211**
**Honeydew color 299**
**Horizontal alignment buttons 143**
**Horizontal Shape Alignment
button 285, 286**
**Horizontal Spread button 285**
**Hot Key column 183**

## I

**Image drop-down menu 149**
**Image Opacity slider 151**
**image palettes, color picker 304**
**image property inspector**
about 148, 149
Aspect Ratio buttons 150
Image drop-down menu 149
Image Opacity slider 151
Image well 150
Image Zoom slider 151
Positioning Offsets 151
**Image well 150**
**Image Zoom slider 151**
**Include Quick Look preview checkbox,
Document Property inspector 317**
**income flow diagram**
amending 74
**InkScape**
URL 88
using, for SVG file conversion 96-99
**inspector bar 167**

**inspector palettes, OmniGraffle workspace**
  about 11
  property inspectors 11
  shortcuts 11
  tips 52, 53
**Inspectors | Hide Inspectors menu**
       **command 298**
**Inspect Style menu 126, 132**
**interest shapes menu command 242**

## J

**Jumps Elsewhere action, action property**
       **inspector 202**
  Application start screen canvas 205, 208
  Canvas dropdown 204
  Center on a Point action 203
  Highlight an Object action 203
  start canvas 205
  Switch to a Specific Canvas 204
  Switch to the Next Canvas action 204
  Switch to the Previous Canvas action 204
  Zoom to Display a Rectangle 203

## K

**Kerning checkbox 144**
**keyboard combination**
  for canvas toolbar 182
**keyboard shortcuts**
  and OmniGraffle 217-221
  Command key (⌘) 218
  Control key (^) 218
  Enter key (↵) 218
  right arrow key (→) 218

## L

**layers**
  ⌘ C keyboard shortcut command 333
  ⌘ V keyboard shortcut command 334
  Action button 333-338
  copying 334, 335
  deleting 336
  duplicating 333
  Edit | Copy menu command 338
  Edit | Cut menu command 338

  Edit | Layers | Duplicate layer menu
    command 333
  Edit | Layers | Layers Settings menu
    command 337
  Edit | Layers menu 333, 335
  Edit | Layers | Move Selection Into Layer
    menu 338
  Edit | Layers | New Layer menu
    command 333
  Edit | Layers | Select All in Layer
    menu 338
  Edit | Paste menu command 334, 338
  Merge Layer Down command 335
  merging 335, 336
  moving 335
  new layer, adding 333
  New Layer button 333
  New Share Layer 333
  rearranging 335
  Select All in Layers command 339
  settings 337
  shapes on 338-340
  shared layers 340-344
  Triangles layer 340
  using 344
  working with 333
**layers, settings**
  locking a layer 338
  printing settings 337, 338
  visibility settings 337
**Layout buttons 211**
**Leading 144**
**Left-to-Right direction button 215**
**Line and Shapes inspector 130**
**Linear Blend 137**
**Line Connection option 173**
**Line Editing preference 182**
**line endings**
  tails and (arrow) heads 122
**Line Hops drop-down menu 123, 124**
**line label controls 164, 165**
**Line Length slider controls 213**
**Lines and Shapes inspector 119**
**Lines and Shapes palette 37**
**Lines and Shapes property**
       **inspector 42, 111, 132**

controls 133
**Lines and Shapes property inspector,
    controls**
  Color button 133
  Corner Control drop-down menu 134
  Corner Radius field 133
  Double Stroke button 133
  Single Stroke button 133
  Stroke checkbox 133
  Stroke end drop-down menu 134
  Stroke Pattern drop-down menu 133
  Thickness field 133
**line shape**
  Bézier lines 121, 122
  favorite line styles 125, 126
  favorite line styles, removing 126
  line, endings 122
  line hoops 123-125
  line labels 126, 128
  line, reversing 123
  line style property inspector 117
  line types 119-121
  midpoints on lines 117-119
  properties 116
**Line Tool 18, 26, 116**
**line, types**
  Bézier 120
  curved 120
  orthogonal 120
  straight 120
**Line type selector 119, 123**
**List button 231**
**list function**
  about 231
  View | List menu command 231
**locking a layer 338**

**M**

**magnet**
  editing, magnet tool used 194-197
  of shape 195
  on each vertex choice 195
**Magnet selection drop-down menu 173, 174**
**magnet tool**
  used, for editing magnets 194-197

**magnifying glass 300**
**Major Grid Spacing controls, Grid Property
    inspector 309**
**major guidelines 274**
**make points editable menu command 243**
**Make Same Height menu command 272**
**Make Same Size menu command 272, 273**
**Make Same Width menu command 271**
**Margin control 145**
**Maximum object rank button 212**
**Merge Layer Down command 335**
**Microsoft Visio Templates**
  importing 100-104
**midpoints**
  on lines 117-119
**Minimum object rank button 212-216**
**Minor Grid Steps, Grid Property
    inspector 309**
**minor steps 274**
**Miter option 134**
**modifier keys, Diagramming Tool**
  ⌘ (command key) 190
  ⌥ (option key) 190
  ⇧ (shift key) 190
  unmodified 190
**mouseless editing 217**
**Move selected shape 10 pixels at a time,
    task 222**
**Move selected shape one pixel at a time,
    task 222**
**Multivibrator.graffle 125**
**My layers canvas 343**

**N**

**natural sized shape 270**
**New Canvas 342**
**New Canvas button 329**
**New Diagram Style button 233**
**New Layer button 333**
**New Share Layer 333**
**New Template button 237**
**Note Property inspector**
  about 320
  Data Key 320, 321
  Data Value 320, 322
**Note Property inspector palette 103**

# O

Object Separation, automatic layout 212
Object Separation controls, automatic
    layout 212
OmniGraffle
  about 6
  advanced presentation mode 260, 261
  advantages 6
  and keyboard shortcuts 217-221
  canvases 325
  ColorSync support 263, 264
  diagram creation, avoiding 6
  diagram objects 7
  diagram styling, ways 267, 268
  layers 333
  overview 5
  presentation, creating 259
  presentation highlight, behavior
    changing 263
  presentation highlight, color changing 262
  presentation, navigating 260
  presentation, starting 259
  presentation, stopping 259
  setting up 7
  similar shapes 288
  using, as presentation tool 259
  workspace 8
  workspace, setting up 345-348
OmniGraffle | Preferences menu
    command 181, 127
OmniGraffle workspace
  canvas 8
  caveat 348
  inspector palettes 11
  setting up 345-348
  stencils 12, 13
Opacity Slider 301
Open button, action property inspector 201
open file action, action browse tool 200
Opens a File action, action property
    inspector 201
Opens a URL action, action property
    inspector 201
outline function
  about 223

Edit | Outlining | Indent menu command
  230
Edit | Outlining | Outdent menu command
  229
outline editing of diagrams, enabling 224
Outline marker 225
people, adding to family tree 227
Outline marker 225

# P

page orientation, Canvas Size Property
    inspector 313
Palette drop-down list 304
Palette | New From File drop-down list 304
patterns palette, color picker 305
pen tool
  using, to create own shapes 184-187
Point of Alignment matrix 285
Positioning Offsets 151
Preference menu 127
presentation
  actions and presentation mode 261
  advanced presentation mode 260, 261
  creating 259
  navigating 260
  stopping 259
printing settings, layers 337, 338
property inspectors
  about 307
  Canvas Size Property inspector 312-315
  Data Property inspector 319, 320
  Document Property inspector 316, 317
  Grid Property inspector 308
  Note Property inspector 320-322

# R

Radial Blend 137
Radial Layout button, automatic
    layout 211, 213, 216
Rank Separation controls, automatic
    layout 212
readme.txt file 101
Remove midpoints button 119
Remove midpoints menu command 119

Reverse the line's connection button 123
Round option 134, 135
rubber stamp tool
  about 193
  used, for replicating shapes 193
Ruler Units drop-down, Canvas Size
    Property inspector 314
Runs a Script action, action property
    inspector 202

## S

Same object rank button 212
sans serif 267
Search Field popup 80
Select All in Layers command 339
Selected Object Rank, automatic layout 212
Selected Object Rank controls, automatic
    layout 212
Selection inspector 289, 292
Selection property inspector 42
Selection Tool 112, 116
Select | Similar Objects menu
    command 290
Set as Default button 238
Set line type drop-down menu 119
Shadow Casting button 141
Shadow checkbox 130, 141
Shadow Color 141
Shadow Fuzziness slider 141
Shadow Offset control 141
Shadow property inspector 43
shadow property inspector, controls
  Behind all Shapes button 141
  Shadow Beneath this Shape button 141
  Shadow Casting button 141
  shadow checkbox 141
  Shadow Color 141
  Shadow Fuzziness slider 141
  Shadow Offset control 141
Shape Collection 24
shape inspector bar 167-169
Shape Repulsion slider controls 213
shapes
  Action button 338

adjusting, with geometry property
    inspector 160-164
aligning, to document grid 275-278
aligning, to each other 284-286
big wedge experiment 244-247
connecting 171-176
copy of existing shape, drawing 113, 114
creating 240
creating, pen tool used 184-187
Edit | Copy menu command 338
Edit | Cut menu command 338
Edit | Layers | Move Selection Into Layer
    menu 338
Edit | Layers | Select All in Layer
    menu 338
Edit | Paste menu command 338
grouping 156
intersect shapes menu command 242
line label closeness, determining 39
line label controls 164-166
make points editable menu command 243
moving, around canvas 47-49
natural sized shape 270, 271
on layers 338
ordering 154-156
re-styling 294-297
replicating, rubber stamp tool used 193
resizing 269, 270
same size, making 271-273
Select All in Layers command 339
selecting, ways 287
shape groups, creating 157, 158
shape groups, resizing 159
shape groups, ungrouping 158, 159
size to fit image 270
subtract shapes menu command 240, 241
text caption, adding 113
Triangles layer 340
union shapes menu command 242
shape style, properties
  shape stroke inspector 132
  stroke, color 132
Shape Tool 112
shared layers
  about 340
  My layers canvas 343

New Canvas 342
new shared layer, creating 341
**Show grid lines checkbox, Grid Property inspector 309**
**Show or Hide Layers action, action property inspector 202**
**similar shapes**
about 288
connected shapes, selecting 291, 292
selecting 288
**Single Stroke button 133**
**Size | Make Natural Size menu command 271**
**size to fit image 270**
**Smart Alignment Guide**
using 66
**Smart Alignment Guides 268-281**
**Smart Distance Guides 268**
**Snap to Grid checkbox 275, 278**
**Snap to Grid checkbox, Grid Property inspector 309, 311**
**Solid 137**
**Square option 134**
**stencil**
built in types 61
creating 83, 84
creating, graphics used 85
defining 60
diagram 59
exporting 99, 100
organizing 105, 106
**stencil based diagram**
about 64
expense buckets, adding 66-69
incoming cash flow 65
rulers, enabling 64
**stencil, creating**
example 89-93
fancy graphics, using 87, 88
InkScape, using for SVG file conversion 96-99
svg Detective, using for SVG file conversion 93-95
third party graphic files, legal side 86, 87
vector based diagramming application, using 85, 86

**Stencil Folders pane, Stencils palette**
Favorite Stencil section 82
Recent Stencils section 81, 82
sections 80
stencil library 81
**Stencil Grid View button 102**
**stencil library**
viewing 60
**Stencil Library Controls, Stencil palette**
Stencil Action button 78, 79
Stencil Search function, using 79, 80
Stencil View Mode buttons 76, 77
**Stencils palette**
Connections 61
Metadata pane 61, 75
overview 75
Stencil Folders 61
Stencil Folders pane 75, 80
Stencil Library Controls 61, 75, 76
Style Tray 61, 75
Style Tray, selected shapes 82
**Stroke checkbox 133**
**Stroke end drop-down menu 134**
**Stroke Pattern drop-down menu 133**
**stroke style button 120**
**style brush tool**
⌘+Z keyboard shortcut command 191
Edit | Undo Brush menu command 191
option key (⌥) 192
used, for style replication 190-192
**Style inspector 24**
**style replication**
style brush tool used 190-192
**Style Tray 190**
**subgraphs**
about 250, 251
Change damaged tire, steps 250
creating 250
experimenting with 250
get new tire, steps 251
replace spare tire, steps 251
shapes, editing 250
ungrouping 250
**subtract shapes menu command 240, 241**
**svg Detective**
using, for SVG file conversion 94, 95

## T

tables 254
tails and (arrow) heads, line endings 122
text caption
   adding to shape 113
Text containment buttons 144
text fitting button 130, 279
text inspector bar 169, 170
Text Offset controls 282
Text Offset dialog box 145
text property inspector 143
   Font button 144
   Horizontal alignment buttons 143
   Kerning checkbox 144
   Leading 144
   Margin control 145
   Text containment buttons 144
   Vertical alignment buttons 143, 144
Text Rotation 145
text shapes 128, 129
Text Tool 34, 126
Thickness field 133
Tool Palette 181
Triangles layer 340
Triple Color Wells 138

## U

UML 63
Ungroup command 104, 158
Unified Modeling Language. See UML
union shapes menu command 242
Unit scale drop-down, Canvas Size Property
   inspector 314
URL action, action browse tool 200
userdata variables, Note Property
   inspector 322

## V

variables 62
Vertical alignment buttons 143, 144
Vertical Shape Alignment button 285, 286

Vertical Spread button 285
View | Canvases menu command 326
View | Display Canvases menu
   command 329
View | List menu command 231
View | Magnets menu command 195, 173
View | Zoom menu command 197
View | Zoom | Zoom In menu
   command 276
visibility settings, layers 337
VisioCafe
   URL 100
visual diagrams, creating
   colors, using 55
   element shape consistency, maintaining 58
   few fonts, using 55
   figure captions, using 57
   focus point, determining 57
   legends, using 57
   lines, selecting 56
   planning 54
   tips 53-58
   titles, using 57
   visual symmetry, caveat 56
   white spaces, handling 58

## W

What You See, Is What You Get. See
   WYSIWYG
Wrap to Shape checkbox 145
WYSIWYG 10

## X

X icon 260

## Z

Zoom button 197, 276, 278
zoom in (⇧+⌥+⌘+=) 197
zoom out (⇧+⌥+⌘+-) 197
Zoom Tool 198

**[PACKT]**
PUBLISHING

**Thank you for buying**
**OmniGraffle 5 Diagramming Essentials**

# About Packt Publishing

Packt, pronounced 'packed', published its first book "*Mastering phpMyAdmin for Effective MySQL Management*" in April 2004 and subsequently continued to specialize in publishing highly focused books on specific technologies and solutions.

Our books and publications share the experiences of your fellow IT professionals in adapting and customizing today's systems, applications, and frameworks. Our solution based books give you the knowledge and power to customize the software and technologies you're using to get the job done. Packt books are more specific and less general than the IT books you have seen in the past. Our unique business model allows us to bring you more focused information, giving you more of what you need to know, and less of what you don't.

Packt is a modern, yet unique publishing company, which focuses on producing quality, cutting-edge books for communities of developers, administrators, and newbies alike. For more information, please visit our website: www.packtpub.com.

# Writing for Packt

We welcome all inquiries from people who are interested in authoring. Book proposals should be sent to author@packtpub.com. If your book idea is still at an early stage and you would like to discuss it first before writing a formal book proposal, contact us; one of our commissioning editors will get in touch with you.

We're not just looking for published authors; if you have strong technical skills but no writing experience, our experienced editors can help you develop a writing career, or simply get some additional reward for your expertise.

[PACKT]
PUBLISHING

## SketchUp 7.1 for Architectural Visualization: Beginner's Guide

ISBN: 978-1-847199-46-1      Paperback: 408 pages

Create stunning photo-realistic and artistic visuals for your SketchUp models

1. Create picture-perfect photo-realistic 3D architectural renders for your SketchUp models

2. Post-process SketchUp output to create digital watercolor and pencil art

3. Follow a professional visualization studio workflow

4. Make the most out of SketchUp with the best free plugins and add-on software to enhance your models

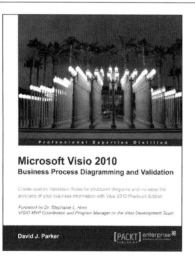

## Microsoft Visio 2010 Business Process Diagramming and Validation

ISBN: 978-1-849680-14-1      Paperback: 344 pages

Create custom Validation Rules for structured diagrams and increase the accuracy of your business information with Visio 2010 Premium Edition

1. Optimize your business information visualization by mastering out-of-the-box, structured diagram functionality with features like the Basic and Cross-Functional Flowcharts

2. Create and analyze custom Validation Rules for structured diagrams using Visio Premium

3. Get to grips with validation logic for Business Process Diagramming with Visio 2010, by using the provided Rules Tools add-in

Please check **www.PacktPub.com** for information on our titles

[PACKT] PUBLISHING

## Blender 3D Architecture, Buildings, and Scenery

ISBN: 978-1-847193-67-4    Paperback: 332 pages

Create photorealistic 3D architectural visualizations of buildings, interiors, and environmental scenery

1. Turn your architectural plans into a model

2. Study modeling, materials, textures, and light basics in Blender

3. Create photo-realistic images in detail

4. Create realistic virtual tours of buildings and scenes

## ASP.NET 3.5 Application Architecture and Design

ISBN: 978-1-847195-50-0    Paperback: 260 pages

Build robust, scalable ASP.NET applications quickly and easily

1. Master the architectural options in ASP.NET to enhance your applications

2. Develop and implement n-tier architecture to allow you to modify a component without disturbing the next one

3. Design scalable and maintainable web applications rapidly

Please check **www.PacktPub.com** for information on our titles